Not Tiger Moms

Not Tiger Moms

REIMAGINING ASIAN AMERICAN MOTHERHOOD

Miliann Kang

UNIVERSITY OF CALIFORNIA PRESS

University of California Press
Oakland, California

Library of Congress Cataloging-in-Publication Data

Names: Kang, Miliann, author.
Title: Not tiger moms : reimagining Asian American motherhood / Miliann Kang.
Description: Oakland, California : University of California Press, [2026] | Includes bibliographical references and index.
Identifiers: LCCN 2026018469 (print) | LCCN 2026018470 (ebook) | ISBN 9780520356283 (cloth) | ISBN 9780520356290 (paperback) | ISBN 9780520976054 (ebook)
Subjects: LCSH: Motherhood—Social aspects—United States. | Mothers—Social aspects—United States. | Asian American women—Social conditions.
Classification: LCC HQ759 .K316 2026 (print) | LCC HQ759 (ebook)
LC record available at https://lccn.loc.gov/2026018469
LC ebook record available at https://lccn.loc.gov/2026018470

GPSR Authorized Representative: Easy Access System Europe, Mustamäe tee 50, 10621 Tallinn, Estonia, gpsr.requests@easproject.com

35 34 33 32 31 30 29 28 27 26
10 9 8 7 6 5 4 3 2 1

This book is dedicated to Asian American mothers—
past, present, future.

Contents

Prologue: Writing the Asian American Mother as the Other

When I was a kid, I didn't know any of the history—my own family history or Asian American history—so of course, I just blamed everything on my mother. I was strange because she was strange. I'm sure my kids feel the same way about me sometimes. . . . When you don't know what to push back against, you push back against the mom.

EUNHEE, interview, Korean American, social worker

To imagine otherwise is not about imagining as the other, but rather, is about imagining the other differently.

KANDICE CHUH, *Imagine Otherwise: On Asian Americanist Critique* (2003)

When it comes to writing the "other," what questions are we not asking? . . . How you grew up, who you grew up with, how you know them. All of this affects what you think is real and whom you think counts as human—which, in turn, affects how you write stories. . . . Why do you want to tell this story?

ALEXANDER CHEE, "How to Unlearn Everything" (2019)

To those of us who identify as Asian American mothers or who were raised by one or who imagine becoming one, *Asian American mother* refers to a specific and complicated person—who despite imperfections, even outright transgressions—is often beloved. Yet, in the public imaginary, the combination of *Asian American* and *mother* is combustible, conjuring a stereotype, a stock figure, an other, or what this book calls a "mother/other." The tragedy of turning a mother into an other is that it makes her a stranger not only to society but to her children and to herself. As Eunhee's heartrending words above imply,[1] if our mothers are made strange, we inherit their strangeness and, in turn, pass it on.

Currently, the particular kind of mother/other that Asian American mothers are most likely to be pegged as goes by the name of "tiger mother."[2] The Asian American mothers whom I interviewed for this book revealed that although many White mothers feel judged by—and compared to—the tiger mother, Asian American mothers such as themselves continue to be judged as tiger mothers, or failed tiger mothers. But as Kandice Chuh's groundbreaking framework makes clear, to "imagine otherwise" is not to imagine as the other but about "imagining the other differently."[3] Thus, this book aims to "imagine motherwise" by thinking beyond the tiger mother but also thinking through this trope, in order to imagine Asian American mothers and all mothers differently

But talking about the tiger mother can be a catch-22. The harder we try to prove we are not tiger mothers, the more we are framed as tiger mothers, just as the more we refuse to be labeled as model minority, the more the label sticks. As with many tropes of motherhood, the tiger mother reveals little about the actual mothers it purports to represent, and much about those who regard them as such. The tiger mother has entrenched itself as a story told about Asian American mothers, and whether or not they identify with this story, it has become something they must constantly adjudicate.

Yet, the tiger mother is only the most recent in a long line of mother/other figures. Many mothers have been cast as mother/others; Asian American mothers have no exclusive claim. At the same time, the ways that they are othered reveal dynamics that are specific to Asian Americans, while linked to other mothers. Parallel to how Black mothers must constantly fend off tropes of "mammy" and "welfare queen," or for Latina mothers, tropes of illegal immigrant "breeders" of "anchor babies," Asian American mothers must constantly contend with the tiger mother label.

This is why it is so hard to talk about the tiger mother and why we cannot *not* talk about the tiger mother. The tiger mother has carried a qualitatively different bite for Asian American mothers than for non-Asian American mothers, varying not just in degree but in kind. The following chapters, however, do not talk only about the tiger mother, but document a range of stories that are told about Asian American mothers, whether as tigers or other kinds of *others*.

These are hard stories to tell, so why tell them? Truth be told, I do not want to tell such stories. When setting out to write a book about Asian American mothering, I did not intend to write about tiger mothering, let alone about strangeness and othering. I wanted to tell stories of progress and celebration—look how far we have come! I wanted to tell the next generation of Asian Americans that if they choose to become mothers, they will write new stories under new circumstances, far different from those of their foremothers. I had hoped to share stories that bore little resemblance to those of my Korean immigrant mother or even to those of myself as an older second-generation Asian American mother whose child has left the nest—and is no longer a child. I did not want to write about an *other* who is me, who is what my own mother was, and who my daughter may one day become—not because of who we are but because of how we are seen, or rather, unseen.

But as I took on the task of researching and writing about Asian American mothering and motherhood writ large, I kept hearing an incessant whisper that turned into a hiss and then an exhortation: "Tell the truth." We are not there yet. And how we get there—or even where we are striving to get—is not at all clear. Figuring out how to understand the truths that Asian American mothers have shared with me, how to tell them, and for whom they will ring true has taken a long time, much too long. Then again, how long is it supposed to take to figure out what it means to be othered as a mother and what this does to mothers, both to those who are othered and to those who do the othering?

I have not figured out how to do full justice to these stories and to those who entrusted me with them, but I know what *not* to do. In writing about how Asian American mothers are othered, I must not further other them by making them into objects, things, data points on a bell curve. Nor must I claim to be giving Asian American mothers a voice, as they are fully capable of speaking for themselves, even though they are rarely given the audience they deserve. In addition, Asian American mothers do not have just one voice or just one experience, but many.

Over the course of conducting this research and writing this book, I have listened to the many different voices of Asian American mothers and have aimed to write about them in a language that is accessible and of interest to many audiences, not only those within academic circles. *Mother/Other* is still mainly a scholarly work of social science, but I have tried to organize it so that those who are interested in the academic debates can engage with them and those less so can skim them. (I have mainly included these scholarly references in the notes and later parts of each chapter, rather than leading with the theoretical arguments and literature review, as in a more traditional academic style.) But I hope readers do not skip these sections entirely, as the book stakes its claims on the groundwork of many Asian American and feminist-of-color scholars, artists, activists, and public intellectuals and aims to give them their much deserved due.

My own mothering stories invariably shape the stories I tell about other mothers, but the purpose of this book is not to recount my own journey through motherhood or, for that matter, to probe the interiority of any one mother's story. At the same time, I know that—alongside the many Asian American mothers whom I interviewed—I have been in constant conversation with a chorus of real and imagined mother figures: the mother I had as a child, the mother I wish I had, the mother I am, the mother I wish I could be. All these mothers loom large, shaping the questions I ask, those I am unwilling to ask, and those I do not yet know to ask.

I am trained as a sociologist, so the questions that I gravitate toward and that drive this book are less about Asian American mothers' individual identities or psychological traits than about the shared social contexts, past and present, that shape their mothering. Thus, I regard each of the mothers that I interviewed not as objects of study but as key informants into the social conditions that shape their mothering. And because many of these conditions are messy and challenging, writing about them is also messy and challenging.

So, in response to Alexander Chee's provocation that opened this chapter—why do I want to tell these stories, and what questions am I not asking? Am I willing to ask not just how Asian American mothers are othered but how we benefit from *not* being the other—or at least, not the most abject other? What do we gain and what do we lose from a racial hierarchy in which we and our children occupy neither the top nor the bottom rung but are somewhere in the middle, the most model of minorities? How have Asian American mothers fueled the tropes about us by performing to type and demanding that our children do the same, whether through the pursuit of grades, sports trophies, music awards or which colleges they get into. How are we complicit in othering ourselves, our children, and other mothers? Is the necessary question not simply how are Asian American mothers othered, but how do we resist othering or fail to?

My fear is that in trying to respond to these questions, this book does not present Asian American mothers—me included—in the most flattering light. But the reason to tell these stories is not to flatter ourselves or to make us look good. It is to shine light on the limited ways that we have been regarded as mothers and to imagine new possibilities for ourselves and for motherhood writ large. This is why it is so hard to tell stories of how Asian American mothers are othered; this is why I want to tell these stories.

Introduction

One Is Not Born, but Rather Becomes, an Asian American Mother

One is not born, but rather becomes, a woman.

SIMONE DE BEAUVOIR, *The Second Sex* (2011)

The Self is the familiar (Europe, the West, "us") and the Other is strange (the Orient, the East, "them").

EDWARD SAID, *Orientalism* (1979)

Mothering is not just gendered but racialized. . . . How do we break mothering free of ideological encapsulation?

EVELYN NAKANO GLENN, *Mothering: Ideology, Experience, and Agency* (1993)

There is not really a conversation about Asian mothers, beyond the stereotype of a tiger mom; there just aren't others. I think rightfully there is a focus on Black mothering or Latina mothering, and both of those are laden with stereotypes as well, but there is actually a conversation. . . . Anti-Asian racism is about erasure, and I think that plays out in Asian American mothering as well.

ALICE, interview, Chinese American, policy advocate

Mother is a loaded term: good or bad, loved or hated, legitimate or illegitimate, but rarely neutral. *Mother* with a capital *M* names a specific person; *mother* with a small *m* designates a social category and the cultural and political meanings attached to it. Mother tongue, mother's milk, motherland, motherlode, Mother Earth. Giver of life; larger than life. *Mother* represents love, nurturance, security, care, connection, and belonging—or the failure to provide or receive these. Mothers are revered, except when they are reviled for not living up to the impossible standards required for reverence or for failing to revere the standards themselves. In this case, they cross the line from *mother* to *mother/other*.

This book argues that what is at stake in the wide-ranging conflicts about motherhood is not simply who qualifies as a good or bad mother but how these qualifications are used to draw boundaries of who belongs and who is *other*. The distinction between deserving mother and undeserving mother/other is not a mere catfight or media spectacle that can be reduced to oversimplified terms such as "mommy wars."[1] Instead, mother/othering wields immense power; it can determine who gets to stay or go, who lives or dies, and whose children live or die.

To paraphrase Simone de Beauvoir's famous edict, women are not born but made. Likewise, mothers are not born but made. However, questions about how mothers—not just women—are made have not been as fully interrogated by feminist scholars, or for that matter, by de Beauvoir herself.[2] This book dives into questions of how motherhood is made in ways that are closely related but not reducible to how womanhood is made. Further, it interrogates not only what makes a mother but what makes a mother into an *other*? Specifically, what makes an Asian American mother, and what makes her into a *mother/other*? These questions are intentional double entendres, asking what are the lived experiences that make an individual into a mother, and what are the collective standards that define *mother* as a socially recognized status? Why are certain mothers excluded from this status, and what broader forms of exclusion does motherhood build upon and further entrench?

Mothers go by many different names: mom, mommy, mummy, mama (or muh-thuh as they say in my home state of Massachusetts). Across Asia and the Asian diaspora, they go by many more: mā, má, maa, mātā, mẹ, imoto, ina, omoni, nanay, umma, to name but a few. How then do all these different terms and the many people they represent, once they arrive on U.S. shores, become encapsulated in a single moniker: Asian American mother? And how has this category been so easily reduced to "tiger mother"?

As a result of Yale law professor Amy Chua's 2011 bestseller *Battle Hymn of the Tiger Mother*, "tiger mother" has not only become code language for achievement-oriented, tough-love parenting, but it has become a catch-all for all Asian American mothers.[3] Chua's book thrust Asian American mothering into the public spotlight, and the light has not been flattering. On the one hand, the tiger mother is just the latest figure in a long line of unsavory gendered and racialized stereotypes of Asian women, from Suzy Wong to Mata Hari, from lotus blossom to dragon lady. On the other hand, there is something new about the tiger mother figure, as it is not merely her sexuality or hypersexuality that is regarded as problematic, but her mothering, or specifically, her *hypermothering*. I focus here on the tiger mother not because it is the only or even the most interesting of the many tropes that have been projected onto Asian American mothers, but because it is currently the most dominant and the most instructive for exploring the stories that circulate around Asian American motherhood.

Far from a benign or complimentary depiction, this book shows how the tiger mother has solidified as a *matritrope*, a widespread representation of a group of mothers that imbues them with shared characteristics based largely but not solely on race. More than merely hurtful stereotypes enacted by individuals, matritropes are powerful ideological weapons that control reproduction to produce widespread racial effects, from excluding certain groups from entering the country to defining limited terms of inclusion for those who enter and stay. Alongside the concept of mother/othering, *matritropes* is meant to provide a broad theoretical frame that is at the same time embedded in the particular histories and experiences of Asian American mothers. In the following chapters, I track not just the specific content of matritropes about "yellow motherhood"—whether prostitutes, mongrels, coolies, criminals, models, or tigers—but what ends they serve—that is, to show not just what they *are* but what they *do*.

The central argument here is that, currently and throughout history, the ideological meanings that are given to the term *Asian American mother* reveal less about the complex lived experiences of the actual persons who embody this category than about a racial imaginary that regards them as a particular kind of *other*. In exploring the multiple meanings of the Asian American mother, this book stakes the following main claims. First, at the collective level, the descriptor *Asian American* shifts the meaning of *mother* from one intimately connected to the self to one who is essentially *other*. Second, *mother* is a core component in constructing the racial category of *Asian American* in all its various forms, from yellow peril to model minority, into that of other. (To say it a different way: the yellow peril cannot exist without perilous yellow motherhood; the model minority is not possible without model maternity.) Third, the various forms of othering to which Asian American mothers are subject are inextricable from but not reducible to the denigration of Black, Latina, Native and Indigenous motherhood and the elevation of (certain versions of) White motherhood. Finally, the contradictory imperatives of Asian American motherhood—that Asian American mothers be good but not too good, high achieving but not overachieving, and that they raise children who can walk this same tightrope—are a setup.

Yet, the kind of othering that Asian American mothers encounter is often hard to contend with, or even recognize, as it often comes in the guise of praise, however faint. The tiger mother is a vivid example, just like the model minority, in that it appears to be a positive stereotype (if such a thing exists). Once when I took issue with the term, the White American mother that I spoke with seemed taken aback: "Wait, you mean, you think it's bad to be called a tiger mom? I know this one Asian American mom—she's perfect, her kids are perfect. I call her TM. I thought it was a compliment."[4] But whatever the intention of those who use the term—including Chua—its effect on Asian American mothers has been far from complimentary.

Heated debates about the tiger mother have revealed and heightened the perception of Asian American mothers as foreign threats, along with magnifying the broader racial constructions of Asian Americans as forever foreigners. As Alice described at the beginning of this chapter, the tiger mother stereotype has contributed to the erasure of Asian American mothers, foreclosing more nuanced conversations such as those about Black and Latina mothering. Further, she emphasized that despite the diversity among Asian American mothers, they have been homogenized as tiger mothers and held to the standards of the highly successful model minority. Her interview further underscored that although the tiger mother has centrally positioned Asian American mothers in debates about motherhood, it has also simultaneously othered them.

Making mothers into the problem is nothing new, but making mothers into each other's main problem is a newly ramped-up political strategy. What better way to distract mothers from the many social problems that they face than to have them face off against each other? In short, although mothers must respond to a whole host of social problems, instead they are often seen as responsible for causing these very problems for themselves, for each other, and for those around them.

While much attention has been given to how the mother is constructed as the other in relation to the child or to the father, the concept of mother/other explores a different set of questions regarding how mothers are constructed as others in relation to each other and to society. In this book, I do not focus on fathers, not because I think fathers are unimportant but because Asian American fatherhood has not generated the same kind of heated public debates and animosity as has Asian American motherhood. Likewise, I do not focus on parents broadly, as this often obscures the fact that many of the debates about parenting are in fact about mothers and mothering.[5] Nonetheless, while I recognize the risks of gender essentialism in focusing only on mothers, it is also possible to think about motherhood beyond normative gender categories. Rather than automatically reinforcing gender binaries and the nuclear, heterosexual, middle-class family structure, *mother* can be a capacious and malleable term. Alongside feminist scholars and the study's participants, this book aims to redefine motherhood beyond its normative meanings and attachments.[6] However, in order to envision different meanings and ways of being mothers, we need to acknowledge what are the prevailing constructions of motherhood, and the histories that have brought us here.

Looking back, the hot-button debates that defined contemporary motherhood at the turn of the 21st century—now seem almost quaint: breastfeeding versus formula, slings versus strollers, dedicated soccer moms versus decadent "wine moms."[7] Today's conflicts about motherhood—and among mothers—have both escalated and shifted to intense political attacks against transgender students, vaccine mandates, undocumented immigration, diversity, equity, and inclusion (DEI) policies, the teaching of banned books and critical race theory, and the right to legal abortion.[8] In the face of such pressing issues, debates about tiger mothering (depicted as tough love versus free-range parenting, emphasis on straight A's versus social and emotional intelligence) seem fairly innocent, even frivolous.

But this book argues otherwise, that there is much more going on here than meets the eye.

Scratch the surface and tiger mothering provides a gateway into examining how motherhood has become increasingly contested yet often overlooked terrain for defining boundaries of othering and belonging. Although it speaks mainly to debates about motherhood in the United States, this book also has relevance for understanding the increasingly exclusionary boundaries of caring, compassion, and citizenship that are being erected and enforced globally. It speaks to questions of home and homelands that continue to pull at those whose mothers migrated from other motherlands and whose claims to belonging, not only as daughters but as mothers in their own right, remain partial and contested, even with the attainment of citizenship papers, diplomas, and professional credentials.

When Daughters of Asian Immigrants Become Asian American Mothers

Caught in a web of seemingly endemic mother-daughter tensions, the second-generation Asian American daughter has been cast as a sympathetic figure, but what happens when this daughter grows up to be an Asian American mother herself? The transition from Asian American daughter to mother is marked by a stark shift from sympathy to antipathy, most dramatically but not solely illustrated in her characterization as tiger mother. While public attention, popular culture, and the racial imaginary have shifted from perceptions of second-generation Asian American women in the role of daughters to that of mothers—as in the attention given to the tiger mother—research and writing on Asian American motherhood still is weighted toward the immigrant generation.

In order to address this gap, this book focuses specifically on second-generation Asian American mothers, those born and/or raised in the United States. In studying the second generation, social science researchers have contributed many important findings and frameworks but have mainly focused on a younger cohort of Asian American students and young adults.[9] Creative writers and humanities scholars have illuminated the often fraught dynamics of Asian American mother-daughter relations but the mothers in question are still often first-generation immigrants, and the daughters are again mostly children or young adults.[10] The focus on Asian immigrant mothers, while important, has tended to reinforce narrow story lines—be that of intergenerational conflict, Confucian family values, or the striving for model minority achievement—foreclosing other concerns about the many outside forces shaping these families.[11] But many of these second-generation children have now grown up to have children of their own, and many of these Asian American daughters are becoming Asian American mothers.

As a result of being cast as the perpetual daughters of immigrants rather than as mothers in their own right, the stories that circulate around Asian American mothers are most often stories about them rather than by them or for them. This book seeks to fill in some of this vacuum by expanding the range of available stories by and for Asian American mothers and also to develop concepts and methods that speak to and from their complex and diverse experiences. Thus, this book maps the many shifting figurations of the Asian American mother/other, to reimagine new possibilities for actual Asian American mothers and their families and communities. But to tell different stories, first, it is necessary to identify and intervene in the stories that have been told.

Theorizing Mothers as Others

Far from a sisterhood—let alone a global one—motherhood has become an intense site of division across racial lines and even within them. The concept of mother/other shows how certain mothers are grouped together as polarizing racialized figures who are perceived simultaneously as undesirable reproducers and as threats to the normative model of the White, middle-class, heterosexual family. My theorization of the mother/other is indebted to sociologist Patricia Hill Collins's important work on "othermothers," which describes strong connections of kin and community care, particularly among Black women. Hill Collins shows that while othermothers are often loving and cherished, they are often called upon to fill in when Black mothers must care for other people's children and are valued more as paid childcare providers than as mothers of their own children.[12] However, this book flips the othermother concept to show how mothers not only rely on many others but are themselves positioned as "others."

The concept of the other has been central in defining Asians and Asian Americans as outsiders, strangers, inassimilable aliens, forever foreigners. Edward Said is one of the foundational theorists who has explored how ideas of "the Orient" are central to constructions of the other. In his groundbreaking book *Orientalism*, the boundaries between "us" and "them" do not merely reflect universal distinctions between what is strange and what is familiar; instead, these boundaries are created according to specific historical contexts and divisions, most notably, that of Orient and Occident. Further, Said argued that the designation of an uncivilized, abject Eastern "other" has served as the necessary foil against which to define a civilized, Western "self."[13] This oppositional framing of East and West positions Asia as inherently foreign and at odds with Europe and America. Much academic work, indeed the field of Asian American Studies, has built on Said's arguments to show that the term *Asian American*, even though it has come into popular parlance, remains to many a contradiction in terms.

But less attention has been given to the specific ways that the combination of *Asian American* and *mother* invokes a very particular kind of Orientalized other, which at times refers to specific individuals and histories but more often is invoked as a vague but nonetheless far-reaching specter. This book builds on Said's and other feminist and Asian American studies scholarship to show that motherhood has become a primary fault line along which these polarities of Asia/America, East/West, and self/other are understood and enforced. I argue that the lines drawn between mother and other follow a very particular logic of *maternal Orientalism* in which ideas about the Orient as a foreign, inassimilable land are irreconcilable with ideas of "the mother" as the embodiment of home, hearth, and homeland. Thus, Orientalist visions of the East are projected onto Asian American mothers to construct them as the other by resuscitating older representations of the "Oriental mother" while circulating new figurations, such as the tiger mother.

But mother/othering does not occur only at the level of representation; it is upheld by a wide range of social institutions, ranging from schools, workplaces, and healthcare providers to families, communities and states. Indeed, motherhood is a powerful and complex social institution in and of itself; it has become one of the central sites of conflict around gender, but it is also ground zero for debates regarding race, class, immigration, and national identity. And controlling the reproduction of Asian American mothers (or potential mothers) has served as a central driver of what I refer to as *reproductive exclusion*, which refers to the policing of borders based on acceptable forms of reproduction and the policing of reproduction of those already within these borders.[14]

Reproductive exclusion builds on the "reproductive justice" (RJ) framework that has challenged and expanded the concept of reproductive rights to move beyond abortion to include "the human right to maintain personal bodily autonomy, have children, not have children, and parent the children we have in safe and sustainable communities," as articulated by one of the leading RJ organizations, SisterSong.[15] Reproductive justice is grounded in Black feminist scholarship and activism but addresses an expansive intersectional approach.[16] Likewise, reproductive exclusion seeks to highlight Asian American feminist interventions while applying them to expand debates concerning reproduction to address not only formal legal exclusion but a long historical legacy of racist and xenophobic movements, institutional marginalization, and cultural misrepresentation that have limited the freedom of Asian Americans to have and raise children.

In short, whereas reproductive justice examines the expansive ways that certain groups are excluded from full *access to* reproduction, reproductive exclusion shows how reproduction itself serves as the *basis for* exclusion. While differentiating these terms, this book places them in close conversation both in terms of theory and praxis. It shows how many Asian American mothers have been powerful actors in struggles for reproductive justice, even as their efforts have faced many obstacles and have often been overlooked.

Expanding on the question posed at the beginning of this chapter by Evelyn Nakano Glenn in one of the foundational studies of mothering, this book asks not only what it would take to break mothering free from the racial and gender ideologies that encapsulate it, but why the very idea of breaking free from these ideologies is so contested, most of all, among mothers themselves? Motherhood is often naturalized and mythologized as a universal calling, but this idealized mother requires a nemesis, an antithesis, an anti-mother, an *other*. But to interrogate the positioning of Asian American mothers as others, it is necessary to ask not only who is relegated to the category but who is defined in opposition to it.

A mother/other is a mirror figure who, through her failures, reveals the "true" meanings of "normative motherhood" as self-sacrifice and self-subjugation to the needs of others, not just her own children but the existing social order.[17] Yet, mothering and mother/othering are not predetermined by some kind of genetic programming that dictates that mothers will care only about themselves and their own children or people like them. Social institutions—from schools to workplaces, to the family and the institution of motherhood itself—play a significant role in pitting mothers against each other for scarce resources, and they can also provide support for mothers to see each other as allies rather than enemies. But rather than attributing children's successes and failures to the quality of schools, access to healthcare, safety from violence, the state of the nation, the state of the environment, or the state of the world, the mother is the first and last to be blamed.

In the mythology of the American dream, society is never to blame, and success is all up to the individual. But who or what makes or breaks this individual? The answer circles back, invariably and incessantly, to the mother. Further, one mother's success or failure is weaponized to discipline and chide another. Is it any wonder, then, that mothers feel pitted against each other? Because they are. But how have Asian American mothers come to be such polarizing figures in these debates? And whose fights are these really? What drives them, who benefits, who gets hurt, and how can they be stopped?

Motherhood as a Central Site of Racialization for Asian Americans

It is not particularly newsworthy to argue that Asian American mothers are often regarded as others. But I hope to make a stronger claim: that centering motherhood offers a different take not just on how Asian Americans are represented but on how the very category of Asian American is produced and reproduced particularly but not solely in its current formulation as model minority. Much attention has been given to the Asian American family as the unit of analysis, but the specific figure of the Asian American *mother*—not just the immigrant but the second-generation mother—needs to be given greater importance and more focused analyses. Because what or who provides the secret sauce behind ongoing Asian American success, if not the Asian American mother? And what metrics shift this success from admirable to threatening, if not the admiration or threat posed by that mother?

While I am concerned with the experiences of each Asian American mother, I see them as pieces of a larger puzzle regarding the social conditions in which Asian American mothers currently mother. The current conditions of Asian American mothering have turned it into a charged site of othering that pits Asian American mothers against other mothers, their own children, and themselves. Yet, Asian American mothers are often represented as a singular group of tiger mothers, often attributing this form of mothering to race and obscuring the ways that it is grounded in the specific temporal and cultural contexts that have made motherhood and its stakes increasingly fraught and competitive, both locally and globally.

As several respondents noted and will be discussed more later, the fear of Chua's tiger mother is inseparable from fears of China. Asian Americans are continually collapsed with Asia, so what happens "over there" is always connected to what happens here and vice versa. In fact, anxieties over motherhood are ramped up because of the collapsing of clear borders between here and there, us and them. But rather than an import from Asia, Chua's brand of mothering is home grown, made in the U.S.A. Nonetheless, just like Asian Americans themselves, tiger mothering and those associated with it are regarded as a foreign element. This book argues that, whether with regard to tiger mothering or any common identifiers attached to Asian American mothers, the source of commonality is not similar ethnic roots in Asian culture but shared racial categorization as Asian Americans and the associated qualifications related to model minority success.

But Asian Americans have not always been the model minority, and Asian American mothers have not only been cast as model reproducers, nor is there any guarantee that this casting will persist. In fact, the two-sidedness of the model minority, its easy flippability from model to menace, has been a core premise of Asian American studies scholarship. This book extends this scholarship to explore how the various constructions of the yellow peril have relied upon historical invocations of various figures of "yellow motherhood"; likewise, the current racialization of Asian Americans as the model minority depends upon the construct of "model minority motherhood."

How, then, is motherhood central to the racialization of Asian Americans as both model and peril? The dictates of model minority inclusion for Asian Americans have been not only to assimilate through hard work and achievement but to produce high-achieving children who will work equally hard and achieve as much, if not more. However, if they overachieve or *because* they overachieve, they are no longer seen as model citizens but quickly morph into the yellow peril. And this drive to achieve—along with its model and peril consequences—is often perceived as an essential attribute of the Asian American family, as cogently articulated by Gary Okihiro:

> The Asian work ethic, family values, self-help, culture and religiosity, and intermarriage—all elements of the model minority—can also be read as components of the yellow peril. Asian workers can be "diligent" and "slavish," "frugal" and "cheap," " upwardly mobile" and "aggressive," while Asian families and communities can be "mutual aid" and "self-serving" institutions, "inclusive" and "exclusive" groupings, "multicultural enclaves" and "balkanized ghettos." Asian religious beliefs can be characterized as "transcendentalism" and "paganism," "filial piety" and "superstition, while intermarriage can indicate "assimilation," "mongrelization," "integration," and "infil-

> tration," and children can be "our second-generation problem" and "our amazing Chinese kids." "Model" can be "perils," and "perils," "models.". . . The yellow peril and the model minority are not poles, denoting opposite representations along a single line, but in fact a circular relationship that moves in either direction.[18]

But I take this argument one step further and ask what determines if the Asian American family and Asian Americans writ large are read as something to model or something to fear? Both model minority and yellow peril are shape-shifting racial categories, and it is not simply the Asian American family but the Asian American *mother* that is regarded as the central force in shaping these shifts. The Asian American mother is the substance on which Asian Americanness depends, but who or what is she?

The Asian American mother is an elusive category that is not only difficult to parse but can seem an oxymoron to some. The irony is that while Asian American mothers themselves constantly grapple with the varied and complex meanings of this identity, those who are *not* Asian American mothers often seem to think they already know what it means to be one. Overriding their complex histories, connections, and commitments, Asian American mothers are often treated as all the same, whether as tiger mothers or other mother/others.

Who or What Is an Asian American Mother, According to Whom?

Asian American mother can refer to an actual person, the various projections imposed onto this person or persons, a demographic box to check, an analytical frame, a racial and gender typology, a political affiliation, a deeply felt self-identification—or all of the above. Recognizing that it can be simultaneously too broad and too narrow, I have chosen to use *Asian American mothers* as the operative term to define the group and the questions that are the focus of this book. But this presents a fundamental contradiction: while attempting to research a group called "Asian American mothers," I call into question what constitutes this group and even the very idea that such a group exists.

The Asian American mother must be broken down into her constituent parts, but she is more than the sum of these parts. She is both a person and a projection, but the former is often subsumed into the latter. (For now, I use *she/her* out of convention, but later I employ *they* and other pronouns to respect individuals' chosen terms, or *it* when referring to the Asian American mother as a figure of the other, and *we* when claiming this identity and making clear my investments in it.) The very need to complicate even the pronouns by which to refer to the Asian American mother—*she/they/it/we*—underscores the existential ambivalence of this person/group/identity/category/figure. In addition to which pronouns, how to even write this category: Asian-American, Asian/American, Asian Pacific Islander American mother?[19] Again, for now, I settle on *Asian American mother*, with the caveat that this is a shorthand for a category that is constantly being redefined by those who claim it. Yet, whoever, whatever, however she is called or calls herself, the Asian American mother is often designated in the position of other by those who position themselves outside this category.

This book aims to be a vehicle to represent Asian American mothers in all their complexity, to show that they are a diverse group of people who are often treated as if they are all the same. While they are relegated to a common racial and gender category, they inhabit and redefine the meaning of this category beyond its narrow dictates. However, their own definitions are often at odds with the meanings that others impute when *mother* is attached to *Asian American* and vice versa.

If this all seems very confusing, it's because it is. But that is the goal of this book: not merely to question what we think that we know about Asian American mothers but to destabilize the category itself. And if defining the term *Asian American mother* is a complicated enterprise in its own right, how much more complicated is trying to operationalize it into a research design and select participants who properly fit its parameters?

The Asian American Mother as Method: Operationalizing a Contested Category

What is an Asian American mother, why study them as a group, and how? The methodological questions that the study of Asian American mothers raise are connected to a long tradition of feminist research that has challenged the idea of women as a fixed, universal category by persistently asking, "Which women?"[20] Likewise, this book destabilizes the category of Asian American mothers by continually raising the question, "Which Asian American mothers are we talking about?"

This book regards *Asian American* and *mother* as signifiers that are always in the process of being defined and contested. At the same time, these signifiers attach to and are claimed by actual persons and groups, and they can, at times, foster shared experiences and identities. Thus, this book seeks a both/and approach: it uses the Asian American mother as a methodological framework, while also appreciating that it is much more than a mode of analysis; it is also a self-identification for a group of people for whom this term carries deep and complex meanings.

Designating Asian American mothers as a category assumes that such a category exists, that those within it are defined by common experiences and that they are separate and distinct from those outside this category. It presupposes that both race and motherhood are central identities, then imposes these bifocal frames to examine lives that are, in fact, much more multidimensional. But even if there are common experiences among Asian American mothers, what accounts for them? Do these commonalities derive from shared roots in Asian culture, or do they emerge through common experiences as immigrants, children of immigrants, and racial and ethnic minorities in the United States? Does simply being grouped together in the same category become the basis for common identification? Rather than assuming any commonalities among Asian American mothers, this research seeks to explain them but also to make clear where they do not exist or are outweighed by differences of class, sexuality, ability, ethnicity, region, religion, politics, and a myriad of other factors.

Because this book emphasizes the everyday lived experiences of growing up Asian American, how these experiences in turn shape motherhood, and conversely, how motherhood shapes the meaning of being Asian American, it has limited the study's participants to second-generation Asian Americans, broadly defined as those who were born and/or raised in the United States. It includes those born in the United States to immigrant parents, as well as the "1.5 generation," who immigrated as children and completed high school in the United States. (In other words, it does not include international students or those who immigrated as adults.[21]) This selection of participants prioritizes shared racial identification *and* acculturation in the United States, as opposed to presupposing commonalities based on place of birth or ethnic and national origin.

This study is based on participant observation and interviews with over one hundred (N=104) second-generation Asian American mothers; they reflect the diversity that makes up Asian America, but they do not fully represent every dimension of this multifaceted group. I have met and talked with these second-generation Asian American mothers in settings across the United States, ranging from Starbucks to the lobby of the Waldorf Astoria, to public housing, to military bases, to the playground of a Chinese-immersion school, to Ivy League admissions tours, to airport lounges. Some of them had infants less than one year old; some had children leaving for college. Some knew they had wanted to be a mother as long as they could remember; some had actively rejected motherhood and came to it only after a conscious struggle to redefine its terms.

The participants included Asian American mothers who were married, divorced, single, or co-parenting. Some were partnered with Asian Americans, others with Whites or people of color. Some identified as cisgender and straight, and some as queer, gender queer, or trans. They worked in a range of jobs including doctor, lawyer, teacher, professor, special education teacher, construction worker, physical trainer, Chinatown non-profit manager, LGBTQ advocate, human resources manager, filmmaker, hospice social worker, and full-time homemaker. Their parents had come to the United States as international students, transnational executives, undocumented workers, wives of U.S. army personnel, refugees, asylum seekers, and recipients of family reunification visas. Some had been adopted as children; some had adopted their children. They identified themselves according to major ethnic groups such as Chinese, Filipina, Indian, Japanese, Korean, or Vietnamese, but also by more specific identifications, such as Hong Kongers, Hakka, Chamorro, or Kānaka Maoli, in addition to broader terms, such as Pacific Islander, Southeast Asian, Desi, mixed race, or pan-Asian. In short, they illustrate the heterogeneity of the complex racial category that goes by the name Asian American.

Interviews were conducted in regions across the country although the bulk of research focused on urban and suburban areas on the East and West Coasts. The sample included variation across age, income, occupation, and educational attainment. Household and family structures included single, married, cohabitating, monogamous, polyamorous, heterosexual, and same-sex partnerships. The research protocol received Institutional Review Board (IRB) approval and involved recruitment through social media, organizational networks, and snowball sampling. Interviews and field notes were coded and analyzed using NVIVO qualitative software and were lightly edited for clarity. In some case, interviews were conducted over several sessions and follow-up emails or calls, which in the longer profiles have been integrated for narrative flow. Although each chapter concentrates on a relatively few number of cases, they reflect themes expressed and supported by many other respondents in the study. The cases were selected both for the kinds of issues they spoke to, as well as their eloquence in speaking to them.

In addition to careful attention to who the participants were and how they were recruited and represented, a range of interdisciplinary methodological approaches guided interpretation of their narratives. Building on literary scholar Laura Kang's work on the Asian woman as method,[22] I propose the Asian American mother as method by treating the Asian American mother not as a set category but as an analytic through which to view the complex operations of motherhood as a site of othering. This methodological approach is also deeply informed by American studies scholar Kandice Chuh's method of subjectless critique—that is, one defined not by its subjects (i.e., those who identify as Asian American) but by the critical interventions of the field of Asian American studies, especially regarding the complex interconnections between Asia and America.[23] While I appreciate Chuh's important interventions, I see potential for possible misunderstandings. To paraphrase responses from students in a course I have taught on Asian American feminisms, it is still so rare for Asian American women to be subjects that we are not yet ready to be subjectless. However, "subjectless critique" does not mean denying Asian American mothers subjectivity. Rather, proposing "the Asian American mother as method" means *both* positioning Asian American mothers as active subjects and moving beyond their subjective experiences to understand the larger historical and social forces shaping them.

Thus, the methodology aims to highlight the macro-level conditions that turn mothers into others, without losing sight of how these conditions are lived at the micro level and felt very personally. The dilemma is that while centering Asian American mothers as subjects, I develop critiques with which they may not agree or may even strongly disagree. This is very tricky ground. It is not asserting that I or any other researcher knows better than the subjects themselves; rather, we are asking a different set of questions. While taking seriously Asian American mothers' experiences and the meanings they give to them, this book places them within larger social conditions even if the interview subjects themselves do not recognize or situate themselves within these conditions. Drawing on the work of several important traditions and scholars, I develop two main approaches to studying the Asian American mother as both subject and method. Each of these approaches is in conversation with several scholars and scholarly traditions.

First, *maternal narrative plenitude* speaks to the goal of excavating historical, literary, ethnographic, and other sources to discover and recover neglected stories related to motherhood and to amplify their scope and significance. Building on Viet Thanh Nguyen's call to develop and promote greater narrative plenitude, I focus on the elaboration of a wider range of stories about motherhood, and especially about Asian American mothers.[24] The reduction of the diverse mothering approaches of Asian American mothers into the singular trope of tiger mothering is but one illustration of the lack of narrative plentitude regarding Asian American mothers. The need for more plentiful stories of Asian American motherhood includes those of individual mothers breaking out of the tiger mold but extends further to breaking free from this and other limited frames for thinking about Asian American mothering. The following chapters seek to expand maternal narrative plenitude not only among current Asian American mothers but to recover stories from the past by mapping historical discourses that I discuss in more detail later as matritropes of yellow motherhood. In charting the often unnamed yet persistently lurking figure of the yellow mother, I read between the lines of official accounts in search of actual Asian American mothers who have lived under the shadow of these tropes. Relying on the pioneering work of Asian American feminist historians and legal scholars who have done the heavy lifting to unearth and analyze a wide range of sources (official documents, newspapers, personal correspondence and testimonies), I use their archives and historiography to piece together the remnants of these yellow mothers, even when they are not referred to as such. I then follow this trail into the present through interviews with Asian American mothers that show how these historical legacies emerge in the current social worlds that they navigate.

This leads to the second approach, *thick narration*, which addresses the gathering and interpreting of texts, interviews and fieldwork to reveal larger social processes, while also centering the narrative process of the participants themselves. Here I draw on anthropologist Clifford Geertz's method of "thick description," which does not simply record details of everyday life through immersion in a particular field site but interprets their significance in relation to the larger social contexts that shape them.[25] I then seek to integrate this "thick" approach with Black studies scholar Saidiya Hartman's method of "close narration," which seeks to "collapse the subject-object divide" and fill the gaps surrounding those—especially Black women—whose stories have been told, and distorted, by others.[26] Attempting to heed Hartman's call to focus on resilience, radical acts, and collective voices, I have tried to present interview transcripts, along with my own field notes, as partial yet meaningful snapshots that are open to multiple interpretations by the researcher, the researched, and the reader.

This interpretive approach is also heavily informed by the "extended case method" developed by sociologist Michael Burawoy, who explains, "The importance of the single case lies in what it tells us about society as a whole rather than about the population of similar cases."[27] Thus, any given case is not representative of a larger sample; each person's story is unique, but at the same time, it links to other stories to reveal patterns of shared experiences stemming from shared social conditions. For example, no two Asian American mothers are the same, but as a group, virtually all Asian American mothers must contend with societal expectations to raise high-achieving model minority children. whether or not they subscribe to these standards themselves. Currently, they encounter these model minority edicts in the shorthand of being referred to as tiger mother. Therefore, the commonality among Asian American mothers is not that they are all tiger mothers but that they all negotiate common perceptions of them as tiger mothers.

In keeping with this extended case method approach, rather than using one case to generalize about other cases, I regard each interview subject both as a unique person and as part of a collective lens through which to examine the wider social contexts relevant to a particular set of concerns. I do not assert that any of these cases can be used to generalize about Asian American mothers as a whole or that I have captured a representative sample. Instead, each case builds upon the particular experiences of each mother to chart the social structures that shape their mothering, and what their impacts are. In this approach, each case is "extended" to connect to larger conditions of mothering and their significance for Asian American mothers, children, and communities.

As Mario Luis Small argues, such "case study logic" differs from "sampling logic" in that "case study logic can be effectively applied to in-depth interview-based studies, such that the latter may be conceived as not small-*sample* studies but multiple-*case* studies"[28] and that "deviant or unique cases are especially interesting because they provide for ways of developing or extending theories."[29] The specific theoretical framework that I seek to develop, from mother/other to a range of related concepts, extends theorizing on racialized and gendered constructions of mothering broadly, while specifically focusing on how Asian American mothers are positioned as others.

The analysis emphasizes the diversity of experiences of Asian American mothers, while showing how this diversity is often ignored, and how this shapes these mothers' experiences and consciousness. It builds on W. E. B. DuBois influential concept of "double consciousness," that of constantly seeing oneself through the eyes of others and how this results in a splitting of self that that is both detrimental but necessary in many circumstances.[30] I argue that this process takes a specific form as *maternal double consciousness*, in which mothers must not only face the disjuncture between how they see themselves and how they are viewed by society, but they must also negotiate this disjuncture for their children. This maternal double consciousness is especially fraught for Asian American mothers, who are often regarded as having outsized influence on their children, while having little control over the conditions in which they are raising them.

Each mother's experiences and stories of negotiating these challenges, while unique, do not emerge in isolation. Further, while Asian American mothers are connected through certain shared histories and circumstances, they have responded to these in very different ways which manifest as very different political positions over such issues as far-ranging as immigration, affirmative action, or the very meaning of motherhood itself. As a qualitative sociologist and interdisciplinary feminist and Asian American studies scholar, I seek to understand the relationships between the past and the present, the individual and the social, the micro and the macro, and how small and seemingly insignificant social encounters accumulate into widespread social patterns. In addition to developing methodological approaches to address these concerns, I have also aimed to link these to theoretical debates and to develop a specific conceptual grammar to speak to them.

An Asian American Maternal Grammar Book

Parsing the gendered racialization of Asian American motherhood and the significance of various Asian American mother figures, real and imagined, requires a more nuanced vocabulary than is currently available. I have attempted to map out a more robust grammar to conceptualize Asian American motherhood, inspired by Hortense Spillers's field-defining article "Mama's Baby, Papa's Maybe: An American Grammar Book," which theorizes a new lexicon to speak about Black motherhood.[31] In addition to Spillers work, the various terms that follow draw upon a rich body of feminist scholarship on motherhood by women of color, with which I engage more fully in subsequent chapters. I do not claim to be the first to coin the following terms, but I aim to define them in original ways, both to assert broad theoretical arguments and to apply them specifically to the study of Asian American motherhood. So far, I have posited *mother/othering* as an expansive term to name a range of social processes that exclude and pathologize certain mothers while elevating and normalizing others; in the additional terms that follow, I further break down its various dimensions and operations.

Matritropes refers to the widespread and often unconscious stories, stereotypes, and myths that represent certain mothers as a homogenous and often disparaged group—especially but not exclusively with regard to their race—along with the mechanisms through which these tropes circulate. Matritropes do not describe real people or groups but name the pejorative terms and dominant characterizations of Asian American motherhood and reproduction from the perspective of those who deploy them as tools of othering. In particular, I focus on the range of matritropes that have constructed "yellow motherhood" as an abject category. Further, it is impossible to speak of "yellow" motherhood separate from other racialized maternal tropes—whether ones that are relatively rarely spoken, such as of "brown" and "red" mothers, or those that are often explicitly called forth, such as of Black mothers. *Matritroping* speaks to the historical and representational processes that render certain mothers as other, building on Spiller's concept of "pornotroping," which maps how Black women's bodies have been simultaneously sexualized and "ungendered"—stripped of both womanhood and motherhood by the violence of slavery that renders them into mere "flesh."[32] While Spiller's pathbreaking analyses of pornotropes showed how processes of "ungendering" rendered Black women as unmothers, I map parallel but distinct processes through which matritropes of Asian American motherhood result in *hypergendering* and the construction of Asian American mothers as *hypermothers.*

Hypermaternity then names two interconnected processes: first, the sense of overidentification, overinvolvement, and general excess that is projected onto certain mothers, and second, the imbuing of mothers and motherhood with outsized influence to control a range of outcomes—from a child's personality to academic performance, to social status. Asian American mothers are widely regarded as uber hyper-mothers in both senses: their overreach and their omnipotence in controlling their children. Currently, Asian American hypermaternity most often refers to an assumed rabid commitment to what Pawan Dhingra calls "hyper education," but it takes on additional dimensions.[33] Specifically, the othering of Asian American mothers draws upon their perceived "hyperness" in a number of areas, including their hypersexuality and hyperfertility.[34] Thus, hypermaternity, like constructions of Asian American motherhood broadly, is not completely separate from constructions of Asian American womanhood but exaggerates and compounds the tropes on which they depend. Hypermaternity imbues mothers with superpowers that no real mothers possess to control and determine their children's fates, and it contrasts with the reality of multiple forms of exclusion that real mothers confront in general, particularly around their reproduction.

Reproductive exclusion encompasses a range of historical and current social structures that limit the reproductive freedom of particular groups and that utilize reproductive control as a central mechanism to enforce their legal and social exclusion. Defined narrowly, reproductive exclusion is an analytical framework that identifies control of biological reproduction as a central force shaping state regulation of borders and entry. A more expansive interpretation of reproductive exclusion includes the ongoing social exclusion of certain groups already living within a country, including naturalized and native-born citizens, in order to limit biological, social, and cultural reproduction based on constructions of race, gender, sexuality, class, disability, and dependency.

Reproduction exclusion connects broad forms of legal and social exclusion that have denigrated the reproduction of women of color while privileging the reproduction of White women; at the same time, reproductive exclusion centers Asian Americans as the targets of specific policies intended to restrict reproduction through control of immigration and citizenship.[35] While recognizing racialized class animosities as a powerful force driving Chinese exclusion and nativist backlash against immigrants broadly, reproductive exclusion foregrounds recent scholarship that has called for more in-depth examination of the multiple intersections shaping Asian exclusion not just at the border but throughout social life.[36] Reproductive exclusion against Asian Americans operates across multiple social institutions in which mothering is enacted and calls forth various forms of labor by mothers to navigate these institutions.

Intersectional maternal labor identifies the many and often invisible forms of embodied and emotional care work in which mothers engage. Expanding beyond its current focus on perinatal labor and delivery, this term encompasses the ongoing and diverse forms of paid and unpaid work required not only to raise children but to resist ongoing forms of reproductive exclusion and mother/othering. Evelyn Nakano Glenn provided the influential framework of "the racial division of paid reproductive labor" to demonstrate how the social reproduction of White women and families institutionalized the servitude of Black women and extracted low-wage service work from immigrant domestics and nannies.[37] Rhacel Parreñas, Catherine Ceniza Choy, and others have examined the work of nurses and domestic workers, many from the Philippines, showing how they are valued for their cheap reproductive labor in caring for others but face barriers when seeking to immigrate with and care for their own children and families.[38] Shaped by these legacies of immigration and work, Asian American mothers negotiate various forms of intersectional maternal labor that involves both paid and unpaid work. At home, it can range from feeding and caring for children and teaching them about homeland customs and languages to countering anti-Asian racism at school to resisting the tiger mother trope. In the workplace, it can include expectations to educate co-workers about Asian cultures, smooth over conflicts, provide ethnic food for work events, and generally play the role of "office mother."

Finally, to *imagine motherwise* is to envision new possibilities for motherhood based not on bonds of sameness but on recognition of shared needs and investments, even and especially across entrenched and escalating divisions. Imagine motherwise responds to Kandice Chuh's call to "imagine otherwise" by centering Asian American studies in its modes of critique rather than solely in shared racial or ethnic identities, as discussed earlier with regard to her concept of subjectless critique.[39] To imagine motherwise likewise asks for a rethinking of motherhood beyond notions of identity to address the structures and practices that encapsulate Asian American motherhood in ideologies of model minority success. To reimagine Asian American motherhood requires challenging the standards not only of tiger mothering but of model minoritization and to understand how they feed off each other. It also requires doing the work of resisting mother/othering and forging new ways of being mothers and envisioning motherhood.

All these concepts build upon important theoretical debates that address motherhood and reproduction writ large, but this book centers their operations with regard to Asian American mothers while developing approaches that extend beyond them. I develop and apply these terms to frame the narratives of Asian American mothers in the subsequent chapters, as follows.

Chapter Organization

This introduction has introduced the book's main arguments and concepts regarding the othering of Asian American mothers and the historical and contemporary processes through which it unfolds. The subsequent chapters are organized to support these arguments, first by focusing on debates about the tiger mother to illustrate these theoretical concepts through the lived experiences of Asian American mothers. Next, I examine the historical contexts of reproductive exclusion that have positioned Asian American mothers as mother/others and how these contexts persist into the present. I then examine current conditions of Asian American mothering, focusing on how mother/othering operates in various sites, mainly (1) laws and policies, (2) family, community and culture, (3) schools, and (4) workplaces. Practices of mothering and othering are grounded in a broad range of historical and contemporary social institutions that not only control motherhood and reproduction but to impose various forms of mother/othering. These institutions operate in distinct but coordinated ways to impose a sense of otherness on Asian American mothers and families. The following chapters show how Asian American mothers negotiate these various institutional sites and how they resist the specific forms of mother/othering that they engender.

Chapter 1—How The Tiger Mother Became Every Asian American Mother

This chapter focuses on the tiger mother as the most well-known iteration in a long line of figurations that have rendered Asian American mothers as others. It explores why it is important to take the tiger mother seriously in all its permutations—as a specific person, book, media spectacle, and parenting style but, most of all, as a matritrope about Asian American motherhood. It shows why it is worth tracking the evolution of the tiger mother as an interesting phenomenon in its own right but also as a rich illustration of mother/othering that significantly impacts the lives of actual Asian American mothers and families in real time.

Chapter 2—No Country for Asian American Mothers

This chapter explores the various historical tropes that have cast Asian American mothers as others, even and especially those born and raised in the United States. Situating the tiger mother as merely the current iteration of a long line of mother/other figures, this chapter focuses on how U.S. laws and institutions have treated Asian American mothers ambivalently as both model reproducers and foreign menaces. It examines how various matritropes have been mobilized to impose different forms of reproductive exclusion that have limited the rights of mothers, families, and racial groups through control of their biological, social, and cultural reproduction. Rather than a linear progression, it examines overlapping and recurring Asian American matritropes from the unassimilable alien mother to the enemy mother, to the model minority mother.

Chapter 3—Mothering Against/With Culture

This chapter traces Asian American women's journeys to and through motherhood and their roots in vastly diverse cultural backgrounds and racialized experiences. Asian American mothers reject the false choice between holding on to essentialized versions of Asian culture versus total assimilation to the dictates of U.S. model minority racialization. Instead, they actively create new cultural identities and practices that are distinctly Asian American. Their everyday choices—ranging from food to language, to community connections—disrupt ideas that Asian American culture is something fixed, let alone passed on to subsequent generations in prescribed ways. Rather, Asian American mothering is an active and varied site for creating new forms of Asian American *cultures*, but constantly against persistent reproductive exclusion and mother/othering.

Chapter 4—Schooling Mother/Others

This chapter addresses how schools and education broadly serve as sites of othering not just of children but of mothers. Shifting the focus from how mothers influence their children's schooling, it examines the powerful influence that schools have on shaping mothers. Building on scholarship on Asian American "hyper education" and "hyperselectivity," this chapter shows how interactions in schools among mothers, teachers, administrators, and students often cast Asian American mothers as hypermothers and reproduce them in these roles. As intricately connected social institutions, schools and motherhood impose a *hidden maternal curriculum* that teaches mothers not only what their acceptable roles are in their children's schools but what kind of mother is acceptable. Through school interactions, Asian American mothers learn that they are collectively regarded as tiger mothers who exceed the boundaries of appropriate involvement in their children's education, but they also find ways to challenge these messages. Just as school is a playground for children to learn about gender, so is it a central site for mothers to learn about motherhood, as well as what it means to be a mother/other.

Chapter 5—Mother/Othering at Work

Mothers do not merely work for a paycheck; they work to claim racial belonging for themselves and their families. Facing more than just a "second shift" of balancing career and domesticity, Asian American mothers feel pressured to constantly prove their worth while countering their otherness. This chapter shows how work-family balance is almost impossible for Asian American women to achieve, as the dictates of model minority reproduction demand that they continue to demonstrate their own high achievement while raising the next generation of high achievers. *Intersectional maternal labor* demands the constant performance of excellence both at home and in the workplace. This labor can elicit high costs even for professional women who meet model minority standards, let alone for those who are perceived as falling short.

Conclusion—From Mother/Othering to Imagining Motherwise

Far from creating a global village, mothers have squared off in an increasingly high-stakes *global mommy wars*. What are the costs of an ongoing failure of imagination in which many mothers view each other as enemies rather than allies? What are the possibilities of reimagining motherhood beyond a zero-sum maternal hunger game? The conclusion applies the book's main arguments to envision possibilities to *imagine motherwise*. Centering Asian American mothering, it argues for terms of belonging beyond normative standards of motherhood and reproduction. Imagining motherwise is a call to support and value all mothers, not because they measure up to model minority standards and raise children who do the same but because of who they are, and aspire to be, in their own right, on their own terms.

1 *How the Tiger Mother Became Every Asian American Mother*

There's all this fear that Asians are taking over. That's why things definitely get put off on the Asian American mother syndrome, almost like they're the other in society. It's like, "Look at the Asian American mothers—they're pushing their children, but they're not really part of us."

NATALIE, interview, Japanese American, professor

Unlike your typical Western overscheduling soccer mom, the Chinese mother believes that 1) schoolwork always comes first; 2) an A-minus is a bad grade; 3) your children must be two years ahead of their classmates in math; 4) you must never compliment your children in public; 5) if your child ever disagrees with a teacher or coach, you must always take the side of the teacher or coach; 6) the only activities your children are permitted to do are those in which they can eventually win a medal; and 7) that medal must be gold.

AMY CHUA, *Battle Hymn of the Tiger Mother* (2011a)

Chua's construction of Chinese American motherhood excludes and attempts to render invisible any version of this identity that does not fit into its highly hierarchical and market driven construction of that position. . . . The equation of Chinese mothers and "tiger mothers" in the public's mind is perhaps now and forever firmly implanted.

JULIA H. LEE, "Model Maternity" (2016)

In Natalie's words above, and as many Asian American mothers interviewed for this book conferred, they are often regarded as *other*, "not really part of us."[1] But who is the "us" against whom Asian American mothers are set apart? For to define an "us," it is necessary to designate a "them," and in order to establish who is an ideal mother, it is necessary to determine a mother/other. The tiger mother serves as a particularly instructive case of how Asian American mothers have come to occupy the position of an especially ambivalent form of maternal other, both model and peril, admired and despised, invisible and hyper-visible, held up yet held apart. Rather than assessing the pros and cons of tiger mothering this chapter is more concerned with asking how is it that so many Asian American mothers are already collectively assumed to fit the bill?

Overriding the vast diversity among Asian American mothers, all too often, one gets elevated—or elevates herself—as spokesperson for *all* Asian American mothers. Case in point: one Chinese American Yale law school professor proclaims herself a tiger mother, and now, all Asian American mothers have to answer to that name. Amy Chua's book and Chua herself gave a name and face to the often unspoken, yet visceral clash between two contrasting models of motherhood: "tough love" approaches geared toward preparing children to compete in a dog-eat-dog world vs. "free range" styles that prioritize secure emotional attachment and find-your-best-self personal fulfillment. Further, by branding the tiger mother as explicitly a "Chinese mother," Chua unleashed a more specific set of anxieties regarding global competition with China and with Asia broadly. Although Chua is Chinese American, the media and public response to the book revealed how she and other Asian Americans were easily lumped together into a singular category of "foreign threat."

Ironically, as Julia H. Lee argues above, although Chua has positioned herself as a representative of Asian American motherhood, she expresses discomfort toward and does not seem to dialogue directly with actual Chinese or Asian American mothers. She adds, "the mothers that Chua most readily identifies as outsiders to her tiger motherhood are the Asian nationals she encounters, whom she describes as ineluctably foreign and vaguely suspicious."[2] Thus, Chua herself has contributed to the othering of Asian American mothers in her own ambivalent and contradictory claims to speak for them. This irony has not been lost on Asian American mothers, who have been left to deal with the consequences of Chua, her book, and the othering it both capitalized on and further fueled.

How has the tiger mother frame positioned Asian Americans at the center of debates not just about what constitutes good or bad mothering but about the value and meaning of motherhood itself? Why did one Asian American mother's memoir escalate into a national and global referendum on motherhood? And while drawing much attention to Asian American mothers, how has it simultaneously contributed to their erasure, marginalization, and othering?

Following, I map the long trail of the tiger mother as an interesting phenomenon in itself, but even more as an entry point to engage in conversation with the Asian American mothers whom I interviewed and as a vivid illustration of key concepts that I will develop throughout this book. After taking a deeper dive into Chua's *Battle Hymn* book and public response, I share commentary from Asian American mothers who offered their various takes on the controversies it engendered. First, Natalie, who was introduced at the beginning of this chapter, described what it means to grapple with being cast as a tiger mother, while Anh shared what it means to be denied this title. Next, I analyze the tiger mother as a telling case study that illustrates the main argument of this book: that mothering and othering are intricately linked processes, in general, and most pointedly with regard to Asian Americans.

What Exactly Is a Tiger Mother, And Who Gets to Decide?

Beyond its origin story, the tiger mom has transformed into a matri-trope of unapologetically hard-driving mothers who are willing to do whatever it takes to ensure their children's success, and this trope wears a decidedly Asian face. Just to be very clear: this book is *not* arguing that the tiger mother is not related to Chua, her book, and the headlines it generated, or that it is not a discernible parenting approach, or that it is not a stereotype—and a racist one at that—but that it is not *only* those things. The heated debates about the tiger mothering are simultaneously the product of a very specific twenty-first-century moment and a long history of negative representations of Asian American women. At the same time, while the tiger mother has come to mean many things to different people, often unmoored from its originator, it is worth tracing it back to its source.

As defined by Chua herself, the tiger mother is synonymous with "the Chinese mother," and antithetical to the "Western" mom. Chua further framed tiger mothering as a clash between "Eastern" (disciplined, academically high-achieving) and "Western" (coddling, feeling-centered) approaches to parenting. This framing was repeated throughout the book's publicity tour, which began with an excerpt in the *Wall Street Journal* under the provocative title "Why Chinese Mothers Are Superior," along with a reader poll asking, "Which style of parenting is best for children—Permissive Western or Demanding Eastern?"[3] Even more striking than the over 35,000 responses it generated is the framing of the question itself: not only does it set up two poles of parenting—indulgent vs. hard-driving—but it racializes these polarities as East versus West. Granted, Chua herself set up this dichotomy between Eastern and Western parenting or at least capitalized on it, but the question remains, why did so many, so easily go along with her claims?

Chua claimed that her book was a memoir, her own personal story, and was not meant as a how-to book or as a representation of all Chinese mothers. However, the U.S. media and public saw it differently—as a judgment or even an attack against Western parenting. In an interview with Katie Couric, prominent blogger Liz Gumbinner observed that Chua's book "struck right at the core of American values even beyond parenting, which is the idea that the pursuit of happiness is somehow illegitimate or less important than the pursuit of achievement and success." Further, she noted that the usually fractious mommy blogosphere was nearly united against tiger mothering, as "it felt literally like a very foreign attack on our value system."[4] In short, Chua's book tapped into broad anxieties about the undermining of "American values"—not to mention U.S. economic, political, and cultural power—and channeled these anxieties into heated debates about mothering. Both the implicit and explicit discourses around tiger mothering centered Asians broadly as emerging threats, both globally and locally, but pinpointed this distorted and homogenizing representation of Asian American motherhood as the source of this threat.

Years removed, whether or not people know Chua or have read her book or are even aware of the media frenzy that surrounded it, they know of the tiger mother. References to the tiger mother are still ubiquitous, as in Jennifer Senior's best-selling book *All Joy and No Fun: The Paradox of Modern Parenthood*, in which she criticizes the ways mothers are held to an "unattainable ideal—whether it's Donna Reed in Hilldale or the 'Tiger Mom'"—thus placing the tiger mother alongside other iconic maternal figures such as the 1950s television housewife.[5] Herein, I believe, lies the immense discomfort with the tiger mother: it is one thing for a White, middle-class, fictional mother to be held up as the ideal; it is an altogether different and far more unsettling proposition when the mother setting the standard is a real-life Asian American one.

Over a decade since the publication of Chua's book, the tiger mother label and the anxieties it triggered have not disappeared. In a retrospective, the *Boston Globe* recounted the "coast-to-coast maternal nervous breakdowns" precipitated by the tiger mother book, noting that even in light of Chua's subsequent provocative writings on political tribalism and the imminent threats to American democracy, "it's 'Tiger Mother' that still stings."[6] But why did the tiger mother wield such a powerful sting? And if so many White middle-class mothers felt stung by the tiger mother, how much more deeply did Asian American mothers feel this sting?

What It Means to Be Perceived as a Tiger Mother

The following quotes capture just a small swath of the varied responses of Asian American mothers to the tiger mother book, its model of success-oriented parenting, and what it means to mother in the shadow of this trope.

> I don't know how many people would, for fear of being ostracized, praise any parts of her [Chua's] parenting. I thought there were kernels of wisdom in there. Such as you have to work very hard to get some things; you have to give up some things. . . . I think children are tougher than we give them credit for.
>
> SUYEON, interview, Korean American, lawyer

> I didn't read it [the Tiger Mom book] but it doesn't take a brain surgeon to figure it out, especially if you've lived part of it. . . . I've had some conversations with my cousins about how insanely abusive our parents were in this tiger mom model. . . . Like one of my cousins had to stand on one foot for hours. So yeah, she made a lot of money and could retire at thirty-five, but she's plagued by health problems and

> has no partner and doesn't even see herself as capable of marriage. So is that successful?
>
> KAREN, interview, Korean American–mixed race, non-profit manager

> My understanding is that she [Chua] was mostly trying to poke fun at herself and present her own situation, herself, and her family. And at the same time, the fact that she did that, it's like, "You're making it very hard for us Asian American women mothers! Because you're presenting this image." . . . Society is so lazy about really spending any time looking at you as an individual; they would much rather have it presented to them and say, "Okay, I already read about this. Because you're Asian, so you are what I just read."
>
> CARA, interview, Chinese American, arts administrator

While Karen labeled Chua and her tiger mother approach as "insanely abusive," Suyeon appreciated parts of the book, especially its recognition of the hard work required to raise high-achieving children but noted that most Asian Americans were hesitant to share this viewpoint out of "fear of being ostracized." Cara felt that Chua had been trying to "poke fun" at herself and had been misrepresented as speaking for all Asian Americans, but nonetheless, had fed into negative stereotypes that made it harder for Asian American mothers to be perceived as individuals.[7] In sum, Asian American mothers in this study had wide-ranging opinions regarding Chua, her book, and the pros and cons of tiger mothering as an approach, but many had the common experience of being tagged as tiger mothers.

It is way past time to listen to what these mothers have to tell us not only about tiger mothering but about the current state of Asian American motherhood and the conditions that render it as an otherhood. The following two mothers, Natalie and Anh, share very different takes on how this trope has come to define them—or not—but in either case, how it has overshadowed many of their own concerns and experiences as Asian American mothers.

Natalie: The (In)Convenience of the "Tiger Mom Thing"

It's a bit too convenient for the media to have this Tiger Mom thing. I don't think it's an Asian mother thing; it's a professional mother thing, a working mother's issue. That's why it's nice to make it otherwise. It's really about society's fear of women who are able to be successful and mothers, and Asian women are seen as very successful—and that can be threatening. . . . But where is it coming from? Would people be so threatened by tiger moms if they didn't feel threatened by China?

As a divorced mother attempting to balance a high-powered career and raising two teenagers, Natalie described the many challenges of being one of the first women of color in a leadership position at her workplace, while trying to stay on top of carpooling and paying bills. She summed up the backlash against tiger mothering as a kind of racial subterfuge, distracting from the many problems confronting U.S. society by stoking fears about Asia and China in particular. Natalie felt that the tiger mother obscures the realities of Asian American mothers like herself who are negotiating complex family situations while working in full-time, demanding jobs. Even more, she saw the "tiger mother thing" as scapegoating Asian and Asian American mothers for fueling the competitiveness and stress that has come to define contemporary motherhood.

Natalie had recently moved to a new city to accept a promotion and start a new chapter of her life as a single mother. Her biggest concern was supporting her two children through these transitions, especially as her daughter was having difficulty making friends at her new school. She noted that although "there was never any eye-pulling or words that were obviously racist," she had a "gnawing feeling" that being one of the only Asian American students at the school was contributing to her daughter's challenges. But when Natalie reached out to the school for support, she was surprised that the teacher instead implied that Natalie herself was the source of her daughter's difficulties. She recounted:

> The teacher just couldn't seem to hear me, that I wasn't there to complain about grades. You want to talk to your child's teacher at school about how they're doing? You have to work hard to not be perceived as "This is an *Asian mother* who just wants her child to succeed." It's a huge generalization. You have to figure out a way to put it to make them believe you and to not make you into the problem. They assumed my real agenda: for my kids to get straight A's and get into Harvard, of course. So I just talked to my daughter about how she could handle it. The school didn't help at all.

In the end, Natalie was left on her own to figure out how to support her children, which she mainly did over conversations at the dinner table—"building connection and just being there, asking them if they had friends, if they enjoyed school, if they were happy. Those are the priorities." Given how clear and committed Natalie was to her priorities as a mother, why did others assume her priorities were not her children's well-being and happiness, but their grades? Natalie immediately offered her take on why others misjudged her: "It's the tiger mother stuff! It's those *Asian* mothers who do this stuff!"

Interestingly, throughout the interview, Natalie self-identified her race in different ways depending on the situation—referring to herself mainly as Japanese or Asian American. However, when describing how others saw her, she used the term "Asian mother" or "Asian tiger mother." This language was telling, revealing how Natalie made a distinction between how she self-identified versus how others perceived her and how the tiger mother figured into this gap. Natalie further noted that the tiger mother term was applied to virtually all Asian American mothers, turning them into a caricature, rather than recognizing them as individuals, let alone understanding them as part of a complex, heterogeneous group. For instance, rather than responding to Natalie's various concerns about her daughter's bumpy entrance into a new school, the teacher seemed to assume that Natalie was interested only in her daughter's grades.

The tiger mother stereotype seemed to provide a ready-made explanation that any problems encountered by her child were a product of pressure from Natalie herself, shutting down any meaningful discussion of problems stemming from the school environment, let alone from racism toward Asian Americans in the broader society. As widespread as these presumptions of tiger mothering have become, they do not apply universally, as not every Asian American mother is presumed to be a tiger mother, and not every Asian American mother wants to distance herself from this stereotype. In fact, some—like Anh—take pride in identifying themselves as tiger mothers and take issue with those who refuse to recognize them as such.

Anh: You Can't Be a Tiger Mother If You're "on the System"

> I ended up having to quit my job after a long leave of absence [due to postpartum complications], and that was when bills started piling up and I had to go on the system. So, it's like, you want to do better, you want to get off assistance, you want to have your own home. I want to move [out of Section 8 housing], but then my rent's gone up six times, my daycare's gone up six times. I think people who don't have that experience think things about people who are in that situation, and I was one of those people! You never think you will be that person who goes on the system. . . . So for me, having the experience has helped me understand things. . . . I actually think I'm a tiger mother, but no one else sees me that way.

Anh described herself as Vietnamese Amerasian, partnered but not married, a medical assistant in training— and an unapologetic tiger mother. In contrast to Natalie, who possessed high academic and professional credentials and saw the tiger mother label as a limiting stereotype, Anh regarded herself as excluded from the tiger mother category due to her reliance on government support. However, rather than simply taking on its popular meaning as pushing children to heights of achievement in academics and extracurricular activities, Anh redefined the meaning of tiger mothering according to her own priorities.

When I asked her why she considered herself to be a tiger mother, Anh did not automatically refer to high aspirations for her son's educational and professional achievement; instead, she offered her own criteria for tiger mothering and how she met them. These ranged from her fierce protectiveness of her children against bullying, her commitment to extended breastfeeding, her insistence on raising her children with a strong sense of their Vietnamese heritage, and her efforts to get off "the system" of government subsidies for housing and childcare. But after struggling with birthing complications with both of her children, working multiple jobs, and trying unsuccessfully to complete her medical assistant training, Anh could not make ends meet, even with public assistance. She lamented that due to these circumstances, no one but herself recognized her as a tiger mother.

For Anh, being a tiger mother spanned a range of values, many of which revolved around instilling "strong family ties and respect for the elders," along with overall respect for Vietnamese culture, especially food. She gave the following account, highlighting the many influences on her mothering: not only her Asian cultural heritage but specific dynamics of her childhood experiences, her current work responsibilities, her son's school and medical providers, and her relationship with her partner and her children's father, Trung, a Vietnamese immigrant.

My son, Sam, says a lot of things—because they're children! He may not see them as hurtful. I said them when I was younger too, but I think his father is most hurt when he says things like "I'm American, not Vietnamese. I don't like Vietnamese cooking." My son went through that big, huge, long phase—they say that it's a children's thing about eating, etc. But he eats a lot of Vietnamese food. And then they go into the school system and it's like "I don't like Vietnamese food!" All of a sudden? When we take him to a Vietnamese restaurant, he loves squid, and when we go to a grocery store, the roast pork with the crispy skin. But then he was in the school and in the daycare and then coming home and eating Vietnamese food, and that started the problem. So, then his father would give in and cook him American food. He would cook Vietnamese food for us and the baby, and Sam would have this separate macaroni and cheese—every day. I'm trying to control everything from at work:

"No, he needs to eat what we cook!"
His father is like, "But he won't eat it."
"Well, if he won't eat it, then it's his decision, but you're not a short-order cook."
"Well, I can't put him to bed hungry."
"Well, he needs to eat what we eat!"

That is my upbringing. Whatever my mother cooked we ate it.

Anh's insistence that her son eat Vietnamese food at home stemmed from a range of mothering concerns and influences: her desire for him to appreciate his culture but also for him to respect those who fed him and not to treat his own parents like "short-order cooks." She wanted Sam to appreciate Vietnamese food, just as she had appreciated her own mother's cooking, and to recognize the labor that went into it.

These struggles over how to feed their children also demonstrated Anh's commitment to co-parent with Trung but also to challenge him when they disagreed. In fact, Anh shared that she was holding off getting married to Trung not simply because of their arguments about food but due to concerns about his family's dynamics, particularly their penchant for gambling. She further emphasized that while she wanted her children to nurture their sense of Vietnamese American identity, she did not want them immersed in all aspects of Vietnamese culture, especially elements related to money and male privilege.

> We almost split many times over the years. It was mainly because his parents, his family, his Vietnamese friends intervening. The women, I guess, really don't have too much to say. It's sort of the men who control the relationship. I've mentioned before the strong family ties—it always seems like somebody is always getting married or dying in Vietnam and therefore they need our money for something. That has been a really big bone of contention.

While seeking to develop a strong sense of pride in her children regarding certain aspects of Vietnamese culture, like food and language, Anh distanced herself from other aspects that she associated with being part of a close Vietnamese community, such as the expectation that women defer to men, especially on financial issues.

Further, Anh did not think there was just one uniform model of mothering in Vietnamese culture, noting that her class background and immigrating at a young age were also significant influences, along with her mixed-race background. She further noted that both her working-class White American father and her Vietnamese immigrant mother, despite many cultural differences, parented in similar "tough-love" ways that were very different from the more emotionally attuned approach of the college-educated parents of some Asian American friends that she grew up with. An incident that illustrated this was when she and her sister were racially bullied at school about their appearance, especially their hair, and neither of her parents intervened.

> So, growing up, we stood out like sore thumbs. We had hair down to my ankles and were getting beat up every day in school.
>
> *By whom?*
> The White girls didn't like it. They would pull your hair. The boys would stick gum in your hair. I think the hair pulling is probably the most out of all the things—tripping you in gym class, whatever, there's whipping the ball at you, you have that kind of thing—but the hair pulling. We used to go home and beg my mother to cut our hair. So, she cut it.
>
> *How old were you?*
> Well, we came here when I was five, so my sister might've been nine or ten, I was probably seven or eight.
>
> *How did your father react?*
> He didn't exactly take their side, but he said he hated long hair. He thinks women should have their hair cut short.

Rather than confronting the school and the students who were pulling their hair, Anh's father took issue with her and her sister's long hair as the problem, and Anh's mother took it into her own hands to cut it. Anh brought up this experience from her childhood in the context of explaining how different she was from her own parents, who despite their racial differences both parented in what she saw as a more working-class, hands-off approach.

Instead of simply referring to her Vietnamese heritage or Asian American identity, Anh situated her more hands-on mothering approach as arising within specific sites of mothering—her son's school, her workplace, and her family and community—and how they were interconnected. Especially regarding her attempts to protect her son from bullying and to raise him bilingually, none of these sites nor the people with whom she interacted within them offered much support. Instead, they contributed to treating her as an *other* regarding various aspects of her mothering, most notably her attempts to teach her son the Vietnamese language.

> The speech and language therapist that came to the house, she was trying to get him to speak and say a word, and I said, "He may not know those in English. He may know those in Vietnamese." They never came out and said, "Don't speak Vietnamese to him." But they said, "Maybe if you spoke English, only one language, it would be easier for him." This was while I was pregnant with my daughter, so there could have been some regression on his part, but they said it was because he was bilingual. They come into your house and question everything—whether there were complications during pregnancy, at birth, after; is there anything going on in the home; does he have hearing difficulty? So, much to our dismay, his father and I, we only spoke English to him so there would be no further evaluation. I do not consider him bilingual now. And my daughter unfortunately was an infant at that time. We never taught her; we never really even tried to teach her. It was really heartbreaking.

When I asked Anh what made giving up on her children's bilingualism so heartbreaking, she paused and took a deep breath. Sharing that she strongly identified as an "Amerasian" of mixed race, she also noted that she had grown up "on the fringes" of both the Vietnamese immigrant community and mainstream American society.

> It still surprises me now that people look at me and they don't see it—they are surprised to find out that I am Vietnamese. Ever since

around the time when the Amerasians came here, my joke was that I was an undercover Vietnamese person. People would say things not knowing I was Vietnamese, then they'd have to warn each other, "She understands you, by the way."

Anh was proud that she had invested a great deal of time and energy in learning the Vietnamese language, and she wanted to pass this fluency on to her son and daughter. This was especially important to her as she felt that both she and her children where not visibly recognizable as Vietnamese, and most people thought they looked "American," which she understood to mean White.

My children look very American, except for their eyes. Well, American people tell me that the children look Asian, and Asian people tell me the kids look American. So it's like, I think they identify with American people because they are around them all the time. But when Sam was younger, I think he might have identified with Asians because he would go up to an Asian-looking person, an adult even, and think that that person was an uncle or relative of some sort and try to speak to them in Vietnamese. And now that time has passed.

For Anh, speaking Vietnamese was a powerful way to assert her Vietnamese identity, rather than being "undercover," and she wanted this for her children as well. Unfortunately, she gave up on raising them bilingually, as she was discouraged by both teachers and medical professionals, and she regretted losing this window of opportunity for them to develop fluency.

Although Anh proudly claimed the mantle of tiger mothering, when explaining what aspects of her mothering qualified her as such, she articulated a very different interpretation from that in mainstream media discourse. But even according to her own revised criteria, she felt disqualified in most people's eyes as a tiger mother by the mere fact of her being in the welfare system. Thus, Anh articulated an understanding of tiger mother status as determined not merely by an individual's mothering style or aspirations for her children but by the degree to which she met externally imposed standards of model minority professional achievement, or at the very least, the model of a self-sufficient, nuclear family unit.

Theorizing Asian American Mothers' Lived Experiences of the Tiger Mother Trope

What can we learn from Natalie's and Anh's stories in response to the questions that the preceding pages have posed about mothering as a site of othering, and what additional questions do they raise? Following, I apply the various concepts that I have developed in this book, grounding them in the examples provided by Natalie and Anh while connecting them to larger scholarly and public debates about Asian American mothers and reproductive politics broadly.

As Natalie noted, Asian American mothers are seen as too successful, but too successful relative to whom? In contrast, Anh shared that she was not successful enough, but again, in comparison to whom? Both Natalie and Anh felt that they were beholden not just as individuals and as mothers but as Asian American mothers to the standards of model minority success that undergird tiger mothering. Further, whether they met or fell short of them, the mere sense that were being held up to the standards of tiger mothering produced not only tensions with other mothers but a sense of being othered from social groups and institutions.

Natalie's account prompts us to ask, why wasn't she believed when she expressed concern about her child's social and emotional challenges? Even if she was concerned about her child's academic success, why was her concern judged as pressure rather than support? How did these encounters shape Natalie as a mother; her relationships with her children, school, and community; and her ability to focus on her career and other commitments? And how do her experiences compare with other Asian American mothers?

The unspoken logic that undergirded the interactions with the teacher at Natalie's children's school seemed to go something like this: Natalie is an Asian American mother; Asian American mothers are tiger mothers; so Natalie must be a tiger mother and she herself must be the source of her daughter's difficulties. But Anh experienced a different kind of subtext, as her reliance on various forms of government support disqualified her for the category of tiger mother, revealing how this status is closely linked to model minority standards of high achievement or at least self-reliance.

Anh's narrative maps uncomfortable territory, as it violates many orthodoxies in Asian American studies, gender studies, sociology, and other fields that privilege narratives of resistance, despite much evidence that Asian Americans position themselves across the political spectrum, and many express conservative views especially with regard to the family.[8] Similar to Anh, rather than resisting being labeled as tiger mothers, a significant number of Asian Americans have embraced the term or aspired to measure up to it, or at the very least, they recognize it as a style of mothering with which they are familiar. But what is the source of this familiarity? How have these standards of tiger mothering circulated and come to be so widely associated with Asian American mothers?

The tiger mother discourse operates as a *matritrope*—that is, a collection of ideologies about motherhood that circulate widely in the form of taken-for-granted stories about specific groups of mothers and their presumed qualities, most often but not always attributed to their race. Both Natalie and Anh commented on how they are held up to the tiger mother, either as its embodiment or its antithesis.

More than just an unfortunate stereotype stemming from one woman's memoir or the media frenzy it generated, the tiger mother lives in the world now as a well-known matritrope about Asian American motherhood. Seen as both admirable and threatening, it is simultaneously a subtype of the larger trope of the model minority and its own distinct trope tied explicitly to motherhood as the driver of hyper-achievement. Matritropes are usually but not always negative, but even when framed in complimentary terms, they are harmful, as they flatten diverse groups and complex experiences into reductive story lines. In some cases, matritropes can be traced to an actual person (such as Chua), but even when this is the case, they transcend their architects to scaffold systems of belief about whole groups of mothers and their associated qualities.

Chua and the tiger mother matritrope illustrate perceptions of Asian American *hypermaternity* in two main ways. First, the tiger mother is seen as hyperinvolved in her children's lives, to the extent of being controlling and abusive. Second, as illustrated by Natalie's account of interactions with her daughter's teacher, the tiger mother trope gives outsized importance to the influence of the Asian American mother: she is imbued with the power to shape not only her children's achievement but to reshape different social institutions in her image and to her advantage. In contrast, Anh's case reveals how the seeming hypervigilance of Asian American mothers in their children's schools is more often a response to conditions that they did not create and have little control over, ranging from bullying to lack of support for bilingual education.

The widespread and enduring circulation of the tiger mother trope reveals how constructions of motherhood are bolstered by and entrenched within structures of reproductive exclusion. Further, just as reproductive justice has been articulated by Black feminist scholars and activists but has broad theoretical relevance, reproductive exclusion is grounded in Asian American feminist scholarship but is not limited to Asian Americans. The tiger mother trope circulates within and further solidifies obdurate, institutionalized forms of reproductive exclusion against Asian American mothers and families, from denial of entry to inability to claim full rights as citizens, which in turn, impose various forms of othering. Natalie experienced reproductive exclusion in subtle ways by teachers and other families at her daughter's schools, while Anh experienced exclusion in more overt forms, from the lack of support of medical professionals to the various forms of discrimination related to the social welfare system. Thus, the tiger mother matritrope and its long reach provide a lens to track the operations of reproductive exclusion across a wide range of social institutions and sites.

Discourses about tiger mothering emerge and are enforced within concrete *sites of mother/othering* ranging from families, communities, schools, and workplaces to the medical establishment and the legal system, This chapter has mapped the tiger mother matritrope through these various sites, showing how mothering and othering operate vis-à-vis each other, as well as in and through these interconnected social institutions. Natalie focused mostly on schools as the main site that shaped the forms of reproductive exclusion and mother/othering that she encountered, whereas Anh focused on a range of sites, from family meals to the offices of school counselors and speech therapists. The tiger mother trope emerges across these varied sites, showing how both mothering and othering are enacted across seemingly distinct and disparate social contexts.

Contending with widespread perceptions that they are tiger mothers thus emerges as a distinct form of Asian American motherwork but also illustrates more broadly the concept of *intersectional maternal labor*, which names the distinct forms of caring labor that mothers enact and negotiate in order to raise families within the structures of race, ethnicity, gender, sexuality, class, ability, and many other intersections. Natalie performed maternal labor in seeking support for her daughter while negotiating the subtle and overt forms of othering from teachers who saw her as a tiger mother. Anh's efforts focused more on negotiating the intersections of class, disability, race, and gender around the labor of cooking and trying to raise her children bilingually and biculturally.

Both Natalie and Anh constantly negotiated mother/othering, but they did not merely acquiesce or assimilate to its terms. Instead, they *imagined motherwise* by questioning how they were perceived, pushing back on these perceptions, and rewriting their own priorities as Asian American mothers. Even if they could not always change their circumstances, whether the institutional pressures of schools to raise their children monolingually or the framing of them as tiger mothers, they envisioned possibilities beyond what was offered them, even when they could not fully realize them.

Challenges of Taking on the Tiger Mother

Asian American mothers were far from united in their attitudes toward this style of mothering, but they were joined together by having to take on the tiger mother in various ways and guises. According to dictionary.com, to *take on* means "to challenge or contend against," as in taking on a bully; but it can also mean "to acquire or assume," as in taking on a new light or taking on new responsibilities. Whether or not they ascribe to this form of mothering, Asian American mothers have had to take on the tiger mother in both these senses.

Likewise, this chapter has taken on the tiger mother based on both meanings. First, it has taken on Chua and her book according to the primary definition of challenging not only what she said but also how she positioned herself—and was positioned—as the authority on Asian American mothers and how they mother. Second, it has examined how Asian American women have had to take on the tiger mother in the sense of having this label imposed on them and then having to respond to it. Thus, this chapter takes on the tiger mother in both senses of the term to explore (1) how Asian American mothers are assumed to fit the tiger mother mold and (2) how they push back against these perceptions and against the trope itself. In other words, it has examined both what it means to be classified as a tiger mother and how Asian American mothers contest being turned into this particular kind of mother/other.

Although I believe that there is much to be learned from tracking the twists and turns (or hisses and meows) of the tiger mother, I sympathize with those mothers—Asian American and others—who are tired of having to think about tiger mothering and would rather take a pass. I hear their concerns and have grappled with many of them myself. By constantly talking and worrying about being seen as tiger mothers, aren't we just pegging ourselves as such? Shouldn't Chua as an Asian American mother herself be held accountable for creating this stereotype and capitalizing on the media attention? And didn't some—maybe many—Asian American and other mothers identify with and applaud the tiger mother, both as a person and a style of mothering? Indeed, hasn't the tiger mother label stuck around so long because there is some truth to it? Stereotypes stick for a reason; evidence can always be found to justify them. *I know this one Asian American mother who . . .*

Indeed, the danger of attempting to deconstruct any racial and gender discourse is that it will further entrench it. Even if it accomplishes the goal of revealing how Asian American mothers have been reduced to a stereotype, the mere fact of having to answer to the name of tiger mother can cause harm in and of itself. Responding to these concerns provides an opportunity to clarify why the tiger mother is an instructive case study and how this book has come, ambivalently, to center it.

At the time Chua's book came out, I had already been researching the topic of Asian American women and mothering for several years and had collected dozens of interviews and hundreds of surveys with Asian American mothers related to their negotiations of work and family responsibilities. At first, I found the frenzy surrounding Chua's book intriguing if somewhat annoying, and I thought it would serve as an interesting hook or footnote to my research. But as the months—and then years—wore on, to my amazement, references to the tiger mother did not fizzle out, but proliferated.

Questions about the specific components, range, and impacts of tiger mothering have now been explored in-depth from different disciplinary perspectives. Psychologists have examined its emotional dimensions and how tiger mothering correlates with children's mental health and the quality of parent-child relationships.[9] Education scholars have focused on its impacts on academic achievement and social and emotional intelligence.[10] Humanities and literature scholars have mapped the flow of the tiger mother discourse, showing its various representations across media, novels, films, and other sources.[11] Recognizing both value and limitations in all these lines of inquiry, I engage with them, while raising a different set of questions.

Tiger mothering is an amorphous and confusing term that encompasses a broad range of practices and beliefs, but my central concern here has *not* been to investigate what exactly it is or who is most likely to practice it and toward what ends. What distinguishes a tiger mother—or any mother/other—is not simply that she does not live up to prevailing standards of motherhood but that she threatens these very standards. These concepts provide frameworks to analyze the varied responses of Asian American mothers to Chua and the tiger mother, highlighting how—contrary to their complex identities, histories, and families—Asian American mothers are often treated as all the same, whether as tiger mothers or other mother/others.

Conclusion

Whatever their particular take on tiger mothering as a parenting approach, almost all the Asian American mothers who participated in this study bristled at how readily they were pegged as its practitioners, despite the fact that their mothering concerns often strongly diverged from those associated with Chua. Debates about tiger mothering have brought to the surface perceptions of Asian American mothers as hypercompetitive foreigners, illuminating how two seemingly disparate discourses—one about the declining global dominance of the United States and the other about mother blame—are in fact closely linked. Further, the tiger mother has raised questions about not only which mothering approaches are superior but which kinds of mothers are desirable and which are positioned as perpetual outsiders. Especially but not only in the guise of the tiger mother, the figure of a mother/other serves as a convenient scapegoat; she can be blamed for everything from children not getting admitted to their dream school to the collapse of the American dream itself.

The tiger mother debate illuminated how current constructions of motherhood have turned it into a competition for far more than college admission slots or social media followers and into an intense site of political and social conflict and, ultimately, othering. Indeed, fights between and about mothers have become a proxy for an expansive "culture wars" in which a range of highly politicized ideological conflicts are increasingly couched in the language of motherhood, family, and reproductive politics writ large.[12]

Emphasizing the heterogeneous experiences of Asian American mothers, the various concepts developed in this chapter show how Asian American mothers are marginalized through structures of reproductive exclusion and homogenized as tiger mothers through matritropes that tell limited stories about them. At the same time, Asian American mothers develop shared experiences through having to perform similar kinds of maternal labor to counter tiger mothering and through collective ways of imagining motherwise beyond this trope. But damaging matritropes did not start with the tiger mother, nor will this be the last. As the following chapter shows, the tiger mother is the culmination of a long line of matritropes that have constructed "yellow motherhood" as an otherhood.

2 *No Country for Asian American Mothers*

My daughter brought me her crayon box and asked me what color she should use to draw me. I said probably yellow. But she looked confused and said, "But why? Aren't you more brown?" Then I thought, "She's right. I have fairly dark skin, so why am I considered yellow?"

JACQUELINE, interview, Chinese American, financial consultant

We say Black women, brown women, White women, but not yellow women. . . . Even as the label of the "yellow woman" fades from contemporary parlance, the Asiatic figure that it denotes still stimulates passion and derision in multiple sectors of everyday life.

ANNE ANLIN CHENG, *Ornamentalism* (2019)

Why is it so hard to say "yellow"—whether in "yellow woman" or "yellow mother"—let alone to claim it as an identity? Instead, why is *yellow* widely considered a slur when applied to Asian Americans as a people or as a race? What does it mean for a mother and child to be categorized as yellow, especially as they are almost never called this by name, at least not to their faces or within earshot. And what does rendering "yellowness" into an unspeakable condition mean for Asian American mothers and their families? As Jacqueline described above, for many Asian American mothers, it is through a child's questioning that the meaning of *yellow* takes on new urgency, making even the selection of a crayon color a complicated act—because Asian American mothers must answer not just the question of "What color am I?" but "What color is my child?" These are questions not just of racial self-identification but of intersectional maternal labor, as they require answers not just for oneself but for the next generation.

As Anne Anlin Cheng writes, merely uttering "yellow woman" makes us cringe, for this term does not refer to a person but to "a figure whose survival is secured through crushing objecthood."[1] Building on Cheng's exposition of the "yellow woman," I argue that the "yellow mother" is also an absent presence, often unnamed and unseen but not unknown. Despite her invisibility or perhaps because of it, the yellow mother emanates a force field that simultaneously attracts and repels—with the combined effect turning her into an *other*. In this chapter, I call out the many alternative names for the yellow mother and how these tropes turn yellow motherhood into an abject condition of *mother/otherhood*. As yellow mothers, Asian American mothers are regarded as transgressing the appropriate boundaries of both motherhood and Americanness and thus, cannot lay claim to a sense of belonging either for themselves or for their children.

Prostitute mother. Coolie mother. Concubine mother. Mongrel mother. Enemy mother. This is not an exhaustive list of the matritropes that have been used to characterize Asian American motherhood. This chapter explores these and other dominant tropes that have been central to constructing the "yellow mother" into a shape-shifting but nonetheless singular kind of *other*. Far from being merely stereotypes held by misguided individuals, matritropes of "yellow motherhood" have wielded far-reaching power, enabling a range of social institutions to confer value on the reproduction of a few "good mothers" while devaluing those who fall outside these parameters.

Tropes stick in people's minds much more readily than names and dates—let alone obscure legal cases and legislative acts—but herein lie their danger. Although the intention is to name and expose them, cataloguing these tropes of Asian maternity runs the risk of reinforcing rather than disrupting them. But in order to understand the current trope of the tiger mother, it is necessary to trace its roots in other tropes of yellowness, no matter how distasteful, that circulate about Asian American motherhood.

Yellow when attached to motherhood conjures multiple yellow peril tropes that equate Asian American mothers with contagious diseases, sexual immorality, or abusive parenting. Any potential for positive associations with *yellow* were long ago overridden by the concept of the Yellow Peril (along with its close cousins the Yellow Terror, the Yellow Specter, and the Yellow Scare), which cast Asians as invading hordes who threatened Western societies and White racial superiority.[2] More recently, the term "yellow fever" designates desire for Asian women that objectifies them as racialized sexual fetishes.[3] This chapter does not capture the full range of yellow-mother matritropes but selects a few key examples from different historical periods and shows how they fuel distinct forms of reproductive exclusion, even as they are connected through common threads of mother/othering.

In short, the catalogue of yellow mother tropes reveals how fears of Asian American women's hypersexuality and hyperfertility have merged into generalized anxieties about their *hypermaternity*. These anxieties then manifest in matritropes of yellow motherhood that have denigrated them as mother/others while justifying structures of reproductive exclusion. Specifically, I focus on the law as a powerful site of mother/othering by examining several landmark legal cases and legislative decisions. The framework of reproductive exclusion highlights these cases not just as acts of jurisprudence but as indexes that link gender, sexuality, race, and immigration into systems of reproductive control. And matritropes of yellow motherhood have served as a potent justification for excluding Asian Americans based on fears of their unbridled reproduction.

Matritropes of yellow motherhood are not accurate representations of actual Asian American mothers and were never meant to be. Instead, they are manifestations of what Colleen Lye calls "Asiatic racial form"—that is, racialized discursive formations that reveal U.S. "racism and racialization's effects."[4] In her aptly titled book *America's Asia*, Lye examines the "yellow peril" and "model minority" as ways that "America" has imagined "Asia" and how these racial forms have been mobilized to further U.S. geopolitical interests in Asia. I draw on Lye's framework to show how discursive constructions of the *Asiatic maternal form* have historically produced racial effects of othering Asian Americans that continue into the present.

Matritropes and reproductive exclusion are not limited to Asian Americans. But at the same time, focusing on Asian Americans centers their status as the first group to be formally excluded from immigration and naturalization based on race and national origin and the ongoing systems of exclusion that have been justified in their name.[5] Focusing on the state as the agent of othering and the law as a critical site in which mother/othering is enacted and institutionalized, this chapter examines key legislative acts and legal cases that have fundamentally shaped Asian exclusion. It relies on the original archival work and historiography of a number of foundational Asian American feminist historians and then builds on their scholarship to analyze the following cases as examples of various forms of reproductive exclusion bolstered by specific matritropes. I also weave in interview quotes from my qualitative research to show how Asian American mothers continue to grapple with these tropes and forms of exclusion in the current day.

First, the 1875 Page Act and the Chinese exclusion era broadly highlight *reproduction exclusion through immigration control* and the matritrope of the *mother/other as inassimilable alien*, which marked Asian women as undesirable reproducers and justified legislation to keep them out. The specter of the unassimilable alien mother brought together three related but distinct tropes that framed Asian American mothers as suspected prostitutes, coolies, and polygamists. This form of reproduction exclusion fueled not only the formal legal exclusion of Asian women from entry but has had long-term impacts on the ongoing construction of Asian American mothers as others. Further, it has consolidated the law as an apparatus for border policing and racial gatekeeping against all mothers and families.

Second, anti-miscegenation laws and their underlying fears of race mixing demonstrate *reproductive exclusion through control of sexual relations* and reveal the trope of the *mongrel mother/other*. Initially, anti-Asian discourses that supported legal prohibitions against interracial relations focused on fears that White men would be seduced by Chinese women, which helped to fuel the passage of the Page Act and the Chinese Exclusion Act and then cement broader Asian exclusion. But the 1955 case of *Naim v. Naim* highlights another kind of fear, that of White women intermarrying with Asian men. The *Naim* case—which attempted but failed to challenge the anti-miscegenation laws that were eventually overturned in the Supreme Court case of *Loving v. Virgina*—shifted the mongrel mother discourse to White women's relationships with Chinese men whose impure sexual unions would result in the reproduction of undesirable mixed-race children.

Third, Executive Order 9066 and the forced internment of Japanese Americans in concentration camps during World War II disclose the matritrope of the *enemy mother/other*, a maternal foe who threatened U.S. security domestically and geopolitically in Asia and the Pacific. This matritrope justified the enactment of *reproduction exclusion through state violence* through the removal, incarceration, and denial of citizenship rights to women, children, and civilians as collateral damage in the waging of war and empire.

Fourth, the prosecutions of Bei Bei Shuai in 2011 and Purvi Patel in 2013 under Indiana feticide laws demonstrate *reproduction exclusion through criminalization* and highlight how matritropes of Asian women as killers of "unborn children" are mobilized to enforce carceral systems of reproductive control.

Examining these matritropes through interdisciplinary and intersectional lenses, I provide an overview of these historical contexts and representations. The examples I have chosen are illustrative, not all-inclusive, based on significant legal acts and historical figures that illuminate these various matritropes, the social conditions in which they emerged, and their effects with regard to enforcing wide-ranging matritropes and ongoing structures of reproductive exclusion.

Tracing Matritropes and Reproductive Exclusion from Past to Present

While organized mostly chronologically in terms of their period of emergence and dominance, this is hardly a linear progress narrative, as one matritrope neither replaces nor improves on earlier ones, nor does one form of reproductive exclusion resolve itself and then disappear. Instead, they ebb and flow, layering onto each other, picking up new iterations. Thus, I attempt to weave together the various matritropes and the different forms of reproductive exclusion that they have supported, showing their impacts on Asian American mothers, but also their connection to other matritropes, particularly those surrounding Black motherhood.

Mammy. Matriarch. Welfare queen. Jezebel. The Black lady. As Patricia Hill Collins writes, the "controlling images" of the doting but ignorant mammy, the emasculating matriarch, the cheating welfare queen, the hypersexual Jezebel, and the proper Black lady are projections of White people's fears of Black sexuality and reproduction and distortions of actual Black women and mothers.[6] Building on Hill Collins, Spillers, and other Black feminist scholars who have exposed these dehumanizing tropes of Black women and mothers as central to constructions of anti-Blackness, this chapter examines matritropes of Asian American motherhood as central to the racialization of Asian Americans, both as yellow peril threats and model minority citizens.

Parallel to how Hill Collins explains that controlling images reveal dominant discourses about Black motherhood while obscuring real Black mothers and their lived experiences, this chapter examines how Asian American mothers have been viewed as other by dominant U.S. society and how they have been treated accordingly by its institutions, especially the legal system. As with controlling images of Black motherhood, matritropes of yellow motherhood do not merely cast aspersions onto Asian American mothers as individuals or as a group, but they imbue them with qualities of otherness that then attach to their families, communities, and race.

Thus, although ideological justifications for reproductive control are imposed onto all women, they take on specific forms for different groups based on the intersections of gender, sexuality, immigration, class and race. The following legal cases illustrate how Asian American mothers or potential mothers have been subject to specific forms of exclusion that draw upon distinct matritropes—from alien outsiders to invading yellow hordes, to contaminated race-mixers, to enemy vipers, to murderers of "unborn children," especially girls.

In uncovering these tropes of yellow motherhood and assessing their impacts on the Asian American mothers who have lived under their shadow, it is necessary to read between the lines of existing historical records. This ground has been laid by the pioneering work of Asian American feminist historians and legal scholars who have recovered a wide range of sources—official documents, newspapers, personal correspondence, and testimonies—through which to trace these yellow mothers, even when they are not referred to as such and even if they have left barely a paper trail.[7] Pathbreaking Asian American studies historians such as Sucheng Chan, Lili Kim, Catherine

Ceniza Choy, Shirley Hune, Erika Lee, Mae Ngai, Gail Nomura, Judy Wu, Ji-yeon Yuh, Judy Yung, and many others have done the meticulous archival work to fill in significant gaps regarding the gendered dimensions of Asian American history from the Page Act and the Chinese exclusion laws to contemporary refugee resettlement, welfare reform, and immigration restriction.[8] Yet, we still need more exploration of the ways that these coalesce into specific forms of *reproductive* exclusion facing not just Asian American women broadly but Asian American *mothers*.

The theoretical framework of reproductive exclusion brings reproduction more centrally into debates about exclusion and, conversely, brings exclusion into debates about reproduction. Specifically, this chapter highlights how control of reproduction has been a central force in shaping histories of Asian exclusion and how legacies of reproductive exclusion continue to shape contemporary debates about gendered and sexual citizenship. While other frameworks focus on exclusion from different forms of reproduction, reproduction exclusion maps how control of reproduction itself functions as the basis of exclusion. Beyond just legal entry, reproductive exclusion shows the ongoing forms of policing boundaries of gendered citizenship, including control of sexuality, population, racial categorization, cultural assimilation, family formation, and economic resources.

As Greg Robinson suggests, exclusion has become a leitmotif in Asian American studies, a core concept that has brought together "collective histories of immigration detention, mass confinement, and citizenship denial" and the struggles of Asian Americans against barriers to legal entry and social acceptance.[9] Reproduction, as a foundational framework in feminist scholarship, galvanizes debates about gender, sexuality, family, reproductive labor, state power, and the economy.[10] How can these two concepts inform each other, and in so doing, how can they bring the contributions of Asian American feminist scholarship more centrally into debates about both reproduction and exclusion? This chapter situates reproductive exclusion historically and offers ways it can be used to reinterpret specific legal cases and legislative debates, focusing on the Chinese exclusion era and the control of legal entry and then moving to ongoing forms of political and social exclusion and the matritropes supporting them.

The Page Act and the Unassimilable Alien Mother: Reproductive Exclusion as Border Control

That in determining whether the immigration of any subject of China, Japan, or any Oriental country, to the United States, is free and voluntary . . . [or] for a term of service within the United States, for lewd and immoral purposes . . . That the importation into the United States of women for the purposes of prostitution is hereby forbidden. . . . Every vessel arriving in the United States may be inspected under the direction of the collector of the port at which it arrives, if he shall have reason to believe that any such obnoxious persons are on board.

PAGE ACT OF 1875, sect. 141

When I attend meetings with social service agencies that serve Chinatown, sometimes I'm shocked by the things people say. It might as well be a hundred and fifty years ago. There are still people who think Chinese men are drunks, the women are prostitutes, and the kids are mistreated. All of that model minority stuff is fairly new, and it's about Asians in Silicon Valley, not here.

ANGELA, interview, Chinese American, social worker

The Page Act of 1875, the first federal law restricting immigration to the United States based on race and national origin, named "Oriental" women potentially immigrating for "lewd and immoral purposes" as one of its main targets for exclusion. Introduced by Representative Horace F. Page of California and signed into law by President Ulysses S. Grant, the Page Act effectively served to codify single Chinese women into law as suspected prostitutes and to implement the system of border inspections to keep "such obnoxious persons" from entering the country. In addition to supposed prostitutes, the Page Act also excluded "coolie" laborers. Further, the implementation of the law at various ports of entry subjected even married Chinese women to invasive interrogation to determine if they were concubines, second wives, or otherwise involved in polygamous relationships, and thus subject to exclusion.

These tropes associating Asian women with prostitution, coolie labor, and polygamy persist in contemporary matritropes of Asian American mothers as progenitors of deviant family forms. As Angela noted in the interview quote above, many of these matritropes never went away, as current fears about contemporary Chinatowns harboring prostitution, abusive families, and substandard living conditions echo discourses of mother/othering from a hundred and fifty years earlier. Even long after the formal end of the exclusion era, discriminatory policies and pejorative beliefs about Asian American women and the families that they might produce as mothers have persisted.

By posing Asiatic motherhood as a danger not only to economic prosperity but to acceptable family relations, democratic ideals, physical health, and the racial purity of the republic, the Page Act serves as a precedent-setting illustration of the connection between matritropes and reproductive exclusion—that is, between ideologies that *other* mothers and the particular forms of exclusion that they engender. While the language of the law did not explicitly name a "prostitute mother," "coolie mother," or "polygamist mother," the rhetoric of the Page Act and the legal mechanisms that it put into place invoked and further entrenched these tropes of Asian women's immoral sexuality, servile labor, and nonnormative family relations. These different tropes merged into a cohesive matritrope of an *unassimilable alien mother* and justified extreme measures to exclude not just Asian women's immigration and labor but their reproduction.[11]

Challenging earlier historical accounts that attributed the drive to exclusion mainly to economic competition, scholarship in Asian American studies has shown that anti-Chinese movements mobilized sentiments that went far beyond perceived threats to the livelihoods of White workers and raised alarms about threats to the White, economically self-sufficient, heteronormative nuclear family.[12] For example, building on the successful passage of the Page Act and expanding on the rhetoric used to secures its passage, in 1876, the U.S. Congress appointed the Joint Special Committee to Investigate Chinese Immigration (henceforth Joint Special Committee), whose innocuous title belied the virulent anti-Chinese sentiments that it collected in over 1,250 pages of testimony from public officials, missionaries, doctors, employers, and residents of San Francisco. The complaints against the Chinese ranged from starvation wages, prostitution, subhuman living conditions, neglect of the sick and dying, and female infanticide to contagious diseases and polygamous unions. Meticulously culling through this trove of documents, legal scholar Kerry Abrams shows how the wide-ranging complaints against the Chinese coalesced to "exclude a group of people by defining them as outside the boundaries of legal marriage."[13]

Building on the research of Abrams and other historians and legal scholars, this chapter focuses on how, in addition to positioning the Chinese as outside the boundaries of legitimate marriage, the Chinese exclusion era solidified tropes of unassimilable alien mothers who would be incapable of upholding the "sacred relation of the family."[14] In other words, the appeal to the reproductive threat posed by not just the Chinese but all Asians provided ideological leverage to institute a system of comprehensive exclusion that not only kept them out but kept them from reproducing. These appeals implicitly conjured the threat of the Asian mother as an unassimilable alien herself and as the progenitor of similarly alien generations to come.

Rather than a single trope, matritropes of the Asian mother as reproducer of unassimilable aliens have incorporated several mother/other figures: (1) the sexually immoral prostitute mother, (2) the polygamist second wife or concubine mother, and (3) the servile and machine-like coolie mother. These three interconnected tropes of yellow mothers as unassimilable aliens fueled the Page Act and then operated more broadly during the era of formal exclusion. These matritropes helped to spin a web of laws that prohibited entry and claims to citizenship and have continued to justify various forms of reproductive exclusion up to the present day.

Prostitute Mothers: Linking Hypersexuality and Hypermaternity

[Chinese women] are bought and sold for prostitution, and are treated worse than dogs. . . . There is not a family, as we understand the honorable and sacred relation of the family tie, among the Chinese in the whole State [of California], or on the entire coast.

JOINT SPECIAL COMMITTEE TO INVESTIGATE CHINESE IMMIGRATION, U.S. Congress (1876)

As mothers and sex workers, we risk exposing ourselves to all kinds of harassment. If you look at the rise in violence across the board, then it's magnified at least twice-fold for massage and sex workers. And then you add to that being a mother and a caregiver.

YIN Q, interview, core organizer for Red Canary Song

China doll. Geisha. Oriental courtesan. Camptown girl. Hooker with a heart of gold. These are various iterations of the prostitute as one of the most timeworn tropes of Asian femininity. But what happens when this hypersexualized representation of Asian womanhood is tied to motherhood? In short, Asian women are cast as prostitutes, and prostitutes are cast as unfit mothers. The result is a particularly hypervisible mother/other, whose presumed perverse sexuality serves as justification for exclusion—first from entering the country and then from full incorporation into the social institutions of legitimate marriage, motherhood, and family.

Just as the figure of the Asian prostitute has persisted in the racial imaginary, the figure of the Asian prostitute mother also lives on in widespread projections of sexual immorality onto Asian American women's bodies and reproduction. Asian women who work in the sex industry are subject to specific forms of racialized and gendered exclusion and violence, especially those who are mothers and caregivers, as Yin Q, organizer with Red Canary Song, a coalition of Asian massage and sex workers and advocates, underscores.[15] Constructions of Asian women as prostitutes have had a long and resistant shelf life, as they are deeply rooted at the nexus of U.S. immigration law and reproductive politics. The Page Act prevented Chinese and other Asian women suspected of engaging in prostitution from immigrating to the United States but even more, it cast suspicions of prostitution onto all Asian women.

The specter of the Asian prostitute generated a moral panic that loomed much larger than the actual prevalence of brothels and sexual commerce. Historian Sucheng Chan asserts that census takers in San Francisco most likely overestimated the number of brothels, as they assumed that any residences where Chinese women lived together were dens of prostitution.[16] Scholars have also shown how, instead of responding to an actual spread of prostitution, the outcry over the influx of Chinese prostitutes was fueled by White women reformers who engaged in anti-prostitution activism to solidify their own racial and class position through claims of moral superiority.[17] Thus, efforts to control prostitution were not concerned solely with controlling prostitution per se but with enforcing a moral order of sexuality and proper family relations, and Asian women were designated as an urgent symbolic threat to this order.

Prior to the Page Act, some evidence suggests that motherhood served to counterbalance presumptions of sexual immorality, allowing some Asian women to gain admission to the country due to having children. For example, in interrogations of Asian women passengers on the steamer *Japan* arriving from Hong Kong in 1874, Rudolph Norwin Piotrowski, immigration commissioner for the State of California, allowed women with children to land but argued that a "lack of children" provided reason to refuse entry, even if the women were married or claimed to be (as their own claims to respectable marriages were often suspect).[18] The passage and enforcement of the Page Act, however, implemented exclusionary measures that went far beyond the banning of suspected prostitutes to discourage virtually all Asian women from entry, not despite but because they were mothers or potential mothers. As historian George Peffer writes, the enforcement of the Page Act involved invasive interviews by U.S. consuls in Hong Kong as well as officials on board vessels and upon arrival at San Francisco ports, which "complicated the immigration of Chinese wives and daughters as well as prostitutes."[19] These increasingly draconian legal restrictions combined with well-founded fears of racial violence to keep many Chinese women from migrating with their husbands or fathers.[20] A combination of factors thus contributed to fewer Asian mothers being able or willing to immigrate. While earlier historical accounts often emphasized Chinese culture and society as discouraging women from migrating in order to raise children or care for elders in the home country, Pfeffer's and other studies have shown that U.S. immigration restrictions served as the major barrier to immigration not just for prostitutes but for all Chinese women.[21]

This chapter builds on this scholarship to show that the policing of prostitution served as a vehicle to exclude not only Chinese women who were wives and daughters but those who were mothers or potential mothers. Further, this trope of Asian women as debased prostitutes fed into other damaging tropes based not only on commercialized sexuality but on sexual relations with multiple partners, thus spawning the next matritrope associating Asian American motherhood and reproduction with polygamy.

Polygamous Mothers: Dishonorable Wives and Deviant Family Structures

They are not the wives of honor. They are not the wives as would be the first wife if they were in China, but they occupied that relation to them here that is common as Americans know as the mistress to the man. If there is one respectable Chinese tested by the requirements of our civilization, the husband who has but one wife, or the wife who has but one husband, whose marriage vows were made in love and fidelity . . . we do not know of it.

FRANK M. PIXLEY, San Francisco lawyer, 1876

My parents are divorced and I call my stepmother by her first name but she really doesn't like it. I mentioned this once to a friend and she made a joke, "Just call her second wife." I don't know if she realized how loaded that is for an Asian woman.

EMMA, interview, Chinese American, full-time homemaker

Concubine. Consort. Second, third, or fourth wife. Harem. These tropes linking immoral Asiatic sexuality and family formation add another dimension to the matritrope of the unassimilable alien mother—that of polygamist. While the exact wording of the Page Act focused on prostitutes as the target of exclusion, in practice, it cast a much wider net to control a range of nonnormative sexual relations, including concubinage, arranged marriages, and polygamy, as well as fears that these deviant sexual unions would invariably produce hordes of children. As articulated above by Frank Pixley in the year after the passage of the Page Act,[22] Asian immigrant women were called upon to prove not just that they were legally married but that they were the first and only wife. And if they could not verify this, they should be excluded not only from entry but from the position of "wives of honor." And while not necessarily named as such, the subtext of these tropes referred to a polygamous mother as the agent not only of infidelity but of uncontrolled fertility—and this trope bore a distinctly Asian face.

As legal scholar Claire A. Smearman argues in "Second Wives' Club: Mapping the Impact of Polygamy in U.S. Immigration Law," efforts to outlaw polygamy were fueled by "predictions that the immoral Chinese, with their tradition of multiple wives and concubines, would pollute the sanctity of the American family."[23] This casting of the Chinese second wife as a pollutant to the "sanctity" of the American family rested on two assumptions: first, that all Chinese families were polygamous, and second, that all proper American families must be monogamous. As Emma noted in the interview quoted above, even in the current day, to call an Asian woman a "second wife" does not immediately suggest divorce and blended stepfamily relations but calls forth loaded notions of Asian families as polygamous and sexually deviant.

While state powers to exclude polygamists were inferred through the Page Act, the Immigration Act of 1891 explicitly made the practice of polygamy grounds for exclusion, which was broadened in 1907 to exclude "persons who admit their belief in the practice of polygamy."[24] These laws tended to treat polygamy as a singular immoral act and were subsequently applied broadly to groups ranging from Chinese immigrants to members of the Church of Jesus Christ of Latter-day Saints, thus failing to recognize the wide variation in practices of non-monogamy.[25] Nonetheless, while the legal apparatus that was subsequently put in place to outlaw polygamous marriages and families would ultimately extend far beyond the Chinese, it gained much of its initial traction due to fears of Orientalized polygamous unions. Here again, the legal measures for Chinese exclusion were both fueled by and helped to fuel a more comprehensive system of reproductive exclusion.

Assumptions about polygamous practices were later extended beyond the Chinese, incorporating tropes of Japanese samurai consorts and Arab harem girls, to feed into matritropes of Asian mothers who reproduced through non-monogamous sexual unions. Still, at least initially, the Chinese figured most prominently in this and other figures of unassimilable alien motherhood—including the next matritrope of the coolie mother.

Coolie Mothers: Hyperfertility and Unfree Labor

But it is not alone in the field of labor that the evils of the Asiatic interloper are felt. He is the ruin of the household. . . . The wreck of the Workingman's family is graphically depicted.

"THE CONSEQUENCES OF COOLIEISM," *The Wasp*, November 7, 1885

No one ever called us coolies but we fit the stereotype. My parents both worked two or three jobs. We lived in an apartment in Chinatown that was like a box. . . . In some ways, we've come really far, but we only got legal status because of the amnesty under Reagan. Families like ours that didn't have money or sponsors or technical skills weren't able to come legally back then. They still aren't wanted now.

REBECCA, interview, Chinese American, financial consultant

Coolie. Cooly. Kuli. Qulī. Unfree laborer. Indentured servant. The Merriam-Webster dictionary defines *coolie* as a "usually offensive" term for "an unskilled laborer or porter usually in or from the Far East hired for low or subsistence wages," whose etymology can be traced to the Hindu or Urdu word *qulī*.[26] A coolie is most often depicted as a single male Asian worker, and the word characterizes Asian workers collectively as a mass of unskilled and unfree laborers. Although a "coolie mother" may not be explicitly named in these discourses, as the agent of propagating these faceless, nameless, dispensable, workers, she emerges as another form of mother/other and another distinct Asiatic racial form. Bound to servile labor, this mother was regarded as incapable of maintaining a proper middle-class, nuclear family, while being endowed with the capacity to hyper-reproduce hordes of illegitimate and machine-like progeny.

In the article "The Consequences of Coolieism,"[27] the coolie mother and the effects she produces are implicitly referred to in placing the coolie threat not only within the "field of labor" but "in the household" and specifically as the "wreck of the Workingman's family." In other words, the reproduction of the coolie household and family depends on the coolie mother. The long arc of the coolie stereotype persists in current perceptions of Chinese immigrant mothers and families. In the interview quoted above, Rebecca shared how her Chinese American parents were relegated to working menial jobs around the clock while living in substandard conditions but could obtain legal status only through an act of "amnesty." Again, while not necessarily named as such, the trope of the coolie mother still lurks in the public racial imaginary as a maternal figuration with the power to reproduce a class of coolies who threaten to take away jobs from those unwilling to work under such debased conditions. Further, the coolie mother has the capacity not simply to pose an economic threat but to birth coolies who have the audacity to stake claims as citizens.

But what is a coolie, and how does this figure merge with motherhood to produce a particular kind of other? Historian Moon-Ho Jung describes the origin of the "coolie" as a false category constructed in opposition to free labor and most often racialized as Asian:

> No one, in the United States or the Caribbean, was really a coolie, but Asian workers were surely racialized as coolies across the world, including in the United States. . . . Coolies were never a people or a legal category. Rather, coolies were a conglomeration of racial imaginings that emerged worldwide in the era of slave emancipation, a product of the imaginers rather than the imagined.[28]

Building on Jung's analysis of the coolie as an imagined threat to White male workers, the figure of the Asian coolie mother likewise tells more about the imaginers of this figure than about those who were imagined as such. As with the coolie, the coolie mother emerges as a distinct kind of other; however, her imaginers are not primarily White male workers but White mothers, or rather, those who imagine White mothers as the progenitors of a superior Western civilization. The coolie mother is thus imagined not solely as an economic competitor but as a racialized reproductive threat to the ideals of White motherhood and nationhood.

The threat of the coolie conjured contradictory perceptions of them as servile but also tirelessly efficient, and this again looped in the coolie mother as the incubator of this unparalleled industriousness. As with Asian laborers broadly, the perceived capacity for endless toil positioned the mothers of these workers as subhuman, rather than superhuman. The coolie mother is regarded not only as surviving on meager wages in servile conditions but as producing offspring destined to live in similar subhuman conditions. Historically, the threat of the coolie has been used to deflect attention away from exploitative labor conditions and instead to blame the exploited laborers themselves, especially if they are foreigners. But if the coolie laborers were so feared and despised, how much more feared was the agent that could reproduce them in hordes: the coolie mother.

Touting the effectiveness of the Chinese Exclusion Act in stemming the influx not just of undesirable coolie laborers but of their families, James D. Phelan, the mayor of San Francisco, penned an article to mobilize support for the extension of the Chinese Exclusion Act when it came up for renewal in 1892:

> The Chinese, by putting a vastly inferior civilization in competition with our own, tend to destroy the population, on whom the perpetuity of free government depends. Without homes and families; patronizing neither school, library, church nor theatre; lawbreakers, addicted to vicious habits; indifferent to sanitary regulations and breeding disease; taking no holidays, respecting no traditional anniversaries, but laboring incessantly, and subsisting on practically nothing for food and clothes, a condition to which they have been inured for centuries, they enter the lists against men who have been brought up by our civilization to family life and civic duty. . . . The Chinese may be good laborers, but they are not good citizens. They may in small numbers benefit individual employers, but they breed the germs of a national disease, which spreads as they spread, and grows as they grow.[29]

Similar to arguments made for the initial passage of the Chinese Exclusion Act, arguments for its extension, such as those given by Mayor Phelan, conceded that "the Chinese may be good laborers," but even though this was an asset to some employers, it would ultimately "destroy the population" if they were allowed to form families. But Chinese men alone could not "breed the germs of a national disease"; they would require Chinese women—more specifically, mothers. Thus, the coolie mother had to be prevented from coming, lest she expand this population that could subsist on "practically nothing" and "labor incessantly" like machines.

While antipathies toward the coolie mother focused on her reproduction both of and with Asian male laborers, the following trope of the mongrel mother centered a different kind of unassimilable mother, one whose cross-racial intimacies would engender undesirable mixed-race progeny who would not merely compete with free laborers but pollute the racial purity of the population.

Mongrel Mothers: Anti-Miscegenation from Chinese Exclusion to *Naim v. Naim*

If we continue to permit the introduction of this strange people, with their peculiar civilization, until they form a considerable part of our population, what is to be the effect upon the American people and Anglo-Saxon civilization? . . . Can they meet halfway, and so merge in a mongrel race, half Chinese and half Caucasian, as to produce a civilization half-pagan, half-Christian, semi-Oriental, altogether mixed, and very bad?

SENATOR JOHN FRANKLIN MILLER, Republican from California, introducing the bill that would become the Chinese Exclusion Act of 1882

Growing up, people saw me as Asian even though my dad was White. It's the same for my kids. There are more mixed-race Asians now, so it doesn't necessarily make you an other—but it certainly doesn't make you White.

HEATHER, interview, mixed-race Chinese and White American, physical therapist

Mongrel. Half-breed. Eurasian. Semi-Oriental. Mixed-race. Miscegenated. To rally support for the 1882 Chinese Exclusion Act, Senator John Franklin Miller rang alarm bells against interracial sexual relations and railed against the "altogether mixed, and very bad" progeny that these unions would produce. Thus, Miller called forth the mongrel mother—the progenitor of a "mongrel race" and a "semi-Oriental" civilization that would threaten the foundation of the American republic. The interview quote from Heather notes that even though there are currently many more people of mixed-race backgrounds like herself, they and their children are still seen as

Asian and hence as outsiders. Even if they are not outrightly othered, they are far from being seen as honorary Whites.

Concerns about race mixing and the growth of a mongrel race have fueled a long history of anti-miscegenation laws in the United States, which have acted in concert with other exclusionary laws to impose yet another dimension of reproductive exclusion, this one focused not only on keeping people out of the country but also away from each other. Anxieties about fostering "mongrel" unions were often implicit in prohibiting the entry of non-White immigrants, but they became increasingly more explicit. Early anti-miscegenation laws focused on Black-White sexual relations and marriages, dating back to laws passed in 1660 in Maryland and Virginia. They were later expanded to include Mexicans, Native Americans, and Asians (also referred to as "Mongolian" or "Malay"), including U.S.-born Asians.[30] In 1861, Nevada became the first state to pass laws prohibiting marriage between Whites and Asians, and fourteen other states passed similar laws.[31] These laws were bolstered by subsequent court cases that have upheld the right of the state to police the boundaries of White racial "purity" and "superiority."[32] Anti-miscegenation laws thus can be regarded as a form of reproductive exclusion that controlled not only who could engage in sexual relations and marriage but what kinds of families they could reproduce and what kinds of citizenship claims they could make.

Echoing the same language used by Senator Miller over eighty years earlier, the 1955 case of *Naim v. Naim* similarly invoked the interests of the state in preventing a mongrel race, in this case, not to exclude them at the border but to prevent intimate relations across racial line and the legitimation of these relations through marriage. This case also showed how the legal apparatus that was put in place to prevent mixed-race unions also served to undermine claims to citizenship and the ability to remain in the country legally and long-term.

While *Loving v. Virginia* is well-known as the landmark 1967 Supreme Court case that struck down anti-miscegenation laws as unconstitutional across the United States, just a little over a decade earlier, the case of *Naim v. Naim* unsuccessfully challenged the very same Virginia Act to Preserve Racial Integrity, which the Lovings successfully overturned. While often treated as a mere footnote to *Loving*, the *Naim* case deserves attention in its own right for it reveals how Asian Americans have been deeply implicated in debates about interracial mixing. The *Naim* case further illustrates how reproductive exclusion operates through complex mechanisms linking anti-miscegenation laws, immigration and citizenship restrictions, and foreign policy.

In 1954, Ham Say Naim, a Chinese cook who served on British and U.S. ships, married Ruby Lamberth, a White woman living in Norfolk, Virginia. Like Mildred and Richard Loving, Ham and Ruby Naim had also sought to subvert the 1924 Virginia laws prohibiting their marriage by going out of state to marry. But unlike the Lovings, who were both native-born U.S. citizens, Ham was a Chinese national and the legal recognition of his marriage would have given him the opportunity to apply for U.S. citizenship. But instead, after a year of marriage, Ruby asked for divorce, writing in a letter, "Ham, this whole mess is just too much for me to try and contend with."[33]

What was the "whole mess" to which Ruby referred? It is impossible to know what was going on inside Ruby's mind or to know fully what makes any person decide to leave a marriage, but an interesting thought exercise would be to ask what factors made this situation too messy for Ruby to contend with. How much did the complications of fighting for legal recognition of their marriage and trying to secure Ham citizenship contribute to her distress? Was Ruby extricating herself not just from her marriage but from the prospect of her and Ham having children together and thus from her becoming the mother of mixed-race children? In short, how much did the sinking realization of all that it would mean for her to take on the identity of an Asian American mother influence her filing for divorce? While it is impossible to know the complex reasons that led Ruby—or any spousal partner—to seek divorce, it is possible to speculate that the "mess" in which she saw herself was not just about the incompatibilities of their personalities but about the legal and social incompatibility of their races. Any new marriage is vulnerable to multiple stressors, but the legal liminality of an interracial marriage would loom heavily on Ruby, let alone the stigma of being perceived as a "yellow mother"—specifically, a mongrel mother of "semi-Oriental" children.

While Ruby's thoughts and intentions are unknowable, those of the judge hearing the case for the Virginia circuit court, Judge Archibald Chapman Buchanan were very clearly articulated in his unexpected decision to deny Ruby's petition for divorce. Instead, he took the much stronger position that the marriage had been illegal in the first place and that the state had the right to annul it. In his decision, Buchanan directly asserted the state's right to regulate marriage for the purposes of guarding against a "mongrel breed":

> The prevention of miscegenetic marriage is a proper governmental objective. . . . We are unable to read in the Fourteenth Amendment to the Constitution, or in any other provision of that great document, any words or any intendment which prohibit the State from enacting legislation to preserve the racial integrity of its citizens, or which denies the power of the State to regulate the marriage relation so that it shall not have a mongrel breed of citizens.[34]

Buchanan's decision declared that the Naim's marriage had been against the law from its inception, arguing that there were no provisions in the Constitution, including the protections of the Fourteenth Amendment, that prohibited the state from making such a declaration. Further, in asserting that it was the government's responsibility to regulate against "miscegenetic" marriage and to prevent a "mongrel breed of citizens," Buchanan's ruling can be understood as an act of reproductive exclusion first, by denying the rights of this mixed-race couple to marry and to claim the rights afforded to marriages that did not cross racial lines. Second, this decision then undermined the conditions necessary for the Naims or any mixed-race couple to successfully have and raise a family together.

Naim appealed his case to the U.S. Supreme Court on the grounds of jurisdiction, asserting that that his foreign citizenship meant his case should be decided by a federal, not a state court.[35] But the Supreme Court did not take up the case, thereby not only refusing to recognize Naim's claims but allowing the discriminatory law to stand. Thus, not only did the law prohibit Ruby Lambert from legally becoming Ruby Naim, but it prevented Ham Naim from marrying a U.S. citizen and claiming the associated benefits not just for himself but for any children they might have had—or wanted. Yet, as distasteful and injurious as this rhetoric of race-mixing may have been, it paled in comparison to matritropes that positioned Asian American mothers not merely as producers of undesirable mongrels but as enemies of the state.

Enemy Mothers: Japanese Americans and Executive Order 9066

A viper is nonetheless a viper wherever the egg is hatched—so a Japanese American, born of Japanese parents—grows up to be a Japanese, not an American.

W. H. ANDERSON, editorial, *Los Angeles Times*, February 2, 1942

My family almost never talked about the internment, but it would come out in stories, like how they had to bury their kimonos and kendo swords in the backyard. Because looking and acting Japanese made you into the enemy. . . . I think they passed on that fear. When I asked them to teach my daughter some Japanese words, they actually discouraged me from teaching her the language.

HELEN, interview, Japanese American, teacher

Published two months after the bombing of Pearl Harbor, the *Los Angeles Times* editorial quoted above voiced the growing public sentiment against Japanese Americans: despite being "hatched" on U.S. soil, they were "vipers," enemies by virtue of blood that would override any allegiances of birth or citizenship.[36] Two weeks later, President Franklin D. Roosevelt issued Executive Order 9066, authorizing the forced removal of roughly 120,000 people of Japanese descent on the West Coast, over half of whom were U.S. citizens, to internment camps. Many of those incarcerated were Japanese American mothers and children.

How did matritropes of Japanese American women as enemy mothers serve as part of the ideological justification of this action? Clearly, the mass incarceration of Japanese Americans cannot be attributed solely to the construction of Japanese American mothers as enemies. Yet, the opinions expressed in the *Los Angeles Times* editorial depicting Japanese Americans as vipers born of vipers prompts the question, Who is it that lays such viperous eggs? As the perceived agent of reproducing an enemy race, both biologically and culturally, the enemy mother is this viper, who not only lays enemy eggs but hatches and raises them into enemy aliens.

Even several generations removed, these strong anti-Japanese sentiments continue to impact Japanese American mothers and families, as those who lived through the internment learned the hard lesson that even citizenship and full acculturation into the American mainstream were not seen as any guarantee of loyalty, whereas visible expressions of Japanese culture provided proof of disloyalty. Helen, a Japanese American mother in California, reported that her family faced strong pressure to cease speaking, eating, and dressing or otherwise appearing Japanese, in a futile attempt to deflect suspicions of enemy allegiances. Many decades later, her parents still were anxious about speaking the Japanese language and passed this anxiety on to not only their children but their grandchildren. Subsequent generations of Japanese American mothers continue to feel an ambient anxiety that they are perceived not just as foreigners but as potential enemies. In this section, I focus on these enemy discourses as they emerged in World War II and the construction of Japanese Americans, including mothers and children, as enemy aliens to justify their incarceration.

In a 1942 congressional hearing, Commanding General John L. DeWitt summed up arguments in the "Final Recommendation" for "Evacuation of Japanese and Other Subversive Persons From the Pacific Coast," based on the widespread belief that Japanese Americans would hold allegiance to Japan, not the United States—or in his words, that "a Jap is a Jap," which encapsulated the report's conclusion: "The Japanese race is an enemy race and while many second and third generation Japanese born on American soil, possessed of American citizenship, have become 'Americanized,' the racial strains are undiluted."[37] Col. Karl Bendetsen, who played a central role in enacting the order, extended this reasoning to rationalize that even young Japanese American children being raised in orphanages should be interned, arguing, "I am determined that if they have one drop of Japanese blood in them, they must go to a camp."[38]

Extremists such as DeWitt and Bendetsen advanced biologically essentialist views of the "Japanese race" as incapable of allegiance to the United States and implicated even orphaned infants as having inherited enemy blood. In line with this reasoning, the implementation of the executive order targeted any person "with 1/16th or more Japanese blood," according to the U.S. National Parks Service, leading to the internment of "over 17,000 children under 10 years old, 2,000 persons over 65 years old, and 1,000 handicapped or infirm persons," resulting in "the largest single forced relocation in U.S. history."[39]

The most extreme call for controlling the reproduction of Japanese American internees came from Representative Jed Johnson (D-Okla.), who proposed in March 1945 that "we should make an appropriation to sterilize the whole outfit."[40] Due to the war's end soon after this proposal was made, it was never actively pursued. But the mere fact that a member of Congress could openly call for such a measure illustrates the extremes that were deemed justifiable by some to neutralize the threat of the enemy mother. Although sterilization was not adopted as a mass policy, individual cases have been documented, such as that of Alice Tanabe Nehira, who testified that her mother was sterilized at Tule Lake.[41] The number of women who were subject to sterilization or to pressure or fears that they would be might be much higher, because like many experiences in the concentration camps, few people talked about what had happened to them.

As with other forms of mother/othering, Japanese American mothers did not acquiesce to being treated as enemy mothers but found ways to resist even within severely constrained circumstances. Issei (first-generation immigrant) mothers spoke out, but they had to tread carefully, especially if they were not citizens. They formed several different mothers' groups (Blue Star Mothers at Amache, the Mothers' Society of Minidoka, and the Mothers of Topaz) and focused on various causes, most notably, protesting the segregation of Nisei (second-generation) men into the 442nd Regiment.

On March 11, 1944, the Mothers of Topaz drafted a petition signed by 1,141 mothers and sent it directly to President Franklin D. Roosevelt and his wife, Eleanor, in addition to other prominent national and military leaders. The petition protested that their sons were willing to risk their lives for the United States but were relegated to segregated units that experienced high casualties, such as the 442nd Regiment.[42] The mothers' public statements acknowledged that in the wake of Japan's aggression, they could understand why first-generation immigrants from Japan such as themselves were categorized as "aliens," but while accepting their own fate, they argued that their children should not be put in the same group with them.

> When the amicable relationship that existed between America and Japan for the last eighty years was broken by the declaration of war, most of us being aliens, we understood why our rights and privileges were curtailed. But we cannot understand why our children who are American citizens were placed in the similar category as we ourselves.[43]

Why would a group of mothers assert (or be advised to assert) that they should be treated as categorically different from their own children? In an effort to prevent their children from being othered, the Mothers of Topaz effectively othered themselves not just as aliens but as enemies whose rights would understandably be curtailed by the exigencies of war.

But even these self-effacing prostrations on behalf of their sons backfired. In response to their petition, Brigadier General Robert H. Dunlop cautioned the Mothers of Topaz to refrain from seeking to intervene in military decisions.[44] Rather than helping their children's cause, Director of the War Relocation Authority Dillon Myer criticized the mothers' behavior as potentially aggravating their children's standing and warned, "I am certain that you want to take no step which would interfere with the progress toward complete restoration of civil rights and the recognition of your children as loyal American citizens."[45] Myer thus issued two thinly veiled warnings: first, the mothers' protests were foolishly jeopardizing their children's chances to have their rights fully recognized; second, even if their children were ultimately recognized as loyal citizens, this would be in spite of, not because of their mothers, who would never be recognized as such.

When mothers are designated as enemy aliens, it comes as no surprise that they would attempt to categorically distinguish themselves from their own families, to prevent their children from being othered based on guilt by association with their own mothers. In other instances, however, Japanese American mothers mistakenly believed that claiming the status of enemy others would allow them *not* to be separated from their children. This erroneous rationale, based on fears that their status as enemy mothers would lead to family separation, influenced many Japanese American mothers to renounce citizenship in an ill-fated attempt to keep their families together.

The case of Fumiko Emily Takei is perhaps one of the best known among these renunciants, largely due to the prominence and efforts of her son, actor and activist George Takei of *Star Trek* fame, who documented his mother's story in his award-winning graphic novel *They Called Us Enemy*.[46] Fumiko had been incarcerated at the concentration camp at Tule Lake, along with her husband and three young children. Based largely on flawed and contradictory information that was circulating at the time, she and many other Japanese Americans reasoned that the best way to prevent their families from being separated into different camps was to renounce their U.S. citizenship. Fumiko explained to her son that her "sole concern was to keep her family safe and intact. It was not the radicals' pressure. It wasn't any notion of doctrine [but] to force Washington to keep Tule Lake a safe haven for her family."[47] However, this decision backfired, as Fumiko's renunciation led her to face deportation to Japan, despite her having U.S. citizenship by birth and being the mother of three native-born U.S.-citizen children.

Fumiko was among over five thousand Japanese Americans who renounced citizenship, and most of them did so for a range of competing reasons. These included anger at the U.S. government, belief that Japan would win the war, pressure from Japanese nationalist groups, fear of being released from the camps to confront public hostility and even violence, or, as in Fumiko's case, a misguided attempt to keep their family together. Whatever their reasons, their subsequent designation as "denaturalized citizens" and "native American aliens" resulted in their exclusion even as native-born citizens.[48]

Rather than recognizing their complex circumstances, lawyers working with the renunciants to restore their citizenship instead prompted them to explain their actions based on a simple, age-old excuse: their parents told them to do it. Coaching the renunciants to attribute their actions to parental pressure, the lawyers posed leading questions such as the following:

> 14. Did your parents apply to be repatriated to Japan because they feared that they being aliens would never again be accepted in the U.S. and because they feared Caucasians were hostile to Japanese?
> 15. Did your parents pressure you to sign an application for repatriation to Japan so that you would not be separated from them?[49]

While this legal approach of focusing on parental pressure ultimately proved effective in creating sympathy toward many renunciants, it did so by solidifying Japanese parents—and, specifically, Japanese American mothers—as possessing inflated power to influence their children's beliefs, actions, and allegiances.

Further, even with restored citizenship, the Japanese American enemy mother would continue to loom as a suspect figure because once an enemy, always an enemy. In 2016, a full seven decades after its initial op-ed claiming that Japanese enemy vipers would hatch enemy eggs, the *Los Angeles Times* again published a justification of the internment in a letter to the editor, which similarly invoked the power of family ties: "Japanese have an extremely strong attachment to family, and even more so back then. First-generation and, to a lesser extent, Japanese here would have been expected to follow the wishes of their elders in Japan."[50] Such statements, while not singling out Japanese mothers directly, nonetheless implicated them as the assumed inculcators of this "strong attachment to family" that would ultimately trump their American citizenship. Thus, despite official apologies and even reparations, the rhetoric of enemy allegiances due to family ties continues to circulate around Japanese Americans. This justification for the mass incarceration of Japanese Americans was not isolated to a single wartime action but laid the foundation for ongoing systems of criminalization and state violence targeting Asian American women's reproduction.

Criminal Mothers: The Feticide Cases of Bei Bei Shuai and Purvi Patel

How far can the right to the life agenda be pushed? In this case, on the back of a young Chinese woman, who was in great emotional distress at the time. Now what that does, it makes Bei Bei Shuai a hostage to an ideological battle. It's almost like a proxy war. Not too many people would admit that.

MIKE MURPHY, Republican, Iowa state senator[51]

What is the proxy war that was being fought through feticide charges against Bei Bei Shuai, the forementioned "young Chinese woman" on whose back it was being fought? How was this war further extended against Purvi Patel, a young Indian American woman, who was also prosecuted under the same Indiana laws soon after? Shuai and Patel were the first two woman to be charged under an Indiana feticide law intended to protect pregnant women against violence, not to prosecute them.[52] The 2019 documentary film *Bei Bei* examined the complex motivations and politics of the case through detailed interviews with key actors, including Mike Murphy, the Republican state senator who had authored the feticide bill on which the charges against them were based, and expressed the above concern that the bill was not serving its stated purpose to protect pregnant women but was being weaponized for political purposes.[53] In both these cases, the figure of the yellow mother emerged not just as an unassimilable alien or a suspected enemy but as an outright criminal. These representations of Asian American women as the ultimate bad mothers—those who murdered their own children—served not just to other Asian American mothers but to bolster structures of reproductive exclusion that could be used to criminalize all mothers for their pregnancy outcomes and reproductive choices.

Indiana is well-known for its restrictive abortion laws, many of which were enacted under former governor Mike Pence, whose record of advancing a conservative anti-abortion agenda in his state helped to propel him into the position of vice president in the first Trump administration. This general background of heightened reproductive control is significant, but what makes the state of Indiana especially noteworthy in the Shuai and Patel cases is that despite having a very small Asian American population, it mobilized state powers to specifically target two Asian American women in these unprecedented feticide prosecutions. As the National Asian Pacific American Women's Forum, a national advocacy group, observed in a report, "With a history of stereotyping Asians as untrustworthy, perfidious foreigners, it is highly probable that racial assumptions played a role in singling out these immigrant women of color for prosecution."[54] Further, their othering as untrustworthy reproductive subjects served to justify and consolidate invasive measures of reproductive control that have had ongoing impacts not only for Asian Americans but for all women, especially women of color.

Bei Bei Shuai

The first Indiana feticide case was against Bei Bei Shuai in 2011, a thirty-four-year-old immigrant from China, who attempted suicide while pregnant, leading to the death of her fetus and to her prosecution and imprisonment.[55] As reported by various news sources, in December 2010, Shuai was eight months pregnant when her boyfriend, Zhiliang Guan, her co-worker at a Chinese restaurant in Indianapolis, informed her that he was married and already had children in China and planned on returning to them. Shuai pleaded with him, but Guan reportedly threw money at her, then left as she wept on her knees in the parking lot. Overcome with despair and in a deep depression, Shuai wrote a suicide note and then swallowed rat poison. Friends managed to get her to the hospital and she survived, but her fetus—delivered by Caesarean section—did not. As Shuai was transferred under heavy sedation to the mental health wing of the Methodist Hospital, the city's homicide branch launched a homicide investigation against her. In an unprecedented move, on March 14, 2011, Shuai was arrested and charged with murder and attempted feticide, for which she faced forty-six to sixty-five years in prison if convicted.

The charges against Shuai sparked heated debate over the rights of pregnant women, underscoring how the interpretation of fetal harm laws in the United States was not only being used to criminalize them but would discourage them from seeking help if they were in crisis or under threat. Eighty advocacy groups (including the National Perinatal Association, the National Alliance on Mental Illness, the American College of Obstetricians and Gynecologists, and the American Nurses Association) filed amicus briefs on Shuai's behalf. Further, lawyers for Shuai questioned "whether it is coincidental that such an aggressive application of a law originally designed to protect pregnant women against violent men should first be applied against a woman who is Chinese."[56]

Linda Pence (no relation to Governor Pence), Shuai's lawyer, speaking at a rally in her support, noted, "This is the first time in Indiana's two-hundred-year history that any woman has been prosecuted for attempting to commit suicide while pregnant. Why does the first woman happen to be a woman of color?"[57] Pence further raised the concern that, as an immigrant, Shuai could face deportation if she was convicted or entered into a plea deal. After 435 days in prison, Shuai was released on bail in 2012. In 2013, she pled guilty to a lesser charge of criminal recklessness in exchange for the murder charge being dropped. But just a few weeks after Shuai's case was settled, the state of Indiana, rather than learning from this misapplication of the feticide law, used the same law to prosecute another Asian American woman for the death of her fetus.

Purvi Patel

The second Indiana feticide case against Purvi Patel, a thirty-three-year-old Indian American woman, accused her of murder after she miscarried and disposed of the fetus. In July 2013, Patel went to a hospital emergency room for heavy bleeding, initially denying that she was pregnant, then admitting to having a miscarriage and placing the stillborn fetus in a garbage dumpster. The presiding judge, Elizabeth Hurley, drew strong criticism for having influenced the proceedings by allowing footage of Patel being interrogated in post-operative recovery and for describing Patel as having "treated the child, literally, as a piece of trash."[58] The state of Indiana found Patel guilty of feticide and child neglect and sentenced her to twenty years in prison, making Patel "the first woman in the U.S. to be charged, convicted and sentenced on a feticide charge."[59]

A coalition of reproductive-rights advocates mobilized in protest. In an amicus brief in support of Patel, Miriam Yeung, executive director of the National Asian Pacific American Women's Forum, argued, "Purvi Patel is being singled out because of myths and racist stereotypes about Asian American women and their pregnancies."[60] Advocates criticized the high-profile trial and media coverage that sensationalized Patel's alleged use of illegal drugs to abort the fetus, despite no evidence of this in the toxicology report. Media sources also highlighted Patel's ethnic background by reporting that she came from a conservative and controlling Hindu immigrant family who prohibited premarital sex. In addition, she was repeatedly questioned about the ethnicity of the man who was the alleged father: "Was he Indian?"[61] In short, Patel was never presumed innocent; she was already guilty in the court of public opinion, and no evidence, certainly not her own testimony, could prove otherwise.

Given the Shuai and Patel cases, it seems no accident that the only two women ever to be charged under the Indiana feticide law were both Asian American, in a state where only two percent of the population is Asian. Both cases drew upon and further solidified representations of Asian mothers as others who practiced sex-selective abortions, abused and neglected children, especially girls, and overall, held less value for human life.[62] Like the previous matritropes, discourses of Asian women as mother/others subjected them to various forms of exclusion, which in these cases, included prosecution by the state, the media, and public opinion.

Ongoing Impacts of Matritropes and Reproductive Exclusion on Asian American Mothers

Aliens, mongrels, enemies, criminals are but a few of the most prominent matritropes of Asian American motherhood that have fueled various forms of reproductive exclusion. From the 1875 Page Act to the criminalization of Asian immigrant women under current feticide laws in Indiana, structures of reproductive exclusion have persisted and expanded to not only control who enters the country but what rights and resources they can access once they are here, specifically with regard to having and raising children as well as claiming full rights as citizens. For example, the specter of the unassimilable alien mother as prostitute, polygamist, and coolie, although originally directed at the Chinese as targets for exclusion from entry, continues to loom over all Asian American mothers and families, casting them as mother/others and subjecting them to varied and persistent forms of reproductive exclusion.

Likewise, the mongrel mother plays out currently in discourses about mixed-race families. At first, the *Naim v. Naim* case seems to reveal little about Asian American motherhood, as it appears to be a story mainly about Ham Say Naim, a Chinese immigrant whose marriage to a White woman was annulled, thereby denying his claim not only to citizenship but foreclosing the possibility of him becoming an Asian American father. The mongrel matritrope, however, extended to the forms of reproductive exclusion that Ham Say Naim experienced, both exclusion from the institution of legal marriage based on anti-miscegenation laws and exclusion from the right to apply for spousal citizenship.[63] Further, if we center Ruby Naim—both her own perspective and how others perceived her—it becomes clear that she raised the specter of the mongrel mother, even without having children. Disparaged as a White woman for marrying a Chinese man, Ruby Naim sought to dissolve the marriage, refusing and then being refused recognition as an Asian American wife, let alone potential mother.

In the end, neither Ruby nor Ham's claims were recognized, as the court decision left in place the Virginia anti-miscegenation law while giving power to the courts to further limit the rights of noncitizens, specifically the Chinese, in enforcing it. The *Naim* case has mainly been examined as an illustration of how anti-miscegenation laws like the Virginia ordinance not only prohibited marriages across Black and White racial lines but also applied to control sexual and marital relations for Asian Americans and foreigners broadly.[64] Through the lens of racial and immigration politics, it further codified Asians as racial outsiders and perpetual foreigners who could not claim citizenship through marriage. But through the lens of gender and sexuality, it raises additional implications. The judge's ruling in the *Naim* case also denied Ruby the right to file for divorce, effectively saying that she had never had the right to choose to marry Ham nor to end the marriage. Although she never became a mother, at least with Ham, the specter of the mongrel mother already cast Ruby Naim as a potential mother/other for having crossed racial lines in her choice of a partner and threatening to procreate with him.

The enemy mother trope went a step further to position Asian Americans not merely as unassimilable outsiders but as enemy infiltrators. The case of the internment of Japanese Americans during World War II, while ostensibly focusing on the outsized influence of the Japanese patriarchal family, also raised the specter of the Japanese American mother as an extremist agent who would instill fanatical Japanese nationalism in her children. Fears of the Japanese American mother/other served not only to justify internment as a form of reproductive exclusion through state violence but also fueled ideological justifications for direct reproductive control, which at the most extreme, included calls for sterilization.

In these conditions, many Japanese Americans sought to distance themselves from their own families, including their parents. Historian Mae Ngai notes that this legal strategy recognized that placing blame on "coercive parents and fanatical pressure groups" would elicit more sympathetic responses to the act of renunciation but at the cost of further entrenching stereotypes of "Japanese culture as extremist, as manifested in patriarchal families and fanatical nationalism."[65] Building on Ngai's analysis, the lens of mother/othering further illuminates how this strategy of blaming Japanese families and culture—even if it did not explicitly name their mothers—served to further other Japanese Americans through the enemy matritrope.

Though often not explicitly named, the language of "one drop of Japanese blood" and an "undiluted" enemy race cast suspicion on an

Asian motherline, which was seen as capable of transmitting enemy blood and loyalties even to second, third, and fourth generations. Overriding the influence of U.S. citizenship and "Americanized" cultural identities, discourses of the enemy mother revealed ongoing constructions of Asians and Asian Americans not merely as unwanted outsiders but as dangerous infiltrators.

While focusing on the emergence of this trope with regard to Japanese Americans, the figure of the enemy mother has deep roots, from suspicions of Black mothers inciting slave rebellions to Native American mothers fomenting frontier raids, to immigrant mothers inculcating dangerous foreign ideologies, whether Communism or Islamic radicalism.[66] Further, specifically with regard to Asian Americans, the construction of a distinctly Asian maternal enemy has emerged in different historical periods with distinct racial effects. Tropes of Vietnamese women and children as covert Viet Cong helped justify high civilian casualties in the escalation of the Vietnam War. The "war on terror" generated support for endless wars in Afghanistan and Iraq based on a sense of an omnipresent, existential threat in part invoked by matritropes of Muslim mothers as hidden-terrorist-cell incubators. These various enemy sympathies have been attributed to a common fault line running deep within the family, and ultimately, they implicate the mother/other as the progenitor of the enemy within.

The mass incarceration of Japanese Americans, while unique in its scale, was nonetheless just one example of the carceral logic that extended from the enemy mother to foster different tropes of the criminal mother. The criminalization of Purvi Patel and Bei Bei Shuai used matritropes of Asian and Asian American women as simultaneously victims and criminals, who, on the one hand, were oppressed by Asian patriarchy and on the other, were oppressing and even harming their own children or potential children.

All these cases seem, at first glance, to be diametrically opposed to the admiration (however grudging) heaped on the tiger mother.

But the various matritropes of Asian and Asian American mothers or their potential reproduction are co-constructed vis-à-vis each other and simultaneously, counter to Black and White mothers. In her analysis of Purvi Patel's case, feminist scholar Priya Kandaswamy writes that in this instance, "it is the choice not to have a baby that is criminalized," as opposed to representations of Black, drug-addicted mothers for whom "the choice to have a child is criminalized," but both depart from the "idealized White subjects" for whom "the fetus emerges as a subject alongside the innocent pregnant woman."[67] In other words, for Black women and other women of color, it is the mother who is criminalized as a threat to her child, whereas for White women, the threat is outside, a predator who would inflict harm on her and her fetus.[68] These contrasting approaches and applications relate specifically to feticide laws but provide a vivid example of how matritropes more broadly are rooted in laws and the coercive powers of the state to enforce processes of mother/othering and reproductive exclusion.

Conclusion

This chapter has examined how a range of matritropes have framed Asian American mothers as prostitutes, polygamists, coolies, mongrels, and murderers, among others, and how these discourses reflect and solidify structures of reproductive exclusion that in turn produce mother/othering. *Reproductive exclusion* names a constellation of social institutions and their wide-ranging effects that have implicitly and explicitly controlled Asian American women's reproduction primarily but not exclusively through legal and state powers. The effects of reproductive exclusion range from prohibiting certain groups from legal entry into the country to controlling the intimate relations of those already within its borders, to positioning them as reproducers of enemy agents, to criminalizing their reproductive choices and outcomes. All these effects are fueled by matritropes of various kinds of mother/others that have served to consolidate and expand state powers into a diffuse yet comprehensive system of reproductive exclusion that has targeted Asian Americans but has then been institutionalized and applied much more widely.

Once the ideological and structural supports are put in place for any matritrope, they can be assigned to other groups. To draw a parallel, the welfare queen was originally rendered as a Black mother, but once created, this figure has been mobilized and harnessed to other groups and agendas, especially the cutting of state supports for mothers and families deemed unworthy.[69] Black feminist scholars have also traced figures such as the "crack baby mama" and the "unwed Black teen mother" that have been mobilized to pathologize Black motherhood and justify carceral approaches to controlling and punishing their reproduction.[70] Likewise, the various matritropes predominantly associated with Asian mothers, from prostitute to model minority, once formulated, can be imposed onto other racial groups. The cases in this chapter are but a few examples of how a range of matritropes provide the ideological underpinnings of the law to institute multiple forms of reproductive exclusion.

The following chapters shift to examine the ongoing legacies of these matritropes in the everyday othering of Asian American mothers in the present day across various sites of mothering from families to schools, to workplaces. These chapters show how reproductive exclusion continues to operate as a fault line that runs through all of these sites, but also how Asian American mothers resist othering and imagine new possibilities for building shared commitments and solidarity across various institutional contexts. The next chapter focuses on culture as a contested but generative site in which Asian American mothers both experience and challenge othering.

3 *Mothering Against/With Culture*

Culture is the essential tool for making other.

LILA ABU-LUGHOD, *Writing Against Culture* (1991)

The limited ways that you can be Chinese in this country, they feel like straitjackets. If you try to break out of a stereotype and do culture in a more complicated way, there's no audience. . . . I was trying to talk [at my daughter's school] about how this is not the Chinese New Year; it has to do with the spring festival and the lunar calendar. I was trying to break it out of "Chinese." Of course, the kids are like, "Huh?". . . But it's not just about moving away from one version of Chineseness; it's about moving toward another.

KAY, interview, Chinese American, writer

What would it take to break "Asian American culture" out of the straitjackets of Chinese New Year and the conspicuous consumption of multiculturalism? What does culture look like from within Asian American families and communities, as opposed to through the gaze of dominant U.S. culture? If culture is the essential tool for "making other," as Lila Abu-Lughod asserts,[1] how is culture also the essential tool for making mothers into others? Additionally, if culture can be a tool for mother/othering, can it be remade into a tool for *mothering against othering*? What meanings of *culture* are Asian American mothers mothering against, and what meanings of *culture* are they mothering with or toward?

Far from simply passing on static versions of Asian culture from ancestral homelands, Asian American mothers are active agents in forging new cultural identities and practices. In the interview quoted above, Kay described her attempts to create a deep and expansive sense of Chinese, Chinese American, and Asian American culture for herself, her children, and her community. This effort included teaching her children the Chinese language, exploring the history of her family's immigration from China, and sharing cultural customs and celebrations with their friends and school. However, the cultural and familial ties she wished to forge for her children were, instead, increasingly eclipsed by the need to have conversations to help them understand the rising animosities toward China and the backlash against Chinese Americans.

While Kay appreciated that many of her and her children's mostly White, liberal, middle-class friends were supportive of "multicultural enrichment," Kay observed that this often translated into a superficial consumption of Chinese culture, particularly food, rather than any sincere understanding of or support for Asian American communities. She recounted a conversation in which people were talking negatively about Chinese food, and her daughter interrupted, saying, "China is not a restaurant." Kay was proud of her daughter for speaking up but also saddened that she had to speak up. Kay described these challenges of addressing anti-Chinese racism while instilling a positive sense of Chinese identity in her children as simultaneously "moving away" from limiting understandings of Chineseness and "moving toward" others.

Like Kay, many Asian American mothers similarly expressed a desire to move away from essentialized performances of Asian culture imposed onto them by mainstream U.S. society and, instead, to move toward claiming and creating their own forms of Asian American culture—or rather, Asian American *cultures*. This chapter frames and explores these simultaneous challenges of mothering not only away from but toward, not only against but with different meanings of culture.

Drawing on understandings of culture as a set of malleable tools that are used in different ways in different settings, the Asian American mothers in this chapter challenge the idea that they merely channel or reject cultural dictates that have been handed down to them across countries and generations. Instead, mothers make and remake culture in the daily work of mothering—from what to name a child, which languages to speak, and which holidays to celebrate to how to pray, to whom, and for what? Questions of culture manifest in big and small decisions—from what to eat for dinner to where to call home and how to claim it as such? Whether or how much to involve immigrant parents and with what expectations—simply as a childcare necessity or in hopes that they will help to foster appreciation and knowledge of different cultural practices? These complex and often emotional negotiations, however, are often reduced to matritropes either of innate filial piety or insurmountable mother-daughter conflict.

In the previous chapter, I mapped the historical emergence of various matritropes, ranging from the hyperfertile yellow mother to the hypercompetitive tiger mother and how they bolster various forms of reproductive exclusion. In this chapter, I show how these processes produce ongoing othering of Asian American mothers and, in turn, how Asian American mothers respond to this othering. In the face of cultural appropriation and othering, Asian American mothers are actively making and remaking culture through their everyday enactments of mothering. Cultural practices within families and communities are central sites of mothering—and mother/othering—which demand that mothers respond to essentialized views of "Asian culture," while creating new articulations of Asian American cultures. This chapter examines how Asian American mothers produce new cultural practices and meanings through their everyday choices in child-rearing, as well as how the range of these choices is limited by the social conditions that construct them as mother/others.

Cultural sociologist Ann Swidler has offered the useful and influential metaphor of thinking about culture as a tool kit, arguing that culture is not a fixed set of traits or values but rather, distinctive ways of doing things. She asserts, "Culture influences action not by providing the ultimate values toward which action is oriented, but by shaping a repertoire or 'tool kit' of habits, skills, and styles from which people construct strategies of action."[2] Expanding on Swidler's concept of culture as tool kit, the framework of mothering with and against culture reveals how Asian American mothers draw upon a range of cultural tools to construct diverse cultural meanings, identities, and practices, ranging from celebrating holidays to raising children. Culture, however, is not a neutral or benign tool kit but one that wields wide-ranging power, especially the power to other.

If, as Abu-Lughod has argued, culture is the basis of othering, then the making and remaking of culture can both challenge and reproduce othering, and specifically, the construction of mothers as others. In her words, "By focusing on particular individuals and their changing relationships, one would necessarily subvert the most problematic connotations of culture: homogeneity, coherence, and timelessness."[3] Taking up Abu-Lughod's call to write against essentialist notions of culture, this chapter refuses to relinquish culture to its most problematic usages and instead aims to write both against and with culture. Writing *against* culture takes the form of narrating the varied ways that Asian American mothers mother against uses of culture as the basis of othering. At the same time, writing *with* culture illuminates how Asian American mothers expand the possibilities of cultural identity and belonging through their mothering.

This chapter thus seeks to capture the very personal nature of Asian American mothering stories while also situating them in shared social conditions—specifically, in definitions of culture and cultural belonging that position them as others. First, Annika, a divorced Indian American healthcare provider, rejected traditional notions of culture while forging a diverse community of collective caregiving and culture-making, yet she still found herself and her multiracial, blended family often cast as others. Next, Leslie, a Taiwanese American graduate student, narrated her efforts to create new meanings of Chinese and Asian American culture and identity for her daughter and family. But her White in-laws and surrounding community often positioned her as a mother/other, ironically, by insisting she was "one of them" and erasing their differences. Finally, Gina, a Chinese American financial consultant, strove to raise her daughter bilingually and biculturally but was discouraged by both teachers and healthcare providers who saw this as contributing to her child's learning disabilities rather than providing valuable cultural competencies. Together, these mothers illuminate how notions of culture are at the root of perceptions of Asian American mothers as mother/others, as well as how mothers are creating and asserting new meanings and forms of Asian American culture that resist othering.

Annika: Redefining What It Means to Be Indian

Whereas many Asian American mothers pushed back against pressures to assimilate into White culture, Annika also felt the need to resist expectations of her Indian American ex-husband, family, and community, especially as a divorced mother raising children and stepchildren in a blended family. She noted, "I think divorce is a very non-Asian thing to do. My parents had a really hard time understanding. It was kind of funny that I followed the rules and it still didn't work! He said, 'I don't feel like I have a wife.' Well, you don't just have a wife. You have a child and a newborn!" Although she described divorce as a "non-Asian thing," she did so with a sense of irony, recognizing but ultimately rejecting the notion that marriage was a nonnegotiable "Asian thing" from which she had departed. At the same time as she challenged this notion, she acknowledged the many struggles involved as she moved away from the cultural values of her Indian immigrant parents and community and how they had influenced her first marriage to Dev, an Indian American physician.

> I wanted [to marry] not only someone Indian but someone from my state! Because in India, a different state means a different language. My parents had really given us a lot of the culture. I was born there and I came over when I was young and would go back for the whole summer. I had a lot of attachments—it was always important to me. Even within the marriage, I was more religious than him [in practicing Hindu traditions].

Despite sharing many aspects of cultural identity, Annika and Dev experienced many tensions in their marriage, and shortly after the birth of their second child, she filed for divorce. Annika explained that as difficult as these experiences had been, they forced her to assert her own needs after years of prioritizing the needs of others, and she started standing up to her ex-husband and to her parents, who pressured her to move near them.

> People who meet [my ex-husband] now, after only having met me say, "I can't believe you were ever married to him." I didn't really establish my own identity until I was in my thirties. I went through the divorce and had to make changes, and my parents said, "We'll buy a condo near our house for you. Just come back." Culturally it would've been great—there's a strong Indian community where they are. But it was a shift from the Asian culture to say, "No, I'm not coming back. This is where my children belong and if they can be happy here, there's no reason for me to come back." Because in my culture, the

> girl leaves with the children, and that's it. So, it's been very hard for my family to understand. My family in India totally doesn't get it—"They [the children] do what? They go back and forth?"

In addition to her parents and relatives questioning her choices, Annika felt that many others did not understand her unconventional custody arrangements. Because her ex-husband lived an hour away, Annika allowed him to spend time with them at her home rather than having her children spend hours commuting.

> The drive is very hard on them and they hate it. I am lucky to be able to do this, but I was always driven by them. It cost me a lot at times. Maybe it's an Asian thing, the pacifier, to really tell their father, "There's no winner in this." He thinks because I see them every day, I'm so lucky. And I said, "I run around like a screaming meemie!" What does he do? He sits in our house watching a movie with them cuddling on his lap.

Although Annika had become more assertive in vocalizing her own needs, this arrangement seemed to meet everyone's needs but her own. Annika conjectured that this prioritizing of the needs of her children and ex-husband could be regarded as an "Asian thing," but then reconsidered. Rather than seeing herself in a passive role, Annika described how she chose to act as a pacifier and to negotiate arrangements that served her and her family best. In doing so, she also actively countered gendered cultural expectations for Asian women by initiating divorce, not going back to her parent's home, and forging her own community to share caregiving and cultural activities. Thus, she demonstrated mothering with certain aspects of culture and against others.

Rather than returning to the community in which she had grown up to be near her parents, Annika chose to raise her children as a single mother in the city where she had established herself professionally and had built a network of support with other Indian American women. In addition to helping each other with childcare, they shared in culture-making practices, from cooking Indian food to applying henna tattoos together. They also did not join established religious or cultural organizations in Indian immigrant communities, instead forming their own collective "culture camp" based in Annika's home.

> I used to run an Indian culture camp inside of my house for years. I'd have about ten kids and we'd celebrate different holidays. Every day it was a curriculum of three or four traditions. It was a lot of work to put together. The three of us kind of ran it together. Meena's kids are close in age with my kids. Sujani's children are younger but she kind of had the time and interest and ability to dedicate to developing the group. So, we had our kids and Indian kids from other Indian families, and the rest were adopted. They all loved it! It was a great opportunity for total immersion.

By forming their own culture camp, Annika and her friends sought to develop their children's cultural connections without becoming members of formal religious or ethnic community organizations. Together they redefined what it means to be Indian and Indian American—as well as Asian and Asian American—on their own terms through a shared sense of culture and community for their children, as well as for themselves.

Through running the camp together, the three women became very close and often socialized and provided informal childcare for each other. While Annika appreciated this sense of extended family, she also became aware of a less desirable dynamic because bystanders often mistook her as the mother of all the children. She bristled when others amalgamated their many different children into one presumed large Indian family, noting in disbelief the assumption that "a group of Indian children must be all mine, even ten of them!" Thus, Annika revealed that her collective caregiving arrangements were read by others through persistent matritropes of Indian women as both hyperfertile and fungible.

While she was often mistaken as the mother of her friends' children, Annika had the opposite problem of not being recognized as the stepmother of her White second husband's children after she remarried. Annika was now co-parenting both with her ex-husband, Dev, and with her new husband, George, who was White and had children from his previous marriage, requiring further renegotiation of familial and cultural ties. Annika struggled with how much she should expect her stepchildren to participate in Indian celebrations and how much she would engage with traditions that were not her own, such as cooking a turkey for Thanksgiving. The work to integrate their different families and cultural practices refocused Annika's attention away from the culture camp and the community of support she had built through it. She reflected, "When I was divorced and single, those were things I could dedicate that amount of time to, but not with remarriage and blending a family and cultures."

Annika especially missed the support from other Indian American mothers as she grappled with how to address issues of racism that were becoming increasingly pronounced as her children grew older. She found herself processing subtle racial comments that her children regularly received in the majority-White community in which they lived. In her attempts to give her children tools to respond to these comments, she often used humor, but she confessed that this approach had backfired, as neither her children nor stepchildren found these incidents or her attempt to make light of them at all funny.

> When my daughter was younger, someone said her skin was like chocolate. I kind of said, "Well, that could be a good thing, I would

> take that as a compliment!" and she was mortally offended. I won't do that again [*laughs*]!

While she was able to laugh off these gaffes with her daughters, Annika felt the stakes were much higher and boundaries less clear in co-parenting her stepchildren.

> We were talking about what people's strengths were, and my stepdaughter goes, "Well, you're Indian," and my kid said to her, "What does that mean?" And she [my stepdaughter] said, "Well, it's special to be Indian." I think she was trying to say that's what made us unique or different, but that's not the same as a skill or strength that she has. So, they called her on it. That kind of stuff, I try to get them to think and talk about it: "It would be an interesting thing to define what it means to be Indian, and what makes you that."

While Annika felt she could explore what it meant to be Indian with her daughters, ranging from teaching them Indian cultural traditions to discussing racism, she was less certain on how to approach these questions with her stepchildren. As part of mothering with culture, Annika understood the importance of sharing cultural practices with all her children, but she also wanted to respect boundaries between her and her stepchildren, set both by her role as a stepmother and by their different cultural backgrounds.

Annika actively created new forms of Asian American culture through the everyday work of mothering in a racial and ethnically mixed and blended family, but she also struggled with subtle and overt forms of othering in the various communities to which they belonged. As a mother—and through her mothering—Annika noted her marginalization from both mainstream U.S. culture and traditional Indian culture, narrating her understandings of "Asian culture" as far from fixed, especially in terms of how it was relayed to the next generation.

Similarly, Leslie negotiated mothering with and against culture as a Taiwanese American mother married to a White man and raising mixed-race children.

Leslie: It Erases My Personal History to Say "You're Just Like Us"

What's in a name? Many Asian Americans go by multiple names: the name their parents call them, the name on their birth certificate, the name bestowed by a supposedly well-meaning teacher or friend to help them "fit in." The decision to adopt an "American name" is often a fraught moment of self-definition for Asian Americans, seeming to mark a stark choice between assimilation and otherness. Add to this that the act of choosing a name carries the weight of defining not just the child's identity but, potentially, those of generations to follow.

Choosing her daughter's name—or rather, creating it—was a deeply intentional act for Leslie, a mixed-race White and Taiwanese American graduate student, who identified herself primarily as Asian American and a woman of color. She and her husband, Thomas, who is White, sought to blend their identities and backgrounds by integrating parts of both their mothers' names to form their child's name— Li An—which they chose to spell and pronounce closer to its Chinese version. But the name, and its symbolism received an ambivalent response from Leslie's Midwestern in-laws, who used a more Americanized pronunciation—Lee Ann—even after much gentle but insistent correction. Further, Leslie recounted how they seemed ill at ease not just with their granddaughter's bicultural name but also with her biracial appearance, voicing anxieties even before Li An was born.

> It wasn't so much the name, but the discussion of what Li An would look like that was troublesome for me. The bigger issue was when I was preg-

nant, my mother-in-law would often say to me things like, "Boy, so the baby's probably going to have dark hair, huh?" Or "Wouldn't blue eyes with dark hair be really pretty?" Thomas's family on his mother's side, it's just a sea of White blond people. And then there's just me. So I'm always in the center of the pictures, to sort of balance it out [*laughs*]. But it's hard. The funny thing is they still don't acknowledge it. I was talking to them over Christmas, and we were discussing identity and I said, "So much of your identity is not just how you identify, it's how you're identified by your society." It's not that easy, you just can't say, "I'm White," and all of a sudden people will treat you like you're White.

While her in-laws saw themselves as welcoming Leslie and Li An into their family, they demonstrated this welcome by treating them as if they were White rather than acknowledging their racial and cultural differences. Leslie also described how they did not admit their unease with these differences, as exhibited by her mother-in-law's reaction to Leslie identifying herself as Asian American and a woman of color in her graduate program bio and other administrative forms.

I mentioned this, and my mother-in-law went, "What? They asked you that?" And when I said my answer was "Yes, I do identify as a woman of color," there was this shocked look on her face, like she couldn't imagine that I would. And I think that they don't see how problematic it is that they don't see it, how it really sort of erases a big part of my own personal history and my own experience to say, "Well, you're just like us."

Leslie's mother-in-law's insistence that she was "just like us" imposed a color-blind approach that overrode Leslie's self-identification as Asian American, a woman of color, and a member of a mixed-race family, as well as the importance she placed on nurturing these identities in her child. Rather than creating a sense of belonging, this color-blind mentality made it more difficult for Leslie to confront their disparaging comments about her family's Taiwanese background.

> [My in-laws] would ask questions about Taiwan and say, "Does your family have this?" And I realized they thought that my mom's family lived on a rice paddy somewhere, and I'd say, "No, Taipei is a city. It's like living in New York."

Leslie felt that she needed to be on constant alert to shield both her daughter and her mother from her in-laws' comments, while she absorbed them.

At the same time, Leslie could see that her mother also struggled with having a grandchild who did not look like her—as did Leslie herself. While her mother and mother-in-law at first seemed to make similar comments about Li An's fair appearance, they then revealed very different concerns beneath these comments.

> My mom, after she saw Li An, looked at her and said, "You've got a White child." And she loves her, but I think it's troubling for her, seeing her grandchildren look very little like her—they don't really resemble her at all. And sort of seeing herself being physically erased from subsequent generations, I can really understand where that's coming from. It's funny because when my mom says it, I interpret it totally differently than when my mother-in-law says it.
>
> *What do you think your mother-in-law's concerns are?*
> My mother-in-law is concerned her eyes are going to turn brown. And I really felt like, what she was trying to say was, "Let's see if we can get the baby to not totally look like you, or to not look Asian."

Leslie understood her mother's concerns about Li An looking like a "White child" as fears about being "erased from subsequent generations," as their familial connection was not immediately visible based on physical resemblance. In contrast, Leslie's mother-in-law seemed less concerned about her relationship with her granddaughter than about her racialized appearance, which she expressed in comments suggesting that Li An's eyes would "turn brown" and that she would look more like Leslie—that is, more Asian.

In addition to comments by her mother and mother-in-law, those made by friends and strangers in public settings further heightened the sense of scrutiny that Leslie felt was directed toward her and her daughter, raising her own complicated feelings about their different racial appearances and positions.

> I struggled with it, too. Talking to a friend of mine after she saw Li An, she said, "Your mother-in-law got her wish," which made me really sad. And it's not an issue for me now, but it was when I was pregnant. I didn't know how to deal with it. I identify so strongly as a woman of color, I didn't know what I would do, giving birth to this child in a privileged racial position.

By asserting that her mother-in-law's wish to have a White grandchild was fulfilled, Leslie's friend positioned Leslie as a racial other, not just in relation to her White in-laws but to her child. Further, these comments placed Li An in a "privileged racial position" different from Leslie, while also questioning Leslie's status as her mother.

Leslie further noted that others would channel the perceived racial differences between her and her child into assumptions that she was not in fact Li An's mother but a paid caregiver, such as in these interactions with a neighbor.

> These new neighbors moved into these condos next door, and the guy is like twenty years old or something, and he was talking to

> Thomas, and he said, "Do you have a nanny?" And Thomas said, "What?" And the guy said, "Oh, I don't know if it's your wife or your nanny, but she said such and such." And he was talking about me! So, I just made a point of saying to him, "I'm the mom, not the nanny!"

When asked why she thought the neighbor mistook her for a nanny, Leslie reflected, "I think that it's hard to sort of tease out what is distinctively Asian American and what is because of my class background, which is very much working-class poor." Thus, she recognized that a combination of class and racial biases possibly influenced the neighbor's assumption that she was the nanny, not the mother of her child, and she further emphasized that gender shaped this misrecognition. Contrasting her experiences with a friend's White husband, she noted:

> I have a friend who is Korean, whose husband is French, and their daughter looks very Korean. And when he goes walking with her, people often stop him and ask him when he adopted her. But I don't get that a lot. I wonder if people are less inclined to think an Asian person has adopted a White child than the flip?

Leslie thus pointed out that although her friend's White husband was also misidentified when out in public with his mixed-race Asian children, he was mistaken as an adoptive rather than biological father, but not as a paid caregiver.

Leslie further observed that this misidentification of mixed-race families was specific to majority White regions of the United States and departed from her own experiences growing up on the West Coast where mixed-race Asian American families were prevalent. Leslie emphasized the diverse constructions of Asian Americanness in different regions of the United States, but these complex self-identifications and relationships were largely erased in her current setting, where she was consistently singled out and othered simply as Asian.

> Many of the people that we knew were Asian American like I am, sort of a hybrid—it's just this very creolized culture and identity. And so I think that has really influenced the way I think about race. But moving here [to the Northeast], it was very different. If people wanted to indicate me, they'd say, "the Asian person." Once I went to get breakfast with my husband and some sorority sister looked over [at me] and said, "Why are there so many Asian people here? Are they trying to fill some sort of quota?"

Having grown up in a racially diverse region of the United States, Leslie was taken aback by these openly racist and publicly vocalized comments that slotted her into a generic category of "Asian people," for which the quota had been filled. The "quota" remark singled out her racial difference and marked her status as other.

While Leslie's experiences of being othered in her extended family and community drew on tropes of Asians and Asian American women ranging from nannies to unassimilable aliens, within the context of her graduate degree program, they took on explicitly model minority inflections. Leslie shared one example in which another graduate student assumed that, simply by virtue of being Asian, she had an innate cultural edge in academics.

> One of my fellow graduate students told me I was very lucky to have come from a culture that valued education. . . . I would do the reading and people would not be doing the reading, and he goes, "You don't understand, you're lucky because you come from a culture that values education." He knew my family was from Taiwan and assumed that they are educated and wealthy, but my mom is very working class.

Growing up without class privilege, Leslie said she "just had to laugh" when people automatically equated being Asian American with academic achievement and professional status. On the contrary, neither Leslie's parents nor siblings, nor many of the Asian American friends with whom she had grown up in her largely working-class community had attended college. By identifying her as "lucky" to have "come from a culture that values education," Leslie's fellow graduate student erased her actual background as a working-class, first-generation college student and the tremendous effort it had taken for her to graduate college and enter a Ph.D. program. He also lumped her into a category of Taiwanese immigrants who he assumed were wealthy and educated.

Conversely, a professor referred to a contrasting set of cultural stereotypes, that Asian women would inevitably put their families before their careers. After she became a mother, Leslie became keenly aware that a different and distinctly gendered cultural discourse about Asian American women kicked in—namely, the assumption that she would prioritize her family over finishing her degree and pursuing an academic career.

> I had one professor who had been very supportive, but when I went on campus with my daughter, she asked me if I was dropping out of the program. And this was a woman who studies women. I was like, "What? Are you kidding me?"

Many women confront biases that they will—and should—put family before career, but as will be discussed further in chapter 5, these draw on particular tropes about Asian American mothers as passive and traditional. This professor's assumption that Leslie would quit her graduate program after becoming a mother discounted Leslie's strong commitment to her career, which was fueled not solely by her race but by class, region, and other dimensions of her family and community.

Rather than modeling a traditional homemaker, Leslie's mother not only worked but, as a single mother, was the primary breadwinner.

> My mom is the manager for a fast-food restaurant. I didn't realize how much we were really struggling, but when I went to college and I had to file financial aid paperwork, I found out how much my mother made, and she made $18,000 the year before. I can't even imagine supporting myself on $18,000, and she had two kids!

Leslie felt that both her fellow graduate student and her professor had made different but equally erroneous assumptions about her, failing to recognize their own racial, gender, and class biases and projecting them onto her. In both cases, they discounted Leslie's prioritizing her degree and continued professional work not in spite of being a mother, but because she saw the role of breadwinner as an inherent part of the responsibilities of motherhood.

Rather than isolated incidents, Leslie described these problematic interactions as reflective of the attitudes of the liberal college town in which she lived, which often failed to actualize its progressive self-image. While recognizing these limitations, Leslie also appreciated her privilege as a graduate student and sought to take full advantage of the resources this afforded. She regularly took her family to various cultural events sponsored by the university but also was critical of how they packaged Asian culture for mainstream consumption.

> We took them to see these Chinese acrobats, and yes, the performances are really amazing, but I wonder what it means when kids associate being Chinese with being, like, circus performers. And we all know that there are all kinds of politics going on behind these shows, and we have no idea how the performers are being treated.

But that's what's available around here, in terms of exposing them to Chinese culture.

Similar to Kay, who opened this chapter, Leslie blanched at these kinds of highly staged cultural performances and was also concerned about their political messages and possible exploitation of the performers. As committed as Leslie was to raising Li An with a strong and positive sense of her Taiwanese identity, she felt constrained by the limited forms of Asian culture available to them. Faced with such constraints, Asian American mothers like Leslie and Kay—and Gina in the following section—forged innovative ways to create their own cultural practices and to share them with their children. Nonetheless, they were often othered in their efforts not only by family and community but by doctors and other care providers.

Gina: Raising Our Daughter Biculturally, Out of Necessity

"We are raising our daughter very biculturally, but it is not so much intentionally as out of necessity. We speak to her half in English and half in Chinese, which the speech therapist is against. She says she's already speech-delayed and it makes it harder for her and harder for other people to understand her." Gina, a financial consultant, described raising her preschool daughter, Emma, in a multigenerational family that included her husband, Wei, his parents who traveled to and from Beijing, and her mother, who visited almost daily. Emma's grandparents and her nanny spoke only Mandarin, so raising Emma bilingually was to them nonnegotiable. Their complex negotiations of family and culture were further complicated by Emma being diagnosed with speech delays and tensions over the best ways to care for her. These tensions coalesced around issues of raising Emma bilingually, because Gina, her mother, in-laws, nanny, and care providers all weighed in differently.

Whereas Emma's speech therapist focused on narrow metrics for measuring her proficiencies, Gina prioritized Emma's broader abilities to communicate and connect with her family and community, which included two sets of grandparents and a nanny who all spoke Mandarin and limited English. Gina explained:

> She may be saying something perfectly fine in Chinese but they don't know, and they just think she can't talk. But we've more or less insisted, because of the family situation, we want her to be able to talk to her grandparents. We've looked for a bilingual preschool but it's tough because we want her to go to school in the neighborhood, and a bilingual speech therapist is also really hard to find.

Gina grappled with the perspective of Emma's care providers, sometimes unspoken and other times stated overtly, that raising her daughter bilingually would add to her disabilities rather than enhance her capabilities. This still widely held monolingual view runs against more inclusive approaches, which recognize the benefits of integrating bilingual and special education. In addition to the discouragement toward raising her child bilingually, Gina felt criticized for the extended family caregiving arrangements and alternative medical choices she made, which she felt were common for Asian American mothers but were seen as strange or foreign to others.

> Both my mom and my husband's parents are very concerned about her and have watched therapy sessions, tried to cook new foods to tempt her to eat and gain weight, etc. My mom especially has sought out advice from alternative medicine. Maybe another aspect of my upbringing that has affected my daughter's care is that I'm more willing to consider alternative therapy like qi gong, acupuncture (more like acupressure—no needles!), herbs, etc., and I'm a little more skeptical that traditional Western medicine holds the answers.

Similar to her efforts at raising her daughter bilingually, Gina's choice of various kinds of alternative medicinal approaches was looked upon skeptically by her daughter's healthcare providers, many of whom actively dissuaded these practices. Gina's sense that her mothering approaches were seen as suspect by educators and healthcare providers was further compounded by criticism from within her family.

Despite her commitment to building strong connections between Emma and her grandparents, tensions often arose in their multigenerational household. These tensions were heightened by the fact that Gina and her husband were providing both sets of parents with various kinds of support, including financial, on top of incorporating them into their childcare arrangements. In fact, Gina named eldercare, simultaneously combined with reliance on elders to help with childcare, as the distinctive issue for Asian American women's caregiving.

> The big issue I think that's really different for Asian American women is eldercare. It's just expected that my in-laws will live with us at some point. There are some frictions between us, but I'm not sure how much of that is cultural and how much is just the same as in-laws everywhere. It's mostly about child-rearing. They are always on her about "Oh, don't touch that." I've accommodated the situation, but we are getting in each other's way a lot when they're here and it has a huge bearing on our lives. We cover their plane ticket and expenses while they are here.

On top of dealing with these family tensions, Gina's sense of otherness was compounded by her friends' judgments about the degree to which her in-laws were involved in their lives.

> I must say that I'm juggling my in-laws more than any of my American friends. When I tell friends that they're staying for six months they're like, "Are you out of your mind!" It really blows their minds.

> My husband's sister is also in the U.S. but they live in the suburbs and it's just more interesting for them to be here in the city; they can walk places rather than being stuck at home. And our financial situation is better.

Accommodating her in-laws needs drove many of Gina and Wei's household decisions, including living near Chinatown for them to be within proximity to a Chinese community and its restaurants and cultural establishments. These arrangements were almost taken for granted by Gina's Chinese in-laws but baffled her non-Chinese friends.

Contrasting sets of cultural values not only caused stress for Gina with her in-laws and friends but spilled over to her relationship with her mother and her husband.

> I think it's because he's the boy, and they cleave to him more. But I take seriously caring for my mother as well, and I'm like, "Hell, I'm not into this. He's the boy and I'm the girl, so my parents are less important." My mom has complained about his parents before, about when they're here, they take precedence. Which is true, but it's hard, because they have no other place to go and she has her own place. But I think there are still other voices going on that she thinks she's somehow less important.

Gina acknowledged how her husband's status as the only son heightened responsibilities to care for his parents, but in addition to gender, she attributed these dynamics to differences in class and country of origin, specifically her husband growing up in China and her own family's immigration from Taiwan.

> I think there is this dichotomy between the Chinese who left China for Taiwan and those who stayed. Those who stayed in China, every-

> one worked! For people like my mom who left for Taiwan, they have more old-fashioned ideas about if you have a child, your top priority is to stay home. Whereas I think a child is your main responsibility, but you can care for them and support them in other ways. My mother communicated this sense of "I don't understand why you're having such a hard time. A baby is a happy thing!" And then she would get in these digs like "Maybe it's because you work." With my in-laws, there is more acceptance of me working.

In their divergent attitudes about her career, Gina noted her in-laws' expectation that she continue to work, as they had both worked full time in China, in contrast to Gina's mother who had been a full-time homemaker in Taiwan. Unlike Leslie, who strongly identified as Taiwanese, Gina only mentioned her mother's Taiwanese background to point out contrasting attitudes about women and work rather than to signal any strong national allegiance. Likewise, she raised differences between China and Taiwan in terms of how she saw these impacting her relationship with her husband.

In addition to mediating conflicts between her mother and her in-laws, Gina also felt that constant negotiations regarding her child's care, parental relations, and finances were wearing on her relationship with her husband. Although they both identified as Chinese American, Wei had been born and raised in Beijing and had come to the United States as an international student. Gina felt that their very different upbringings produced equally different expectations regarding his responsibilities for childcare and domestic work, as well as how to communicate about these responsibilities with their parents and nanny.

> I don't know if it's because he's smart or lazy, but my husband pretty much stays out of it [*laughs*]. He does quite a lot. He does more than

> most fathers, and I'm more resigned now to the differences between what the father gives compared to the mother. He just doesn't notice or worry about things the way I do. Like, with doing something about her delays, he's just coasting along, saying everything's fine, and I'm the one pushing and doing things to get her diagnosed and get support. He's mostly willing to do what I tell him—but I have to ask. We are also financially supporting my mother, and that's one of the main things that's kept me from staying at home.

Thus, not only did Gina's mother and in-laws have different expectations about her working, but their different cultural, class, and immigration backgrounds impacted Gina and Wei's marriage and careers. Later chapters discuss work-family issues in greater detail, but for now, it is worth noting that Gina was not only caught between the much-discussed "cultural contradictions of motherhood" between employed and full-time mothers,[4] but she also felt beholden to different cultural standards for mothers in transnational contexts spanning China, Taiwan, and the United States.

Further complicating their extended family and caregiving arrangements, Gina and her husband employed a full-time nanny, Ying, to help with childcare, eldercare, and domestic work. Their negotiations with and around Ying's role reflected a range of factors that were in part cultural—such as wanting someone who could cook certain foods and speak Mandarin—but were not solely cultural, as they significantly reflected the contractual relationship between employer and employee. The terms of this relationship were further complicated by the involvement of other family members, especially Gina's mother.

> There have been some conflicts with my mom involving the nanny. There's something about Asian women working for each other. In Western culture, the boundaries between employer and employee

are very clear, but here they get blurred. Like my mom gives Ying her old coats and other things that you might do more for a friend, but then she'll let it rip when she has any issues with her. There's a lot of stuff around feeding. Emma is underweight, and my mom feels like Ying isn't paying enough attention to making her eat, like she'll take her out to the park and my mom will be like, "How can she eat if you're out?" Ying will explain, "I did bring a banana," and my mom sees that as talking back. This is not the first blowup. She [my mother] always has this feeling that she knows best, and she does help a lot, so she feels like she can just tell off the nanny, "We don't need you. I can do better than you, damn it!" She doesn't realize the situation this puts me in. I don't want her to take care of Emma full-time, and I don't even think she's physically capable of doing it.

Exhausted with constantly negotiating care arrangements among her mother, in-laws, nanny, and husband, Gina expressed a desire to cut back from work and spend more time with her daughter. However, this desire was stifled by the fact that her extended family was dependent on her high earnings as well as her own reluctance to step away from a career she had fought so hard to succeed in. At the same time, Gina did not try merely to fit herself into others' cultural expectations but instead tried to define her own values and how they influenced her mothering, including how she balanced her work and family responsibilities.

As an Asian American mother, Gina mothered against understandings of culture that positioned her as a mother/other, actively resisting speech therapists and other healthcare providers who discouraged her from raising her daughter bilingually. Gina navigated the conflicting value systems not only of teachers and doctors but of her husband, in-laws, and own mother, all within a larger U.S. cultural discourse that readily judged her and her mothering as not only different but foreign and strange. Faced with being designated as a mother/other, she sought ways to define her own cultural values of mothering, which included raising her daughter bilingually and forging strong ties to multigenerational family members, care providers, and the larger communities in which she chose to live and mother.

Challenges of Mothering With/Against Culture

The seemingly prosaic, everyday activities of mothering accumulate into the cultural building blocks of home and family, but they are framed by competing cultural meanings and expectations. Mothers find themselves pulled in different directions regarding cultural assimilation to the dominant White culture, preservation of homeland cultures, or assertion of new cultural practices and identities. Like Annika, Leslie, and Gina, many Asian American mothers do not simply preserve the cultural heritages of their parents and homeland but they adapt them into new and diverse articulations of Asian American cultures. Whether related to food, language, celebrations, or customs, Asian American mothers do not just socialize their children into pre-existing cultural beliefs and practices, but they are active architects of new cultural forms. While creating meaningful cultural practices for their families and communities, their efforts are often undermined by dominant cultural discourses that position them and their families as others, both in relation to dominant U.S. culture and to their homeland culture.

The sense of being othered within their own families and communities is especially complicated for Asian American women with White partners. Various studies have noted the high rates of intermarriage between Asian American women and White men.[5] In addition, interracial relationships and intermarriage have traditionally been considered indicators of high levels of cultural assimilation.[6] But the mere fact of intermarriage does not predict how race and racial differences will influence cultural practices within these families.[7] The assumption that intermarriage with White partners is an automatic indicator of Anglo-conformity does not hold up for Leslie, Annika, and other mothers in mixed-raced families who strongly assert cultural identities as Asian Americans and as people of color, both for themselves and their children. However, while their partners, extended families, and communities often saw themselves as embracing racial and cultural diversity, they often did not understand what it meant to be Asian American and contributed to dynamics of othering, either intentionally or unintentionally.

In Annika's example, she invested considerable intersectional maternal labor in her efforts at active culture-making, and in doing so, she demonstrated that marriage to co-ethnics is not an automatic sign of conformity to traditional cultural values, whether from Asian homelands or within immigrant ethnic communities, nor is intermarriage necessarily an indicator of assimilation or desire to assimilate. Her account of mothering with certain forms of culture, such as forming a culture camp, while mothering against others, such as refusing to conform to expectations that she stay in an unhappy marriage, underscores that there is no such thing as one unified Indian culture. For that matter, there is no singular Chinese, Vietnamese, or any other national culture, let alone one that encompasses all Asian Americans across their vast ethnic and national histories and cultures.

Instead, what constitutes "authentic" culture is always highly contested and politicized. In the case of India, feminist theorist Banu Subramaniam demonstrates how, precisely because no such unified shared Indian culture has ever existed, it has been manufactured through various political projects, most currently the state's mobilization of Hindu fundamentalism in the service of "national integration."[8] Even if there were agreement (which there is not) that a common culture had existed at some point in India or other Asian homelands, culture is constantly being reshaped through immigration. Immigrants themselves remake culture, as do the "contexts of reception" in which they settle, which includes the level of acceptance by the mainstream society, the formation of ethnic enclaves, and the forging of transnational connections through return travel, social media, and person-to-person communications.[9]

In Annika's case, her marriage to another Indian American was influenced by her desire for a shared culture based both on religion and region, but she soon realized that these commonalities did not translate into shared cultural values, let alone marital compatibility or commitment. At the same time, her divorce did not signal a rejection of traditional cultural values but rather a renegotiation of culture and ties with her family and community. In constructing new family arrangements after divorce and remarriage, Annika did not cut off from the culture she had grown up with; instead, she recomposed it, primarily through the ways she introduced it to her children. Rather than turning to formal religious or community organizations, Annika and her friends created their own culture camp, engaging their own and other children in various traditions without attaching these to strict cultural belief systems or practices. These mothers illuminate a larger trend in which Asian Americans are increasingly adopting informal approaches to cultural practices rather than joining established religious or ethnic organizations. Scholars generally agree that second- and later-generation Asian Americans tend to be less religious than the first generation but also point out that Asian American religious practices can be quite complex.[10] However, statistics such as weekly worship service attendance do not account for other measures of religious practice, such as ancestor worship, home altars, attendance at temple-sponsored Lunar New Year celebrations, and practices that may be more associated with ethnic identity than specific religious affiliations.

At the same time, efforts by Asian American mothers to carve out new cultural meanings were made into targets for othering, which in their case most often took the form of racialized comments directed at both them and their children. In Leslie's case, mother/othering took multiple forms: assumptions by neighbors that she was her child's nanny, interactions with in-laws that feigned colorblindness while fixating on phenotypical and cultural differences, comments by peers that attributed academic success to an innate cultural edge, and expectations that motherhood would take priority over graduate study and careers.

These incidents contributed not only to a climate of racial microaggressions but also to a pattern of mother/othering that fostered hypervigilance and the need to strongly assert herself as an Asian American, a woman of color, and most pointedly, the mother of her own child. Because Li An was still young at the time of the interview, Leslie had not yet talked extensively with her daughter about confronting racism. But Leslie was anticipating and preparing for these conversations. She actively sought out various cultural activities, but was frustrated by the limited options, such as performances by Chinese acrobats, which were objectifying and highly politicized with strong anti-communist rhetoric. Most painful to Leslie was the sense that, despite her efforts to cultivate a sense of her rich cultural identities as a mother in a Taiwanese, Chinese American, Asian American, and mixed-race family and her attempts to share these with her daughter, many people, including her close friends and even her mother treated Li An as a "White child."

In this context, the seemingly simple act of choosing a child's name becomes laden with meaning. Leslie's decision to choose a recognizably Asian first name for her daughter is especially significant because women's ethnic identities often get erased if they marry someone with a European surname, for children still often take their father's last name even if mothers keep their own.[11] In addition, the choice of children's names influences how they interact with various social worlds outside their family, especially schools and then workplaces. This can have serious consequences. For example, studies have found that perceptions of an ethnic or racial name resulted in disparity in callbacks on resumés among job seekers, especially for those perceived as Black or Latinx.[12]

Asian Americans also encounter discrimination based on names and attract teasing and other forms of discrimination.[13] In one notable example, following the September 11 attacks, South Asian men were the least likely to receive callbacks for job interviews, and perceptions of them as "foreigners" mushroomed into blatant racism and xenophobia.[14] Some scholars have counterargued that names have little impact on overall life chances, since college education, professional status, and other resources outweigh bias toward ethnic-sounding names.[15] But there is no doubt that the contested meanings and consequences of an ethnic-sounding name added weight to Leslie's act of creating a name for her daughter that integrated family backgrounds across racial and cultural differences, while being recognizably Asian. Through the small but profound act of naming a child, Asian American mothers like Leslie assert their own cultural heritage for themselves and their children. A discernibly Asian name can be especially significant for mixed-race children and families, whose race and ethnicity are not easily identifiable based on physical appearance.

Indeed, racialized perceptions and misperceptions of phenotypical differences called forth particularly noxious forms of othering in which Asian American mothers in interracial families had their ties to their children called into question.[16] For Leslie, comments by a neighbor about her being a nanny imposed a sense of otherness between her and her own child. Further, such comments often assumed a desire to claim White racial privilege that ignored Leslie's strong identification as a woman of color and her desire to pass this identity onto her daughter.

Finally, some mothers, like Gina, sought to integrate not only the cultural heritage of immigrant parents but the immigrant parents themselves into their households. Far from a monolithic sense of

Chineseness, Gina negotiated the different ways of being Chinese embodied by her mother, in-laws, and nanny and incorporated all of them into their expansive Chinese American family. Gina was strongly committed to raising her daughter bilingually, for practical reasons such as communicating with various caregivers, but more to forge connections with her larger family and ethnic community. Gina described how various providers failed to comprehend bilingualism as a necessity, let alone an asset.

Many Asian American mothers felt similarly caught between their immigrant parents and the opinions of healthcare and education professionals. Gina's case shows how mothers of color with special-needs children face heightened perceptions of cultural otherness that can lead to questioning of their overall ability to care for their children.[17] One study noted that "nearly three quarters of Asian-Americans used at least one type of complementary and alternative medicine in the past 12 months, which was significantly higher than the national prevalence rate."[18] However, while they were much more likely to use alternative medicine, they were also more likely to express concerns that Western doctors denigrated Eastern health approaches, which led them to "withhold or avoid disclosing information about their cultural practices."[19]

Stories such as Gina's show that this sense of being judged for incorporating "Chinese medicine" still persists into the second generation. Due to her professional and class resources, Gina was relatively protected from fears that her daughter could be removed from her care due to these decisions, but the historical legacies of children of color being removed from families due to supposedly backward cultural approaches to medicine, education, and parenting continues to cast a long shadow.[20] Thus, even highly resourced and assimilated mothers like Gina are not exempt from long-standing matritropes and pressures of mother/othering and their negative consequences for them and their children.

Contrary to perceptions of Asian American mothers as conduits of an immutable, inscrutable Asian culture, Asian American mothers are actively constructing new cultural identities and practices. However, framing Asian American mothering through the lens of culture may understandably make some apprehensive, as cultural arguments about families, especially those that essentialize culture based on race, have done great damage. Concepts such as the "culture of poverty" have placed the blame for poverty and its transmission from one generation to the next on the moral failure and cultural values of families, particularly Black families, rather than on the conditions in which they live.[21] Such uses of culture should indeed be written against, and many scholars have strongly done so. For example, as discussed earlier, representations of Black mothering as a dysfunctional "matriarchal culture" have been critiqued by feminist and family scholars who have shown the strengths of Black cultural practices of extended kinship and community care.[22] At the same time, scholars of Black motherhood and Black mothers themselves have not simply dismissed culture but have engaged in the work of opposing pathologizing cultural narratives. Likewise, Asian American mothers are also reclaiming culture, recognizing its operations not only in making others but in resisting othering.

Mothering with and against culture moves beyond the binary of either enculturating the next generation into the traditions of the ancestors or acculturating to the norms of the dominant culture.[23] Rather than treating culture and cultural identities as if they are automatically dictated by immigrant parents or overseas ancestors or ethnic enclaves, this chapter has shown how culture is lived within families and across generations. In narrating their mothering stories, Leslie, Annika, and Gina reveal that culture both writes and is rewritten through everyday choices as quotidian and complex as what to name a child and what to feed them; whom to marry or divorce; and how to integrate grandparents, in-laws, and nannies into family living and care arrangements, or not. In short, Asian American mothers' intersectional maternal labor is shaped by their cultural aspirations for how to live and what to live for.

Conclusion

Rather than discount culture due to fears of replicating its misuses, culture should be treated with the rigorous and careful attention that it requires. This chapter has shown that culture can be fluid, heterogenous, and contextual rather than static, uniform, or universal. The stories narrated here show how Asian American mothers expand the cultural repertoires of what it means to be Asian American outside of the cultural dictates of model minority racialization. Thus, they challenge culture as the basis of othering by developing new cultural formations that serve as tools for anti-othering, even as these tools are often developed as necessary responses to othering.

Mothering with culture involves making choices about what to eat, which holidays to celebrate, what languages to speak, where to live, which values to live by, and which to pass on. At the same time, mothering against culture necessitates resistance to and hyperawareness of problematic framings of Asian culture that are imposed onto Asian Americans, particularly onto Asian American mothers, children, and families. While culture can serve as the tool for making mothers into others, the claiming and creating of new cultural identities and practices are also the basis for resistance to othering. In mapping new cultural directions for themselves, their families, and their communities, Asian American mothers are simultaneously remapping the terrain of what it means to be Asian American.

The next chapter shifts the focus of the making and remaking of culture from homes, families, and communities to schools and schoolyards and the complex social relations that revolve around them. Building on this chapter's framework of mothering with and against culture, the following chapter shows how the institutional context of schools forces mothers to push against mother/othering and reproductive exclusion but also calls forth Asian American mothers' efforts to mother with and toward alternative visions for their children's education.

4 *Schooling Mother/Others*

Public schools now are so different from when we were raised. Because of all the budget cuts, the private schools are at least one year ahead. When my son was starting first grade, he was doing multiplication and division, but teachers thought he was too active and wanted him to be on ADHD medication! I said, "No, I think he's probably just bored." So, I gave him my own package to work on. They actually made copies, but then they reported us for overworking our kids! The school we're at—there are a lot of Asians, a lot of Koreans, a lot of Chinese families, so others just see a lot of tiger mothers.

MINDY, interview, Chinese American, physician

"What is learned in school?". . . An examination of schooling and its sociological ties to the family and the workplace can illuminate the social and political functions of schools.

HENRY A. GIROUX AND ANTHONY PENNA, "Social Education in the Classroom: The Dynamics of the Hidden Curriculum" (1979)

What mothers learn in school relates not just to their children's schooling but to their own. Mothers are schooled in what roles they are expected to play and not play. They learn where they and their families stand in the social hierarchy inside the school and how this standing is inseparable from the social order outside of school. In short, they learn which mothers belong and which are *other*. Just as mothering is not something innate but must be learned, so othering and being othered are not intrinsic traits but acquired knowledge, and much of this knowledge is acquired in schools. This chapter recognizes the immense socializing power of schools not just on students but on mothers, shifting the focus from how mothers influence their children's schooling to how their children's schools influence mothers.

Previous chapters have discussed how the tiger mother construct builds on a long history of matritropes that have cast Asian American mothers as reproducers of foreign and undesirable families. This chapter demonstrates not merely how these processes play out in schools but how schools play an active role in constructing Asian American mothers as outsiders and in enacting mother/othering more broadly. Mother/othering in schools takes many forms, which this chapter examines through the concept of a *hidden maternal curriculum*. Reframing Giroux and Penna's question above, this chapter builds on the concept of the hidden curriculum to ask not just what is learned in school but what mothers learn in school. And what can we learn by looking more closely at schools as sites not just for educating children but for schooling mothers?

Scholarship on the hidden curriculum has challenged the idea that schools are meritocratic, democratic institutions, revealing instead how educational systems actively create and reproduce social divisions.[1] Beyond the hidden curriculum for children, this chapter shows how schools enact a hidden maternal curriculum that reproduces hierarchies among mothers inside schools and that in turn shapes their social positions outside school. This hidden maternal curriculum impacts all mothers but imparts specific lessons to and about Asian American mothers. Schools often position Asian American mothers in the role of hypermothers—specifically as tiger mothers—who are relentless in their pursuit of their children's high academic achievement. But Asian American mothers articulate and enact a different kind of hypermothering that is called forth not by dreams of hyperachievement but by hypervigilance to othering.

Mindy, quoted above, provided a rich account of how Asian American mothers are othered in school through a diffuse yet powerful hidden maternal curriculum that influences not only how they mother but how they are perceived as mothers. She shared how she was committed to sending her children to the local public schools but voiced concerns that the U.S. public education system was falling behind on multiple fronts, from infrastructure to quality of instruction. Notably, her point of reference was not China or other Asian countries but private schools in her neighborhood that had better resources and academic outcomes. Rather than pulling her children out of the public school system, Mindy decided to become more actively involved. As a physician, she drew on her strong math and science background to assess and address weaknesses in the school's math curriculum, in hopes of benefiting her own children and the school as a whole. She rearranged her work schedule and even cut back on the number of patients she was seeing in order to volunteer at the school.

Her efforts, however, were not appreciated. On top of her concerns being disregarded, her increased involvement brought unwelcome scrutiny to her family, including unsolicited and unsubstantiated comments that her son had ADHD. What Mindy ended up learning in school was that she was not valued as an involved parent whose time, energy, and skills were assets to an under-resourced school, but instead, that she was regarded as a major part of the problem, one of a "lot of tiger mothers" who overworked their children and increased competition and stress for teachers and other families.

Whether or not they ascribe to this pressurized, high-achievement style of mothering, Asian American mothers have been collectively painted in the tiger mother stripe. The reductive framing of

Asian American mothers as tiger mothers does a disservice to their many concerns about schooling, ranging from the safety of the social environment to the lack of diversity in the curriculum, to racial microaggressions, to the declining investment in the U.S. education system, especially public schools. In contrast to the tiger mother stereotype, the strongest common concerns among the Asian American mothers interviewed for this book were not about their children gaining admission into Ivy League colleges but about claiming a sense of belonging for their children—and for themselves—in the schools they were attending right now.

Focusing on the narratives of three Asian American mothers—Althea, Kyra, and Tae—this chapter examines schools as sites of mother/othering that demand complex and often exhausting forms of intersectional maternal labor. Each of these mothers held a vision of education beyond the formal curriculum, ranging from homeland visits to learning cultural traditions, to developing strong racial, gender, and sexual identities. Instead, they found much of their energy devoted to managing a hidden maternal curriculum of mother/othering that was imposed not only through formal school policies but also through informal interactions in sites such as playgrounds, holiday events, school bathrooms, and classrooms.

While their experiences and the narratives through which they make meaning of them are distinctly personal, these three women express commonalities with many Asian American mothers who encountered schools as sites of othering. Many mothers found themselves unwitting participants in school policies and interactions that othered them while also implicating them in othering other mothers. Although they made choices about how they contributed to or challenged mother/othering at school, beyond their individual actions, they confronted an entrenched hidden maternal curriculum throughout the institutional level of schools—from field trips to field days, to fields extending far beyond the schoolyard.

In illustrating how the hidden maternal curriculum operates to further mother/othering, this chapter develops three related concepts to examine motherhood and schools as closely intertwined social institutions that reinforce each other's power to reproduce social divisions and inequality. First, *educational maternal labor* recognizes that the gendered work that mothers do in schools is indeed work, whether paid or unpaid, and requires skills, time, material resources, and emotional management. Second, *maternal agency* recognizes that the socialization of mothers by schools is not a one-way process but that mothers make choices to participate in or resist the hidden maternal curriculum. Third, *hypermothering* speaks to the specific constructions of Asian American mothers as fueling the hypercompetitiveness that has become a defining factor in both education and motherhood.

Theorizing the Hidden Maternal Curriculum of Mother/Othering

The hidden curriculum is the unofficial learning transmitted through informal channels rather than through formal instruction.[2] It is sometimes referred to as things that are "caught not taught" in schools—that is, knowledge that is absorbed even when it is not openly instructed or even acknowledged.[3] It is well established that schools act as agents of socialization that reinforce social norms and hierarchies among students; this chapter theorizes a parallel *hidden maternal curriculum* of unspoken rules and roles that validate certain mothers and marginalize others, all the while consolidating the power of both schools and motherhood as institutions that perpetuate othering.

Research on the hidden curriculum has mainly focused on the reproduction of class inequality, wherein schools reinforce social stratification between elites and non-elites.[4] This emphasis is captured in the evocative title of Paul Willis's influential book *Learning to Labor:*

How Working-Class Kids Get Working-Class Jobs.[5] Riffing on Willis, I considered titling this chapter, "Learning to Mother: How Model Minority Mothers Raise Model Minority Children." While somewhat catchy, this title would be inaccurate (not to mention derivative) and would further confine Asian American mothering to the model minority and tiger mother frames. Instead, through their involvement in their children's schools, Asian American mothers in this study are keenly aware of how model minority racialization shapes perceptions of them as tiger mothers, but they also find ways to challenge the imposition of this matritrope. Thus, the hidden maternal curriculum and learning to mother are frameworks that can be useful in understanding Asian American mothers' educational concerns and the forms of labor that they perform in schools but must also be used with care in order to not further homogenize them.

Further, it is important to recognize ongoing critiques of the concept of the hidden curriculum, which some regard as focusing too much on informal learning and distracting from the many problems in the official school curriculum, such as censorship of books, failure to teach about histories of slavery and genocide, and substandard instruction in math, science, and many other areas. Scholars focusing on race have especially focused attention on how a hidden curriculum in schools criminalizes Black children, leading to greater disciplinary strictness that is justified by ideologies of Black criminality.[6] Even when Black students are not overtly policed, as Prudence Carter demonstrates in *Keepin' It Real*, they are subjected to a "culture of power" through which schools impart "rules, tastes, appreciations and styles for success that are fashioned by the dominant social classes whose members are mainly White, middle- and upper-class."[7] Dawn Dow's *Mothering While Black* and Riché Barnes's *Raising the Race* demonstrate how Black mothers must teach their children to avoid racial bias, criminalization, and violence while simultaneously striving to instill in them a positive sense of Black racial identity.[8]

While Asian American mothers are not exempt from these fears for their children's physical safety, most do not have to negotiate the same level of concern about their children being subject to institutionalized violence and criminalization on a daily basis. The concept of the hidden maternal curriculum does not ignore the many differences between the kinds of concerns that Black mothers and Asian American mothers confront in schools but emphasizes how schools operate as sites of mother/othering for many different racial groups, although in very distinct ways. The ways that Black mothers must contend with the trope of the welfare queen is qualitatively different from how Asian American mothers grapple with the tiger mother trope, but both reveal how matritropes manifest not simply as annoying stereotypes but through far-reaching policies and interactions that have a profound impact not just on children but on mothers.

Specifically for Asian Americans, the formal curriculum largely omits Asian American history and contemporary issues, perpetuating the belief that Asian Americans are a marginal group and ignoring their contributions and critical perspectives.[9] These critiques of the concrete and visible problems in the curriculum, however, need not be seen as separate from the hidden messaging transmitted to and about mothers. Instead, the hidden maternal curriculum can provide another lens to critique aspects of both formal and informal school curriculum by underscoring that not just students but also mothers and families are constantly being shaped by what is taught in schools.

The trope of Asian American mothers as tiger mothers emerges in the context of schools to construct them as hypercompetitive threats in the eyes of others, while demanding their hypervigilance to subtle and overt ways that they and their children are othered. Thus, hypermothering is simultaneously imposed on and enacted by them. The conditions that produce the "hyperness" of Asian

Americans in parenting and education have been illuminated in Pawan Dhingra's *Hyper Education: Why Good Schools, Good Grades, and Good Behavior Are Not Enough*, which explores what drives certain Asian American parents to invest heavily in their children's education beyond formal schooling. Dhingra shows how shared experiences of migration and education lead certain ethnic groups to cluster around specific activities, such as Indian Americans in spelling bees, to give their children an edge in the face of racial discrimination and global competition. These activities, however, also take on importance as instilling moral values of hard work and discipline while building connections to co-ethnic communities.[10]

The larger conditions that contribute to hypermothering are also illuminated by Jennifer Lee and Min Zhou's *The Asian American Achievement Paradox*, which examines the "hyper-selectivity" that pre-sorts for Asian immigrants who already possess high educational credentials or seek to attain them as international students.[11] The emphasis on education that these immigrants pass on to their children does not derive solely from Asian cultural values but is powerfully shaped by U.S. immigration policies based on the 1965 Immigration and Nationality Act and subsequent legislation. Further, the "success frame" that both demands and naturalizes Asian American educational and professional accomplishments also fosters an "achievement paradox" in which Asian Americans who do not excel are regarded as failures. Hyper education and hyper-selectivity provide the context for hypermothering, and these are all fostered by the positioning of Asian Americans as model minority. But these processes do not happen automatically; they are enacted in specific institutional sites—in this case, schools—by a range of actors, including teachers, administrators, students, and mothers.

The hidden curriculum has served as a generative framework to understand schools as institutions that reproduce social class and inequality. The hidden *maternal* curriculum expands this framework to address schools as sites for a broad range of social processes related not just to class but to race, gender, sexuality, and especially, reproduction. Similarly, in *Women Without Class: Girls, Race, and Identity*, Julie Bettie examined a broad range of school-related activities to show how class identities are not just about class but are constructed in relation to race, ethnicity, gender, and sexuality. Further, these identities are not fixed but are constantly claimed or contested through active "class performances" in everyday interactions among students, teachers, and administrators.[12] Likewise, mothers engage in *maternal performances* of different social identities that are not innate but are validated or invalidated in specific sites of mothering, in this case, schools. While learned and enacted at school, the hidden maternal curriculum that mothers absorb about themselves and other mothers reverberates beyond the schoolyard to address much larger debates about race, families, and educational achievement and how these all define boundaries of belonging and otherness. In turn, schools call forth specific forms of maternal labor in which mothers negotiate not just their children's education but their own as mothers.

Asian American Mothers Negotiating the Hidden Maternal Curriculum

The specific hidden maternal curriculum that Asian American mothers must negotiate is how to support various aspects of their children's schooling while constantly grappling with mother/othering, especially through racialized and gendered constructions of them as tiger mothers. Each mother's narrative that follows is a deeply personal account but also illuminates theoretical and public debates in which Asian American mothers are constructed as others within schools and through school-related activities and interactions. More broadly, they reveal how normative models of motherhood and family are valorized and how departures from these models are denigrated through a hidden maternal curriculum of mother/othering.

Althea: Excuse Me, I'm a Minority!

Althea, a Filipina American financial consultant, found herself in awkward interactions with a group of White mothers at her son Angelo's elementary school who assumed that she shared their negative views of racial minorities. Rather than seeing this an indication that they recognized and accepted her as an Asian American or that they conferred "honorary" Whiteness upon her, she felt that they erased both her Asianness and her non-Whiteness in order to feel comfortable around her. This included freely voicing their beliefs about racial dynamics at the school and assuming she agreed with them.

> I think that at some point they forget I'm Asian. I always think that this is a very odd thing to say, or am I totally clueless? But I've experienced it so many times, more often than I would like. Somebody would say something offhand not realizing that I'm there. It's like, "You're denigrating minorities, and excuse me, I'm a minority!" The reason I know this is there was an incident not too long ago. One of the moms, she was talking about how the high school is going down the tubes. So here I am eavesdropping—does she know anything academically or something like that? No, no. She says, "All these minorities!" Then—it was so funny—one of my friends was like, "Oh no, it doesn't include you!"

Despite describing this interaction as "funny," Althea was clearly not amused, as she realized her tenuous inclusion was predicated on other mothers believing that the term *minority* "doesn't include you" and assuming that she would concur by not identifying with or as such. Her friend, by attempting to smooth over the awkward interaction by reassuring Althea that she was exempt from the disparaging remarks, instead put her in an uncomfortable position; not only was Althea othered, but she was faced with a choice between confronting these mothers or letting it slide, thereby tacitly validating the othering of "all these minorities" and separating herself from them. Althea thus showed how routine playground interactions could turn quickly into fraught racial encounters, eliciting feelings ranging from discomfort to anger, to guilt—all of which she found draining and alienating.

At first, Althea thought these mothers' comments stemmed from their concerns about academic standards, but on further reflection, she attributed them to the school's changing racial demographics. Speculating about the motivations of the mother who made the remark, Althea said, "I think in her mind, the more White people the better [*laughs*]. I think that's what it is. Really, I don't know, but it seems to me that that's where it's coming from—*who will my child play with?*" In other words, Althea surmised that the negative views toward minorities held by these White mothers at her son's school were not based on the school's educational standard, its formal curriculum, but on its hidden curriculum—that is, what their children would learn and who they would become by playing with more diverse peers. In turn, these anxieties extended to what kind of peers the mothers themselves would have to "play" with—or refuse to.

Althea further observed that the reason these White mothers did not see her as a member of a U.S. racial minority was that they perceived her as a foreigner. Explaining how she picked up on this perception, she noted how they often commented on her fluency in English.

> They're surprised by that—"She speaks so very well!" Because I speak like them, they think we share the same ideas or whatever. They always say, "Oh, you speak English better than I do!" It's very odd. They hear but don't really see me. I'm really the only Asian in the group.

By commenting on her command of English, the mothers at her son's school indicated a presumption that English was not Althea's first language. Not only did they assume that Althea shared their negative views toward the increasing number of "minorities" at the school, but they assumed that she was a foreigner who did not identify with or as a racial minority, let alone as a person of color or as Asian American.

Indeed, Althea herself admitted that she was not fully comfortable claiming these identity terms, as she had spent most of her childhood in the Philippines and even after years of living in the United States, she still most strongly identified as Filipina. Althea described her immigration experience as "atypical," as she had neither come with her parents as a child nor alone as an international student. Instead, she went back and forth between the two countries to attend private schools in the Northeast and then a prestigious liberal arts college. After graduation, she had been torn about returning to the Philippines but then found a job in the financial sector, where she met and married her husband, Bill. In fact, it was not until she gave birth to her son, Angelo, that she felt rooted to life in the United States and decided to become a citizen.

After they had Angelo, Althea and Bill decided to move from the city to the suburb where he had been raised, as his extended family lived nearby and the school district was highly regarded. Because most of Althea's family members lived in the Philippines, she was grateful for support from Bill's family, especially her sister-in-law, Susan, who was a full-time homemaker and had children around the same age as Angelo. Since Susan had generously offered to help with pickups and host Angelo for afterschool playdates, Althea leaned toward sending her son to the same private preschool attended by his cousins. But she started to have second thoughts as she initiated the application and realized spots at the preschool were highly competitive, noting, "I think there is even an application process for babies!" After an off-putting interview, which she felt was geared toward assessing how well she could "fit in with the elites," she decided to look elsewhere.

At first, finding a Filipina childcare provider had not been a priority for Althea, but she started to think more consciously about how the choices she made about her son's education and caregiving arrangements broadly would impact his racial and cultural identity. So, when the opportunity unexpectedly presented itself to place Angelo at a home-based preschool run by Flor, a Filipina immigrant, Althea seized on it. Explaining her decision, she laughed: "It all came down to food!" and then she elaborated.

> The last person we met just happened to be Filipina. I wouldn't have known it from her name; she took her husband's name. Right then, it was like love at first sight! She grew up in the same province that my parents grew up in, so her method of cooking was so familiar. I don't know how to cook it, so she would make me food, too. My son is actually very, very, picky, and my husband and I made a pact: "Okay, there are many battles, but we're not going to battle about food. We just want dinner to be dinner." He just has a limited palate, but with Flor, you have no choice, you eat this! He had to expand. She doesn't spoil. Like I said, she'll make food, and you don't want to eat it, well you kind of have to [*laughs*].

In addition to educating her son's palate to embrace Filipino food, Flor's small preschool was very appealing to Althea for other reasons. In contrast to the very structured programs she had previously explored, Althea approved of Flor's no-frills but warm approach to early childhood learning.

> Not terribly strict, she just doesn't take any nonsense. It's very practical to me. She had a schedule, and you go by it and she doesn't handhold or anything like that. She's very caring, lots of hugs—they

> love it. She lives across from the park, so they're always out if it's a nice day. Very safe, because they just walk. She's lived there forever so she has her little playground in the back. In the summer, she has her little pool. She's like, "They're children! We don't necessarily have to teach them anything. We have books in here, let them read!"

Rather than seeing preschool as an opportunity to gain an educational edge or connect to elite social networks, Althea prioritized a family-like environment in which her son would feel loved and learn about Filipino culture. This warm, familial setting also assuaged her guilt about working long hours, and she felt deeply indebted to Flor, both for the care she provided to Angelo and the support she gave to Althea to focus on her demanding career in the financial sector.

> I worked really long hours, and I was just telling my husband, our son was with Flor until age five. So, the entirety of the time, because of the commute, I spent an hour with him in the morning and an hour at night. That was it. The rest of the time it was all Flor! Thanks to her taking care of him, he completely relates and is so very proud of being Filipino. I kept my name and all of that good stuff, so for the longest time, Angelo thought that he was full Filipino. His father would say, "Honey, yes, you're half-Filipino and half-White. You're also from Ireland. You're American." But really until age five, age six, he was always saying, "I'm Filipino!"

After her son moved on to the public elementary school, Althea felt tremendous gratitude toward Flor and kept in touch with her for years but then lost contact. In retrospect, Althea was surprised at how close they had been, noting that she and Flor came from very different class backgrounds.

> I was surprised with my reaction as well because I can't say I get along with all Filipinos in general here in the States, because I was brought up very, very, differently. Her way of seeing things, we didn't always agree, because as I said we are all very argumentative [*laughs*]. That's what I liked about her. She's very direct, so she told me this is how much she charges, take it or leave it. So, I was like, "Okay!" She would have problems with other parents not paying on time or what not. That has never ever been an issue for us. She never increased. She actually told us, "I never increase yours, because I know yours will come in."

Althea acknowledged that although she felt close to Flor and was very grateful for her support both in educating her son about their Filipino heritage and enabling Althea to focus on her career, in the end, their relationship was ultimately based on her son's education and care needs. And after Angelo was no longer attending her preschool, they drifted apart.

Althea also underscored that while she felt very fortunate to have found a preschool in which her son could develop a positive sense of his Filipino identity, she did not indiscriminately value all aspects of Filipino culture, nor did she prioritize these cultural aspects in all her educational choices for her son. In fact, she intentionally distanced herself from certain parts of Filipino culture with which she had been raised, particularly related to Catholic schooling.

> We were very devout Catholic growing up and now I'm anti-Catholic. So, I'm going kind of opposite. My son has not been baptized, and my sister has heard of that—they wanted to kidnap him when we're asleep and have a priest baptize him. I was like, "Don't you dare!" [*laughs*] Many of our traditions were around being Catholic—actually, my husband also grew up Catholic, he's Irish, and is now atheist. We both went to Catholic school, so it's a deliberate choice: "No, he's not doing that!"

What were your reasons for leaving Catholicism?

I've always been pro-choice, not so much that I'm for abortion—in fact, I would rather work towards women not having to go through that. But it's a choice. As a woman, as a couple, as a human being, there should be a safe way for me, whatever decision we come up with. It doesn't make sense—it's scary, scary, scary—this group of people who would have control over women's bodies.

Thus, while strongly identifying as a Filipina, Althea also rejected elements of Filipino culture—namely, the strong influence of Catholicism and its associated beliefs on abortion and women's bodily autonomy. Her disagreements with Catholicism, in turn, influenced her choices not just about her own religious practices but about her son's education. Not wanting him to attend Catholic school, Althea and her husband decided first to enroll Angelo in Flor's preschool and then in a highly regarded and diverse public school.

Despite interactions with other mothers at the school, such as the discussion about "minorities" and being treated as a foreigner, Althea felt mostly positive about the public school, especially its diversity with regard to race, but much less positive with regard to gender. In fact, she noted that her son had experienced more negative interactions around gender than race. She described him as a "sensitive soul" whose interests set him apart from other boys his age.

His class is very colorful, from Asian, to African, to Portuguese, to anything. He gets along with everybody.

Has he experienced any bullying or teasing?

In terms of his race or color of his skin? No. He gets teased more about his interest in dance—"Only girls do dance." He's fine with that now, but at first, he said, "I don't understand why I'm being teased." I was like, "Dearest, we know that's not true. Either you're going to let it affect

> you, or you just say, 'Well, you're not so bright!'" I love dance for him because he's so fit. I'd rather him do that than baseball, where you stand for hours on end not really moving. I think it's very healthy for him. I just want him to learn so that he can enjoy it. . . . I'm sure there are better teachers I could find for him, but he likes this one. His pace could go a lot faster, but he's doing his thing. He likes the girls—because the boys tend to roughhouse. They like sports; he's not into sports.

With regard to extracurricular activities, not only did Althea encourage Angelo to pursue dance instead of sports, but she did not push him to excel or seek out the best instructors. Instead, she focused on his enjoyment of movement and the friendships he developed with children of all genders.

Although Althea felt that the school was very "colorful" with students from many different backgrounds, as Angelo grew older, she was concerned that he had no Filipino friends at school and they did not live near a Filipino community. She wanted him to develop a sense of being Filipino beyond food and the other aspects of cultural identity that Flor had helped him learn, and for him to have a direct connection to her homeland and her family. Thus, she and her husband made a commitment to prioritize regular trips back to the Philippines to enrich his educational experiences while making sure he kept up with his formal schooling.

> When my son was born, we made a pact that we'd go home regularly to the Philippines. So, our first trip when he was two and a half, we stayed for four weeks. We've been doing that up until recently. I would die if we went in the summer. I cannot deal with the heat anymore. So we go during school, usually around winter vacation, January, February, when the weather is nice, and he can go out and do things. When it's that time, and we know that we are going home, we always talk to the teacher beforehand and say this is what we will do.

> And they'll be like, "Oh, he'll learn more from this trip than he would otherwise." They'd be very open to give me a packet.

Althea believed that her son's formal schooling was adequate, but the informal curriculum was missing a more global understanding of both "his place in the world" as well as "his place in the family," and she was committed to regular trips to the Philippines to fill these gaps. In addition, because her mother had passed, Althea wanted to stay connected to her father, her extended family, and her homeland, as she felt that learning about family history and cultural traditions was important not only for her son but for herself as a mother.

> With my mom having passed away, I just don't know who to model, which is kind of sad. It's very hard. Whatever traditions that my mom may have done, or my ancestors, became more of a practical thing for my dad since now he's in charge of all of these things. His way of doing things, I know, is very different from what my mom did, but I can't remember what my mom did. That's one thing I like about my family. I may not have seen someone literally for fifteen years and when I came home it's like I never left. It's such a cliché, but once it happens to you, it's like, on the flight back I think, "Good god, wherever you were before, that spot is still here for you." It's really quite amazing and I'm very thankful for it.

These visits home were clearly very important to Althea, nourishing her as a mother and reinforcing her expansive vision for educating Angelo in various ways, both in and out of formal schooling.

But as much as she made sure that he kept pace with his assignments and timed their winter visit to overlap with as many school vacation days as possible, Angelo still ended up missing a significant number of school days. As he moved into higher grade levels, his absences began to draw criticism—not so much from teachers or administrators, who were generally supportive, but from other mothers.

> Actually, the teachers always come back and say, "Wow, he's more advanced now with the curriculum than we are!" But other moms would say, "You're getting special treatment." And I would tell them, "I just asked, and they said yes." I made sure he went through all his stuff, and trust me, there's lots of time. We have a bit of structure. Academically, he has to do what needs to be done.

While aware of the critical comments by other parents toward Angelo's absences, Althea strongly believed these trips were of huge benefit to her son in developing his understanding not only of Filipino culture but also claiming his identity as mixed race. She observed that while he was often marginalized in the United States for not meeting the ideals of White masculinity in his appearance or interests, in the Philippines he received much positive attention for his distinctive looks, his dancing ability, and his Americanness.

> When we go back to the Philippines, the first thing that they say is "You should be on TV!" Apparently being biracial and his accent are all very big things. I think he likes the attention. He gets spoiled. He's the youngest, so whatever he wants to do, he gets to do. I don't know how this is going to change and what middle school is going to do, but he's very proud of his coloring, his stature—he's kind of tiny. He says he likes it that way. He actually looks like me—he looks Filipino, dark skin. But there is that thing that he looks mixed. We have a contest to see who's going to get darker faster, because in the winter we both lament, "Ah, we're so light." [*laughs*]

In addition to fostering pride in his Filipino and mixed-race identity, Althea appreciated that these homeland visits strengthened their relationship as mother and son and reinforced cultural values that she held dear, such as respect for elders. She emphasized that these values had to be taught and were not intrinsic traits that all Filipinos naturally possessed.

In fact, Althea questioned what it meant to be culturally Filipino, as the country encompasses such a wide range of people and traditions.

> I can't say what is distinctly Filipino or what is something I just want to do. What would be distinctly Filipino: playing mahjong? [*laughs*] Angelo knows how—he's actually pretty good. Does that make him Filipino? My pride and joy is that he is very respectful, but those are *my* hard-and-fast rules, not everyone's. I see it in his cousins as they get older—they talk back, and you can see Angelo hear something and he looks at me, eyes bulging, saying, "I can't believe they said that!" I don't let him get away with that. The cousins are older, not really his age, so there's that. I'm sure that will happen when he's thirteen [*laughs*] but right now, it is lovely. People just love him because he never talks back.

Althea regarded respect for elders not as a universal aspect of Filipino culture, let alone of all Asian cultures, but as a quality that had to be taught and learned both in and out of school. Further, she saw this sense of respect as fluid, something that would likely recede as he became a teenager. Because she understood cultural values as needing to be fostered, she valued their trips home as an important part of his education in the broadest possible sense, including offering opportunities for him to learn through work and strengthening his commitment to attending college.

> The way I grew up, everybody goes to college. You just can't even *not* think about it. It's just what you do. My husband, on the other hand, here in America, it's like, "Oh, you don't have to if you don't want to."

> But we talk about it openly to him: "This is what your father thinks, and this is what I think." Right now, he's thinking, "I can't imagine not going to college. I *have* to go to college." It might change. I have this fear of the teenage years that all these lovely things are just going to flip and disappear. . . . A family member in the Philippines owns an export business that, when he is fifteen or sixteen, I may let him go there for a summer so he can learn the business a little bit. He would love it.

Althea noted that trips home to the Philippines normalized expectations that he should attend college and that he should also engage in paid work as a teenager, which many of his friends at home did not.

Althea had many resources to draw upon to give Angelo meaningful and varied learning experiences, and she recognized these privileges, but she was still anxious about what the future held. "I'm not looking forward to what middle school and high school will be like." When asked to elaborate on these fears, she summed up: "All that pressure, I've never subscribed to it." Concerned about the pressurized academic environment Angelo would encounter as he grew older, Althea saw grounding her son in his cultural background, family, history, and job opportunities in the Philippines as essential elements of his broader education.

At the same time, she did not want him to confine his interests and relationships to other Filipinos. She regretted having made this choice herself, lamenting that while she had attended a diverse liberal arts college, she had rarely ventured outside a small circle of Filipina friends, and she saw this as a pattern among other Asians and Asian Americans.

> This could be overgeneralizing but from looking at people that I know that are Asian, they seek out other Asians. I see it as a cocoon, which I don't necessarily embrace. . . . In college, the Filipinos were all together and it was actually quite bad. They would all speak in

> their—*our* language. There would be ten of us in this big dining hall, and everyone would be looking at us. It's true. We just all gravitated towards each other and were all very close. But because of that, in a way, I missed having a multicultural experience in college. My roommates were Filipina; it was just the Filipinas.

Althea both cherished and regretted socializing mainly with other Filipinas in college instead of taking the opportunity to connect with more diverse students. At the same time, she took note of her current situation as the reverse of her college one, with her now being the only Filipina and only Asian in her family, workplace, community, and child's school. While she chided herself and other Filipinas as cliquish, Althea dearly missed those close connections, especially as she had no close Filipina friends nearby who were mothers.

Revisiting the dynamics among the mothers at her son's school, Althea surmised that her conditional acceptance by this group of White mothers was premised on their "forgetting" that she was Asian or a racial minority, and this sense of being overlooked for who she was transmitted a sense of otherness. Many Asian American mothers shared this sense of being other as accruing from seemingly insignificant but frequent interactions, ranging from playground conversations about school demographics to complaints about absences due to homeland visits. But for other mothers, such as Kyra, the hidden maternal curriculum came into bold relief around a specific charged incident at their children's schools that crystallized their positions as mother/others.

Kyra: They See Me as the Anti-Christmas Mom

As an educational consultant, Kyra confronted a particular form of mother/othering through a hidden curriculum that dismissed her concerns both as a mother and an educational professional with expertise in diversity, equity, and inclusion. She found herself othered on two different but related counts: first, as one of the only South Asian mothers in her children's predominantly White elementary school; second, as a trained consultant with expertise to critique the school's lack of diversity in curriculum and programming. These came together around her sense of not being able to bring her expertise to address concerns at her own children's school.

> That's been an odd feeling, to know so much about critiques of sexism, or racism, or class, and yet actually not be able to be in the schools doing anything . . . to actually really get in there and apply some of the insights I can bring to bear upon school reform in ways that would benefit my own kids and other kids.

Like many Asian American mothers, the othering that Kyra experienced often took the form of an "odd feeling," but then it took more solid form around a particular incident. The underlying tensions that Kyra had sensed as both a mother and an educational consultant came to a head around concerns involving the school's lack of sensitivity around holiday programming.

> In a nutshell, it was just a regular mandated part of the public school day and nobody questioned it but me. It was holiday time, December 22, what was normally library visiting day, where the kids would go and pick up their books because it's been determined that *literacy* is important for young children. And they replaced it with *shopping time* for holiday gifts. The PTA sanctioned this event; they thought it up; and they ordered tons of plastic goods, like Scooby Doo pencil sharpeners, Power Puff Girls erasers, and mugs that say this and that. So, it's a profit-making enterprise. And they think it's all good; they're funding the PTA and they're helping busy families get their holiday shopping done! And never was there an interrogation over what

holiday was this, whose holiday was this? My objection is that even if it is your holiday, perhaps you wouldn't expect your five-year-old to be shopping for gifts for other people when they don't know how to count money.

Kyra's reservations about the holiday fundraising event were based on multiple concerns: in addition to focusing narrowly on the celebration of Christmas, the event substituted library and reading time with a product-themed shopping fair. Not only did it exclude those who celebrated different holidays, but it turned students into consumers, without considering whether their families had resources or interest in consuming these products. Thus, Kyra's concerns were not only as a mother of a child attending the school but as an educator critiquing the lack of awareness of socioeconomic and cultural differences in the school's programs. Both sets of concerns—as a mother and educator—required her to invest significant maternal labor in attempting to get the school to respond.

> I wasn't sure what to do, so I ended up just sitting in the library with my son on that day reading books by ourselves. I felt that I needed to make clear to him and to the school that I didn't support the event. So that just set me off on a whole thing. It was a long, protracted process where we had to call meetings, and I did research and brought it in and talked about different holidays and how even Christmas was never a commercial holiday, until recently. That was really challenging but we made our point. Now they have a charitable focus, and the kids make self-portraits and those are their gifts. And we suggested things to the art and music teachers to celebrate the season very broadly.

Although Kyra felt that she was able to institute a positive, if minor, change at the school, she had to galvanize support from other parents in order to bring this about. The hidden maternal curriculum that Kyra learned from this incident was that her own concerns were not enough to merit a response.

> It was eye-opening. It made me realize, as much as I think I'm so hip to issues of diversity and social justice, that it was having kids that has shown me how this stuff works in the so-called real world. . . . I think that public schools in particular are really challenged right now to step up and deal with issues of multiculturalism and everything we know about what are some of the better ways to educate kids. As I move through the school system and I read it culturally as an institution, I really think about what it would feel like to not have the resources that I've had to understand what's going on there.

Although strongly committed to both her work and family, Kyra struggled to integrate her personal and professional commitments and apply them toward improving not just her own children's school but the wider public education system. However, she did not attribute her strong commitments in the field of education simply to being Indian or South Asian but to her own educational background and expertise.

> I've never been to India. I don't really have a South Asian sensibility as much as I really have an Asian American sensibility in the political, pan-ethnic sense. . . . I've come to claim the larger Asian American rubric, to understand there is a cultural depth and background to the construction of my family. I understand now how much of my personal struggles around the right way to have family or how I felt growing up, it is very much what we have theorized in Asian American studies. So, for the most part, my sense of ethnicity has been the one crafted by being educated basically in an ethnic studies model.

Notably, Kyra did not ascribe her strong commitment to education, both for herself and her children, to her Indian identity and culture, but neither did she discount the power of culture. Her educational training gave her tools to situate her family of origin in historical and social contexts, which in turn, enabled her to choose which aspects of her cultural background to claim and which to challenge.

The aspects of culture that she most strongly critiqued revolved around gender, but here, she also did not essentialize gender inequality as an innate part of "old world" cultures. Instead, she noted how gender roles were shaped by specific immigration histories and family dynamics. Although her parents followed a traditional model of breadwinning father and stay-at-home mother, Kyra was adamant about not attributing this arrangement to being Indian. Instead, she situated her family within the broader migration history of the Indian diaspora and the historical construction of the racial category of Asian Americans. At the same time, she saw her parents and herself as complex individuals. This was especially true with regard to her mother, with whom Kyra shared a very close but complicated relationship. Kyra acknowledged that while she did not want to confine her mother to a traditional maternal role, she had benefited from her mother's willingness to take on this role both in Kyra's childhood and now, as a grandmother who contributed much to afterschool care.

> So, I have a lot of conflicted feelings about using my mother. I say "using" very specifically for that reason. It is often instrumental. It hasn't necessarily brought us closer in our mother-daughter relationship. She's there because I can't be there. It has allowed me to further my own career. All of these years, I've sort of had this traditional grandmother type who didn't question—like some Americanized grandmothers are saying they're on the golf tour, they're traveling, they have rejected that role of child-rearing and all-for-the-kids, but my mother has always made herself available in that way.

Kyra's conflicted feelings about "using" her mother stemmed from her recognition that not only did her children benefit from having such an involved grandmother, but Kyra's and her husband's ability to focus on their careers was being subsidized by her mother filling in for childcare and educational gaps. In addition, she was aware that she was resorting to an individualized solution of relying on her mother to compensate for the public education system, rather than holding the school district accountable for after-school programming and transportation.

As both an educator and a daughter, Kyra felt these contradictions most poignantly when she was able to participate in educational and professional activities due to her mother's support, but in so doing, felt that she was denying her mother opportunities for her own enrichment.

> A few times I've been running off to a lecture and I've realized my mother would most benefit from this lecture; she would be more interested in it. There is a funny way in which I am aware of this, but I rely on this traditional this-is-an-Asian-mother framework; this is this grandmotherly person who says this is her role in life. But the other part of me says she should be going out to the same lectures and doing the same things I'm doing.

Kyra was acutely aware of the many contradictions in her mothering, her work, and her commitments regarding education and how these impacted not just her children's schooling but her own, while limiting her mother's ability to engage in adult learning activities. Kyra also noted that schools as institutions were benefitting from the unpaid labor of mothers and the paid and unpaid labor of other caregivers—in this case, her own mother.

Kyra had been aware of various shortcoming at her children's schools and the hidden messages they conveyed about mothers and their relative standing, but she could no longer ignore them after the holiday shopping fair incident.

> It just became so clear that they see me as the anti-Christmas mom, not as an educator. I have to be honest that some of our relationships never recovered after this. I had this kind of insight where I thought it doesn't matter what people say; it comes down to what institutions actually do.

Kyra used this insight regarding what institutions were actually willing to do to take a hard look at her children's school and her own ability to impact their schooling, given her work responsibilities. She also reassessed her reliance on her mother, who was transitioning from providing childcare and educational support for Kyra's children to needing care herself. A few years later, Kyra and her family made the decision to move to a school district that was more in line with her values as an educator, as a mother, and as a daughter.

These changes were precipitated by Kyra's encounter with the hidden maternal curriculum at her children's school that dictated what cultures were celebrated and what role mothers were expected to play in celebrating them. In some ways, Tae encountered similar struggles in her attempts to make her child's school more attentive to issues of racial, gender, and sexual diversity. But on top of not having their concerns as a mother and LGBTQ advocate acknowledged, Tae was often not recognized as a mother at all.

Tae: I Do Expect a Mother's Day Card

Through small and often taken-for-granted actions, such as drawing Mother's Day cards for only one mother or sharing information about field trips with only one parent, schools and school-sponsored activities enforce a hidden curriculum that defines contemporary motherhood according to traditional gender and sexual norms. As a gender queer Korean American mother working as an LGBTQ advocate, Tae described how they were often illegible as a mother to those who equated motherhood with femininity and who only saw the possibility of having one mother in a family.

> My relationship to gender is fluid. I present pretty masculine but I also have a lot of feminine traits. In relation to my then partner, she was very feminine so people automatically assumed that because of her femininity, that she was the mother. . . . The teachers assume that they are going to talk to the other parent who is more feminine, and I have to insert myself and say, "Hey, I want to know information about what is happening in the classroom. I want to know when the field trip is happening.". . . I think they recognize me more as a parent but the whole idea of what a mother represents, I kind of have to be very vocal about "Oh, I am the *mother*!" I initiate being there on Mother's Day; I initiate telling the teachers at school that I do expect a Mother's Day card!

Both Tae and their former partner, Lisa, self-identified as mothers, but teachers and parents at the school often could not comprehend this and instead, relegated Tae to the role of "parent" or a father-like figure. She not only had to initiate receiving a Mother's Day card but had to constantly demand to be recognized as a mother.

> It's hard to figure out whether or not people are being really PC about it: "Oh, you are gender queer? Maybe you have a different identity? What do you feel about your *parenting* experience?" Or they just feel so awkward that they just don't talk about it. It is hard to know exactly why it doesn't come up unless I initiate it, but the fact that I have to initiate it in the space and say, "Hey, I do feel like a mom. It is important. It is very important for me." In the school that my child goes

> to, there is a PTA and so forth and there is this expectation that—it is very gendered—the moms are going to participate in the classrooms, and the dads are going to do carnival day but they are not necessarily engaged in the day-to-day details of the classroom. Like, literally, at the beginning of the school year I have to sniff the teacher down and say, "This is my expectation of communication with me. This is how our family structure works." And I have to kind of also pull out the law, saying that as the custodial parent, it is your responsibility to communicate with me.

Although certain situations necessitated asserting rights as a custodial parent, in most instances, Tae did not prefer to be called a parent, instead strongly claiming their identity as a mother and as gender queer, alongside their full range of racial, sexual, and other identities. Tae did not regard these identities as in contradiction but often had to challenge others who did.

> I identify as queer, gender queer, woman-loving woman, although I struggle with that term because I don't always identify as a woman, but I think it is the closest identity that works for me. I think that boxing myself in the binary doesn't work for me particularly, so gender queer allows an umbrella term, to not be specific but yet be specific. I identify as Korean American. I was born in Korea and I grew up and was raised in and nurtured in America. I would probably put gender queer Korean American first as my identity, as Asian American itself is a complicated identity, so that is why I said "kinda Asian American."

Just as they used *gender queer* as an umbrella term that could hold many complex identities, Tae sought to expand the term *mother* to embrace their fullest identities with regard to gender and sexuality but also positioning themselves as "kinda" on the edge of fixed racial categories such as Asian American.

While Tae was committed to expanding the boundaries of motherhood beyond normative feminine traits and family structures, they nonetheless found that attaching to traditional indicators of motherhood was often necessary to be socially recognized as a mother.

> I think the representation of what a mother is [influences] how you get marked in public and by people in society—for instance, going to parent groups and so forth. I am not a traditional-looking mother but yet, I interact and have very similar feelings about nursing and caretaking and not being able to sleep like other mothers, and I also did give birth to a child. So, I feel connected with the mothers, but there is always that gap.

Although Tae did not regard birthing and nursing as universal or necessary criteria for claiming motherhood, these normative maternal experiences were what others recognized, putting Tae in the position of emphasizing them to assert their status as a mother. But these assertions caused conflict with Lisa, Tae's former partner, who had not birthed or nursed their child.

> The part that I think that made it more hard was that because my former partner wasn't the bio parent, there was this expectation in our relationship for me to step back because she didn't have the same recognition, because she didn't have the biological experience of carrying the child. So not only did society not give me recognition of being a mother, she wanted me to step back and not be a mother. Now that we are separated, that space—because she is not physically next to me anymore—doesn't happen as much.

Lisa and Tae's conflicts over claiming the role of mother were not merely personal incompatibilities. Rather, they were pitted against each other by normative constructions of motherhood that allowed only one of them to be recognized as the mother. Thus, they were made to compete against each other, and because Lisa was more recognizable as a mother based on her femininity, Tae was put in the position of appealing to biological ties with their child and status as a birth mother. These contradictions about who was recognized as not just *a* mother but *the* mother arose in and were intensified by the school context. At the same time, these interactions had tremendous personal consequences, as the conflicts that arose at school significantly impacted their relationship outside of school, eventually contributing to their separation.

Further, the ways that mothers were recognized, or not recognized, at school influenced Tae's relationship not just with their former partner but with their child, Blake. To counter negative messages conveyed about Tae as a mother, Tae regularly initiated conversations with Blake, ranging from discussions about gender pronouns to the fluidity of gender and sexual identities.

> I am just not assuming that my child is going to be heterosexual. I am not assuming my child's gender. I am also giving my child language to be able to feel the fluidity of identity in general via pronouns, via sexuality, via how people present. We talk gender all the time because she is like, "Why do you say them and theirs?" and then she is like, 'Well, I am a girl,' and I am like, "Ok, that is fine, [*laughs*] but you know that that is not the only choice, like there are all these other options. Today you may feel this way and maybe tomorrow or maybe a year from now you may feel different, but it will still be fine and it's all fluid." So, we just try to make it kind of an everyday conversation.

Tae fostered open conversations with their child about why Tae preferred *they/their* pronouns and why Blake preferred *she/her* pronouns, and these talks expanded to address the very meaning and possibilities of gender and sexual identities. Tae was deeply committed to these conversations as a rewarding part of their mothering but the constant work of countering negative messages about Tae as a mother took a toll.

Tae noted that while these messages were communicated in different social settings, school stood out as the site with the highest stakes. As with many heated debates about gender identity, those related specifically to motherhood came to a head in various settings, but most pointedly around the highly contested space of the school bathroom.

> When we are in restaurants or public places where I don't necessarily know people—let's say we are at the movies or at a store and the clerk comes up to us—it is those kinds of moments. But often at school, that is the really hard one . . . I remember one of the earliest conversations was in the bathroom—we were going to the bathroom and Blake was like, "Why did that grandma give you that dirty look?" And between you and me, the grandma was washing her hands but we were in the bathroom stall so I know she was listening to us the whole time [*laughs*] and I was like, "I don't know why she gave me a dirty look. What do you think?" And she [my child] was like, "I think she thought that you were in the wrong bathroom." And I was like, "Well, do you think I am in the wrong bathroom?" And she goes, "No, mama!" So that it is an everyday kind of experience, when things come up and we talk about it. Like we slow down and we just unpack it a little so that she has the words and she has the ability to be curious about it and not feel like "Oh, that is a taboo conversation."

In addition to fostering open communication in general, Tae talked specifically with Blake about their own gender identities and about larger gender dynamics at the school. Tae recounted this conversation about the pressure for children to designate boyfriends and girlfriends and to declare "crushes" from a very early age.

> Around third grade there was this kind of conversation where you just pick somebody that day to be your boyfriend. And I was like, "What does that mean? Why do you need to have a boyfriend?" And my child started naming all these people and was like, "Gretchen has a crush on him, and she thinks he is really cute," and all this stuff. I was just trying to see if there was some real feeling behind it as opposed to just replicating everybody's feelings—and there wasn't. It was just like "I have a crush on him." So, I was like, "Do you want to hold his hand? Do you want to talk to him?" And she was like, "No, I never want to talk to him ever!" [*laughs*] So I told her, "You don't have to practice these types of relationships and I want you to have real feelings behind them." The backpiece is when I talk to the other parents, it really irritates me when I see two kids standing next to each other and people are like, "Look, they are going to be boyfriend and girlfriend. It's so cute!" And so, sexualizing our kids prior to their age is just the most inappropriate yet the most accepted thing in America and in a lot of countries.

Tae's observations revealed how the hidden curriculum in schools about sexuality emerged among adults but was carried over to children. While approaching these conversations with humor, Tae expressed both irritation and fatigue in having to constantly address them.

Even and especially in a school and community that saw themselves as progressive, Tae bumped up against a hidden maternal curriculum that was even harder to challenge, as many teachers and parents were often unaware of their normative assumptions about motherhood and did not see themselves as part of the problem.

> What is really complicated about this community is that it says, "Oh we are liberal, we accept everybody, we want to do social justice," but when it really plays out on the day-to-day ground level, gender is a

> really hard pill for people to swallow so far as being able to be transgressive. For instance, the teacher was like, "Oh, we are into social justice and we want to make sure that we tell a different story about Thanksgiving, and we do mindfulness in the classroom, and we do yoga." But when it comes to gender, I can see how they reflect their own family structure: "This is a girl, and this is a boy, these are things we do, and we go to church." It is very structured, so when connecting with me as a person who doesn't fit in one of those boxes, I can personally feel the inconsistency of communications and values. I think when you are really asking somebody to be an ally towards the queer people of color community, I don't necessarily see folks moving forward in that way.

Tae called out teachers, parents and community for giving lip service to a range of social justice concerns, but in the end, for reinforcing normative values and social hierarchies, especially but not limited to motherhood. The effort necessary for Tae to be recognized by and at the school as not simply a custodial parent but as a gender queer Korean American *mother* attests to a hidden maternal curriculum that defines motherhood not only through biologically defined reproductive capacities but through constant performances of femininity and heteronormativity and social recognition of these displays.

Resisting the Hidden Maternal Curriculum of Mother/Othering

What Asian American mothers learn in schools is that, like Althea, they can be included on the fringes of White mothering groups, contingent on their tolerance of racist comments and suppression of their own views and cultural identities. They learn that model minority stereotypes confer certain benefits, like being able to negotiate prolonged absences from school, as teachers are predisposed to trust that they will help their children make up missed assignments. They learn, like Kyra, that they are expected to do the work of hosting holiday celebrations and fundraisers without questioning which holidays are being celebrated or for what purposes funds are being raised. They learn, like Tae, that if they are unable or unwilling to conform to not only to model minority standards but to gender and sexual norms, they are not only marginalized from other mothers but are not recognized as mothers at all. All these lessons add up to a hidden maternal curriculum that is often invisible yet pervasive.

Schools are widely recognized as one of the primary agents of socialization, and some would argue that—depending on students' ages and peer groups—schools and the relationships they foster can have even greater influence on students than their own families.[13] The concept of a hidden maternal curriculum reveals schools to be complex social institutions that shape and are shaped by those who teach, learn, and parent within them. Just as students are inculcated with forms of knowledge outside the official curriculum of schools, mothers encounter a hidden maternal curriculum. This curriculum, however, is not merely imposed by the school but is negotiated in complex ways through maternal agency, as mothers make choices about which lessons they absorb and what they do with them.

As education scholar Debbie Epstein argues, the overemphasis on socialization has overlooked how children actively respond to both the formal and informal curriculum in schools, and "the hidden curriculum in schools is produced not just by those 'responsible for school arrangements' but also by those others participating in those arrangements."[14] This participation or refusal to participate in the hidden curriculum pertains not only to students and administrators but also to mothers. In Althea's case, she made choices to forego the selective interview process at one preschool, while embracing a more positive hidden maternal curriculum offered by Flor that included teaching her son Angelo about Filipino culture and supporting Althea as a working mother. Once Angelo moved to public school, however, Althea could not choose the kinds of comments to which she was subjected regarding minorities at the school, but she did exercise her agency as to how to respond.

Sociologist Barrie Thorne has discussed the "gender play" that occurs at schools, especially on playgrounds, as imparting myriad messages for children about what it means to be a girl or boy. But Thorne also demonstrates the many choices children make about drawing gender boundaries or breaking them through mundane activities such as "forming lines, choosing seats, teasing, gossiping, seeking access to or avoiding particular activities."[15] Similarly, whether in choosing which mothers to talk to on the playground, what kind of fundraisers to plan, or how to respect preferred pronouns, mothers engage in forms of *maternal gender play* through which they identify with certain mothers and distance themselves from others. Schools thus serve as "playgrounds" not just for children but also for mothers, who enact, enforce, and sometimes resist the larger social relations in which the school is embedded. Just like children's play, the parameters of mothers' play are established by the school but constantly negotiated by mothers themselves.

These negotiations between mothers and schools require substantial work. Educational maternal labor in schools involves both the work of supporting children's academic and extracurricular activities and navigating the social contexts of schools and other educational institutions with which they intersect. This labor requires constant negotiations about how and how much mothers should be involved in their children's school lives and in the social life of their schools beyond their children's own needs. These negotiations become even more complicated when mothers' paid work overlaps with their unpaid work. In Kyra's case, her maternal labor overlapped with her professional employment, but she struggled to apply her credentials as an educational consultant in diversity, equity, and inclusion to address these same issues in her children's school. Tae's maternal labor took the form of educating not just their own child about gender diversity but also instructing teachers and other families. In addition, Tae put in much work simply getting the school to follow through with official policies, such as appropriate communication about field trip forms, let alone unofficial practices, such as Mother's Day activities and cards that recognize and celebrate two mothers.

Schools shape not only the kind of work that mothers engage in regarding their children's schooling but also the kind of mothers they are perceived to be, both in and out of school. Criticisms of Mindy's attempts to strengthen the substandard math curriculum, described at the beginning of this chapter, led not just to her being labeled a tiger mother but to racializing her and all Asian American mothers as such. The message that they were overstepping their bounds also arose in extracurricular activities, such as the pushback Kyra received for challenging the holiday event.

Beyond the official school curriculum and events, the hidden maternal curriculum broadcasts messages to and by mothers not just as individuals but according to social standards of mothering—and the consequences of departing from them. But concerns related to the hidden curriculum about parenting in schools most often focuses on low-income, teen, or single mothers. These parenting education programs are often developed in response to beliefs that low- and higher-income families engage in very different forms of parenting and that early interventions are needed to educate low-income mothers to improve their children's learning outcomes.[16] A study by Maia Cucchiara, Erin Cassar, and Monica Clark found that parenting education programs offered in U.S. public school districts, which enroll hundreds of thousands of participants each year, are primarily focused on keeping "at-risk" mothers in school or on developing individual parenting skills to foster discipline and academic success.

Noting that these programs rarely addressed the challenges that parents faced in their larger social environments, the study concluded:

> Thus, the "hidden curriculum" of parenting education conveyed the message that good parenting should be unaffected by the challenges of poverty. The mothers, however, struggled to provide for their children in conditions of extreme scarcity, making it difficult for them to focus on other parenting issues.

While Cucchiara, Cassar, and Clark focused on a very different group of mothers than those in this book, their study is useful in helping to reveal parallel beliefs about Asian American mothers who are assumed not to be poor and undereducated but highly successful.[17] Superficially, the implicit lessons imparted to these two different groups of mothers appear very dissimilar, but they provide mirror images of mothers' presumed influence on their children's education. While the hidden curriculum of parenting education in most public schools attributes children's failures to having low-income mothers of color, the hidden maternal curriculum that collectively frames Asian American mothers as tiger mothers has become the default explanation for the presumed success of Asian American students. In addition to overstating the influence of mothers on their children's academic performance, both versions of the hidden maternal curriculum instill racially inflected beliefs about specific groups of mothers, whether the presumption of maternal negligence of low-income mothers of color or the hyper-involvement of Asian American mothers. In turn, mothers pick up on the messaging from schools that define standards of appropriate mothering and judge whether they meet them.

For Asian American mothers, this hidden messaging can often be mixed. In particular, the tiger mother stereotype simultaneously closes some doors against Asian American mothers while opening others. Drawing on her own educational and professional resources,

Althea was not penalized for her son's long absences during their visits to the Philippines and was even able to negotiate with the teachers for educational provisions to allow Angelo to keep at pace with the class. But other mothers at the school implied that she was receiving "special treatment" and if any of them had reported her, Althea might have been subject to accusations of truancy and negligent parenting, similar to those often imposed on low-income mothers and mothers of color, who are far more likely to face surveillance and discipline if their children miss school.[18] Here the tiger mother and model minority stereotypes could coalesce in contradictory ways, both working for and against Asian American mothers like Althea in their interactions with schools.

Model minority assumptions that Asians are inherently strongly committed to education provided reassurance to teachers that Angelo would not fall behind in school, and these unacknowledged privileges have similarities to those that education sociologist Jennie Germann Molz uses to describe parents in the "world schooling" movement. She writes that families that travel in the name of their children "learning to feel global" often overestimate their contributions as global citizens while underplaying the class, racial, and citizenship privileges that allow them to travel freely while reinforcing privatized and exclusive educational initiatives.[19] Likewise, Althea invested many resources in travel to her homeland in order to develop a positive sense of ethnic identity for her son, but her efforts cannot be separated from the complex history of the Philippines as a former American colony and the ongoing disparities in wealth and power between the two countries. In addition to the class resources that these trips required, they reinforced her family's privileges as U.S. citizens and in her son's case, as mixed race in a country where lighter skin confers higher status.[20] Thus, Althea's trips home, while supporting her mothering in various meaningful ways and requiring significant investments of educational maternal labor, also reinforced various forms of maternal privilege.

Likewise, for Kyra, the model minority and tiger mother stereotypes worked in concert but also in opposition. Both stereotypes positioned her as a mother whose children were expected to excel, but the tiger mother trope added a perception of her as someone who excessively meddled in school affairs. Kyra's efforts to broaden the holiday celebration were not solely on behalf of her son but reflected her professional commitment to fostering inclusive learning environments for all students.[21] Her concerns about the school's product-themed fundraiser also drew attention to the creeping commercialization of school events that has become ubiquitous and normalized.[22] Her experiences countered presumptions that increased parental involvement in school is welcomed and benefits students and the schools.[23] Increasingly, the social capital that parents build with school officials and other families through school activities are being leveraged politically to influence school policies and practices.[24] Kyra, however, demonstrates how parental involvement results in different returns for different mothers. Although Kyra wanted the school to benefit from her educational expertise, her investments in educational maternal labor instead resulted in her being othered as a particular kind of hyper-mother, the "anti-Christmas mom."

These mothers' interactions with school officials and other mothers worked to impose lines of belonging and non-belonging around multiple forms of difference, including race, class, gender, sexuality, and marital status—all of which were subsumed into constructions of motherhood. Further, these lines of belonging transferred to children's relationships with their mothers and with each other. In particular, the casual sexualization of children's friendships into budding romances that Tae reported as commonplace in their child's school are consistent with findings by scholars on how young girls are sexualized from a very early age. The kinds of everyday sexualization of children described by Tae are consistent with and precursors to the heteronormative policing documented in C. J. Pascoe's *Dude,*

You're a Fag: Masculinity and Sexuality in High School, which uncovered how schools are central actors in policing the "informal and formal institutional ordering of gender and sexuality" through a diffuse but ever-present "fag discourse" that marks the boundaries of masculinity and heterosexuality in schools.[25] Similarly, this chapter reveals parallel but distinct maternal discourses, which operate through a hidden maternal curriculum that enforces normative femininity and motherhood. As with gender and sexuality broadly, mothers are simultaneously socialized into conforming to these maternal discourses, while also serving as socializing agents.

The next chapter addresses the "motherhood penalty" that negatively affects mothers' advancement at the workplace. But in this current chapter, it is important to acknowledge that motherhood also confers many privileges, at least for those who meet the dominant cultural standards of good motherhood. *Motherhood privilege* includes many forms of status conferred on mothers that enable them to claim strong connections to their children and to access resources to care for them. The most basic of these privileges is to be recognized as a mother to begin with but extends to other forms of privilege, from utilizing policies such as childcare leave to receiving social gestures such as having a door opened or seat given to them, to having maternal qualities such as being patient and nurturing projected onto them. These forms of maternal privilege are most accessible and advantageous for heterosexual, married, middle-class, White suburban mothers, but even among those who do not check all these boxes, the very ability to be recognized as a mother confers unacknowledged privileges that may not initially register as such. The examples in this chapter include the privilege to enter a bathroom with a child, to receive information about field trips, and to celebrate religious holidays publicly. But for those who are regarded as mother/others, these mundane activities become fraught, especially but not only at schools, and even receiving a Mother's Day card cannot be taken for granted. Schools elevate these maternal privileges for some and deny them for others, turning everyday pickups and drop-offs at school into high-stakes encounters for mothers, especially those who must fight to be recognized as such.

Conclusion

I have strongly argued in this book against any universal mothering experiences—let alone regarding the many varied approaches to children's schooling. But I would venture that almost every mother can recount an incident of their child returning from school either glowing from an encouraging comment or broken-hearted from a wounding remark, whether from a teacher, parent, or another child. I would also venture that most mothers can recount a similarly supportive or wounding comment they received at school—not about their child but about them as a mother. While many mothers encounter a hidden maternal curriculum that teaches them that they are not good enough, what is particular to mothers of color is that this kind of learning is often directed toward them not as individuals but as metonyms of a racial group. For Asian American mothers, this often takes the form of being cast as a tiger mother, and just like other dimensions of the model minority, this casting is double-edged: complimentary in one moment, derisive in the next.

The main lesson of the hidden maternal curriculum is to hold mothers responsible for their children's schooling outcomes, but there are many other lessons that schools teach mothers. Whether they are blamed for their children's failures or praised for their successes, the underlying message is the same: mothers are assessed according to how their children perform at school academically, emotionally, socially. But some mothers are graded more harshly than others. The perceived shortcomings of Black, Indigenous, and Latinx mothers have become the default explanation for their children struggling in school, detracting from the structural conditions that stand in the way of their children's success. These conditions range from crumbling school buildings to racial biases of teachers, to dangerous or substandard living conditions that undermine students' ability to concentrate on schoolwork.

Conversely, the attribution of Asian American students' academic success to tiger mothering naturalizes high achievement rather than examining what factors are at play when and if it is achieved. Further, the heated debates about tiger mothering leave little room to address the myriad concerns expressed by Asian American mothers that go far beyond grades and college admissions. What most Asian American mothers identified as the most important things to learn in school are the importance of claiming belonging both for their children and themselves and the relentless maternal labor of staking these claims. These lessons are not just learned in school but transfer over to the workplace, which offers its own specific curriculum with regard to mother/othering.

5 *Mother/Othering at Work*

Asian-Americans surveyed reported that they had encountered pressures to play traditionally feminine roles such as office mother or dutiful daughter at much higher rates than other women, . . . suggesting that the stereotype that Asian-American women are more feminine than Whites is also a stereotype that they should be more feminine.

JOAN WILLIAMS, KATHERINE PHILLIPS, AND ERIKA HALL, *Double Jeopardy? Gender in Science* (2014)

There's no doubt my focus did change after having a child, and work is clearly a second priority. So, I'm not really interested in this upward trajectory. It's kind of this Asian American thing against this woman thing—I just don't want to work that hard anymore. But nobody around me seems to want to accept that.

JILL, interview, Chinese American, financial consultant

I'm a lawyer, and I still have a hard time getting my kids' teachers or doctors or other parents to take me seriously. I could never quit my job, not because of the money but because it keeps people from writing me off as just another pushy Asian mom.

GRACE, interview, Korean American, lawyer

The *Double Jeopardy* report quoted above documents the combined impact of racial and gender stereotypes for Asian American women;[1] this chapter examines the *triple jeopardy* of being an Asian American, a woman, and a mother: a combination that adds up to not just heavier burdens but to a distinct form of othering based on racial constructions of motherhood. As articulated above by Jill, a financial consultant at a leading investment bank and the mother of a preschool child, the "Asian American thing" of hard work and achievement is often pitted against the "woman thing" of motherhood and family. But rather than being one or the other, her efforts to excel in her career while also being an attentive and involved mother are both an "Asian American" and a "woman thing," or more precisely, an "Asian American mother thing."

Whereas Jill sought to ease these pressures by cutting back from work, Grace countered that she felt the need to maintain her professional status as a lawyer in order to be taken seriously as an Asian American mother. Their contrasting negotiations reveal that Asian American mothers are not a monolithic group; there is no single Asian American version of "opting out" of the workplace—or not—let alone of negotiating the various competing responsibilities of work and family. However, there are common factors that shape specific challenges for Asian American working mothers and how they experience the workplace as a site of othering.

The challenges that Asian American mothers confront in the workplace are distinct from those confronted by Asian American women who are not mothers, by mothers of different racial groups, and by Asian American men. At the same time, while Asian American mothers face additional and specific burdens, these cannot be completely separated from the challenges that define gender, race, and motherhood more broadly. In short, the experiences of mother/othering at work that this chapter addresses reflect both the very particular social locations of the Asian American mothers who shared them and a broader pattern of gendered racialization that frames the reproduction of Asian Americans as simultaneously model citizens and foreign threats. Model minority racialization dictates that Asian American mothers must continue to meet high standards of productivity for themselves while reproducing the next generation of hard-working, self-sufficient model minority subjects. Further, they must fulfill these multigenerational standards of high achievement while being careful not to appear to be stepping out of line or taking over at work or in the various spaces in which they interact as working mothers.

A broad range scholarship and public debate has shown how many mothers (and fathers) feel caught between the competing demands of work and family. Many mothers must manage conflicts between paid work and unpaid caregiving responsibilities and must negotiate between these competing pulls. But what are the specific challenges that Asian American mothers face? And what do these challenges reveal about the workplace as a social institution that not only requires paid labor but also shapes many forms of unpaid labor and how they are performed and valued?

The conceptual vocabulary of "work-family conflict," "second shift," "opting out," "mommy track," "maternal wall," and the "motherhood penalty," among others, has productively named and drawn attention to various challenges related to motherhood and paid employment.[2] But these terms also have their limitations. They oftentimes draw too-stark divisions between paid and unpaid work and fail to recognize how they overlap, as workplaces rely on both paid work and unpaid emotional labor, and families rely on both paid care providers (ranging from nannies and domestics to teachers and nurses) and unpaid work by mothers, fathers, friends, and relatives. The distinct pressures that Asian American mothers describe are not unrelated to these concepts but they also go beyond them and require different or expanded frameworks. As Sharon Hays theorized, many women experience "cultural contradictions of motherhood" between the values of succeeding in a competitive work environment and those of creating a nurturing home and family life.[3] However, Asian American mothers confront distinct versions of Hays's cultural contradictions based not just on their individual circumstances or the general contradictions between paid work and unpaid family responsibilities, but as members of a specific racial group.

Cultural constructions of Asian American women as high-achieving supermoms reveal distinctly gendered articulations of model minority racialization that play out in the workplace. Asian American mothers negotiate contradictory gendered and racialized stereotypes: as Asian women, they are expected to be quiet and passive, but as mothers, they are assumed to be hard-driving tiger moms who prioritize their children's success above all else. Both stereotypes come together in the workplace to produce specific forms of othering for Asian American working mothers.

The concept of mother/othering illuminates the workplace as a site where boundaries of belonging and exclusion are enforced, contested, and potentially redrawn. Mother/othering plays out in the workplace through matritopes and structures of reproductive exclusion that impose distinct forms of maternal intersectional labor. These terms capture processes that build on but go beyond racial stereotypes that Asian Americans are industrious but lack creativity, gender stereotypes that women are team players but not leaders, and maternal stereotypes that mothers are less committed to—and should be less committed to—their careers.

Many Asian American mothers thus feel that they have to constantly prove their value both at work and at home. For them, work-family balance is made harder to achieve and is based on different standards and responsibilities. These include intensive involvement with their children by way of education and extracurricular activities, as well as equipping them to face anti-Asian racism and xenophobia. In addition, as discussed in chapter 3, many Asian American mothers are also caring for parents and extended families. But if they withdraw from their careers in order to manage these responsibilities, they are rarely praised as devoted stay-at-home mothers. Instead, they face a range of matritropes discussed earlier, from the hypersexualized prostitute mother to the overzealous tiger mother. Building on these earlier chapters, this chapter shows how historical legacies of exclusion carry over into current tropes that regularly cast Asian American mothers as both unfit caregivers and as uncommitted workers.

In their negotiations of work and family responsibilities, Asian American mothers not only confront the current model minority racial construction but also the wide-ranging historical matritropes that continue to cast their reproduction as threatening and problematic. These tropes eclipse the complex and varied work and family negotiations that pressure Asian American mothers to measure and prove their value not only through their own high achievement but their children's.

Asian American women have the highest levels of college-degree attainment of any racial and gender group, surpassing Asian American men and both White women and men.[4] Yet, many of them do not fulfill the subsequent professional success that this statistic would suggest. In the corporate world, *Forbes* reports that among all racial and gender groups, Asian American women are least likely to hold positions within three reporting levels of the CEO or to have supervisory responsibilities.[5] Asian women are the fastest-growing group in the labor force, but they make up less than 1 percent of corporate leaders in the Fortune 500.[6] Yet, they are often seen as passive and lacking leadership qualities and confront a "bamboo ceiling" based on both race and gender, where they are passed over for promotions or do not receive salaries commensurate with their qualifications.[7] These reports show the presence of specific barriers for Asian American women in the workplace, but more attention needs to be paid to how these barriers are compounded by their becoming mothers.

This chapter explores the distinct set of work and family challenges that Asian American mothers face as well as their strategies to negotiate these intersecting challenges. Although many of the challenges that they confront are also faced by other mothers, other women, and other Asian Americans, when taken in totality they reflect the specificities of a range of barriers and forms of othering distinct to Asian American mothers. To examine the work-family interface as a site of mother/othering, this chapter focuses on three Asian American mothers whose stories reveal the deep cultural contradictions that influence Asian American motherhood and produce distinct forms of othering. Madeline, a divorced mother of two children, confronted sexual harassment that led to her termination in a corporate managerial position. Her experience illustrates how racialized sexualization of Asian American women in the workplace does not go away because they become mothers, but rather, takes on distinct forms that not only block advancement but create job insecurity. Amy, on the other hand, achieved a high level of success in the male-dominated field of surgery but experienced mother/othering for not meeting normative family expectations and also for not fulfilling the role of the "quiet Asian woman." Finally, Winnie, a forensic psychologist, similar to the respondents in the *Double Jeopardy* report cited above, encountered expectations that she should perform various kinds of "office mother" roles. She not only had to work while mothering her two children, but she also had to engage in unpaid labor to mother her colleagues at work.

These interviews reveal that, for many Asian Americans, work is not just a paycheck but the price of the ticket for model minority belonging. But for Asian American mothers, model minority standards require not only achieving success for oneself but raising the next generation of successful Asian American students and professionals. However, when they invest great effort in their careers, Asian American mothers are more likely to be seen as threatening the status quo than to be rewarded with leadership positions, promotions, or raises, let alone to be lauded as highly engaged mothers who simultaneously support their families as breadwinners.

Madeline: They Want You to Do Everything

Madeline was eager to share her story about how sexual harassment combined with new motherhood set her up for retaliation and termination at her workplace. She wanted others to learn and benefit from her struggles, as she thought it likely that other Asian American mothers confronted similar challenges that crossed the line from a merely unsupportive workplace to one that engaged in active discrimination.

> I was one of the key witnesses [in a sexual harassment suit], and because of that I was pretty much terminated. . . . There are just so many things I could share with you because I feel like I've been all over the place. I'm also the kind of person who likes to share with others because I don't want other people to flounder. Other folks have gone through this.

Madeline was not sexually harassed as a mother, but motherhood made her more vulnerable to a climate of sexual harassment in her workplace and to penalties for standing up against it.

Madeline grew up in a small town on the East Coast, where her immigrant parents worked in Chinese restaurants until they were able to save enough to open their own: "They did the very traditional, very small-business kind of thing—they weren't professionals; they weren't college-educated." Highly motivated, Madeline excelled in school, earned a full college scholarship, obtained an MBA at a top business school, and then landed a high-paying managerial job at a

Fortune 500 company. Rather than feeling discriminated against as an Asian American woman, she felt, at least early in her career, that it worked in her favor to be a woman of color in a White, male-dominated field: "I think it opened doors for me, even getting into college and getting scholarships and internships." At first, Madeline said that she had benefited from diversity programs, but she clarified that these programs, over time, either disappeared or no longer included Asian Americans.

Although initially she had seen many opportunities for herself in the corporate sector, Madeline's view of her prospects began to sour. "I didn't fit what they were looking for, which was very, very rigid." Despite having earned a managerial position, she felt that she was not respected, as people routinely asked her to perform secretarial tasks. Further, she noticed how this was part of a pattern, as she saw other Asian American women being similarly treated, while other Asian American men or White women managers did not receive these same requests.

> There was another Asian American woman, a lawyer—she came to the same company where I was and was a manager, but she was treated like the coordinator-secretary-handyperson. I heard after a year she got laid off because she didn't know how to pack well. What a company! They wanted you to do everything. It was crazy. They wanted you to know how to Xerox, to collate, to pack fifty boxes to send off to a conference. . . .
>
> *Why do you think you were both treated this way?*
> I don't know if it was being Asian American or a woman. I just hear so much that there's still the glass ceiling for women.

The *glass ceiling* commonly refers to barriers to advancement into upper-level executive and managerial positions, especially for women but also for racial minorities. However, in Madeline's case and that of her colleague, although both had achieved promotion to managers, they were not afforded the same authority and respect as others in comparable roles. Not only were they expected to take on menial tasks outside of their job descriptions, but they were negatively evaluated if they did not perform these tasks well.

Despite these experiences, at the time, Madeline did not feel that she was being discriminated against as an Asian American woman. "I'm not the kind of person that's experienced a lot of prejudice or bias. If anything, if it is there, sometimes I'm not really able to pick up on it quickly." It was only later that she recognized patterns in which she and her Asian American women colleagues were treated differently than others in comparable leadership positions. Further, Madeline noted specific discriminatory practices related to those who were mothers, which she noticed only after she became a mother herself.

Although she had been ambivalent about motherhood for herself, Madeline said that she had been very committed to supporting mothers that she supervised. Thus, she was surprised and disappointed when she did not received similar support when she had a child. Describing herself as an "older mother," Madeline said that she had been "intensely career-focused" until her late thirties and that she probably would not have met her husband but for connections through work. After they married and in anticipation of having children, they decided to move to the suburbs, commuting to their jobs in the city. When she gave birth to her child, she fought hard for a four-month leave, which even though unpaid, seemed to provoke much resentment from her boss and co-workers. Despite these challenges, Madeline felt that she and her husband transitioned well to managing their new work-family responsibilities, as did their infant daughter, who spent many hours in the car with them.

> Crazy traffic, people going eighty miles an hour, but my daughter traveled well in the car, never threw up, not fussy, easy kid. Her legs would be bobbing up and down to the beat of the music, perfectly happy, and we'd be sharing oranges in the front seat. We really did that commute well. But we were tired, certainly in bed by ten o'clock.

While Madeline felt that she was doing a good job handling her new responsibilities as a working mother, her supervisors disagreed. When she returned to work, she felt that she was immediately asked to pick up a very heavy work schedule, which was difficult to manage with a new baby and a long commute. After returning from maternity leave, she received her first negative performance evaluation.

Madeline, however, noted that this increased workload and negative evaluation were not due to her inability to do her job well as a new mother, although they were disguised as such. Instead, she felt that they coincided with her testifying in a suit brought by another Asian American woman colleague against a supervisor, alleging a pattern of sexual harassment against Asian American women and other women of color.

> It was [my colleague's] immediate boss that was doing the sexual harassment. She asked for me to be interviewed. . . . It really didn't take me that long to decide to participate. It was kind of like this is the truth, I'm not going to be fearful and say I'm not going to be a witness for you because I might lose my job. Basically, I was on a business trip and had dinner with him. When we were at dinner, he started talking about his sexual experiences with different ethnic groups of women and which was better, and it was the same thing he had said to her. It was something you and I would never talk about and share with a coworker! He mentioned one of his sexual partners was Asian. He was saying things about different ethnic women, how they were in terms of being passionate or sexual. It was curious that the woman

> who filed the harassment suit was Asian and I was an Asian woman. This is a man who is a senior vice president. He was White.

Madeline's colleague ended up battling the case for several years, during which she was moved to another position at the company and eventually left after settling the case out of court.

During the period in which Madeline was supporting her colleague's sexual harassment suit, she began to experience another kind of discrimination: not only had she been the target of sexual harassment, but she then experienced retaliation for testifying against it. Madeline's immediate boss, a White woman who was close to the supervisor that Madeline had testified against, reassigned her duties and then gave her a negative performance review.

> I got assigned this job that everyone had done nothing for, and all of a sudden, it was a priority. I feel like I did a good job, but the thing was, she wrote this job performance review, and there were a lot of gaps in it or things that weren't accurate.

Madeline decided to file a suit alleging retaliation due to her sexual harassment testimony, and after months of negotiations, her company offered her a severance package in exchange for dropping the suit. She said that she saw the writing on the wall and decided to take the package and leave, as her colleague had done.

Although Madeline expressed pride in her participation in the suit and claimed that she was "happy to leave," she also acknowledged that this incident precipitated a "chaotic time" in her life.

> I was always ordering take out, I could barely even do laundry, I was snappish with my kids. I finally got divorced, and I was on unemployment for a little while. I started substitute teaching because someone

> else who I liked, a woman lawyer who's a stay-at-home mom now, very active PTO-type person, started substitute teaching and brought it up. And I said, "Maybe I can do that."

In the years following her termination, Madeline's life was unsettled by divorce, moving to another city, leaving her corporate career, and becoming a teacher. But she also felt that her new line of work and work-family arrangements allowed her more time with her children and enabled them to have closer relationships.

> I found out I love teaching! I realize most people would not want to live this way. It's almost like living on the edge. I live very frugally—I drive an old car, I don't want a lot of things. I made a lot of money as a single woman, and as a married couple, we had a beautiful home. So I know that whole thing. And I do not want that. . . . I felt like I could not live like that and be a role model to my own kids.

In addition to finding her passion in teaching, Madeline expressed pride that she had fought back against abuses in her workplace, left an unsupportive marriage, and rejected an upscale lifestyle—in effect, shedding the various trappings associated with model minority success. She summed up her experiences positively but also was honest about her struggles and regrets.

> My kids I feel are terrific [but] I wish I could start my whole mothering thing over again. I feel like I did my best, you know. Honestly, as they say, no one ever teaches you anything about being a parent, no one teaches you how to be a marriage partner, nobody teaches you anything. . . . People think divorce is bad, my finances are bad, but I don't think of it as bad at all. I think it's actually showing I have courage and strength to do what needs to be done. If I had done anything else, the consequences would be a lot worse. Totally miserable in my

> mind, not living my life. So when you talk about balancing work and mothering, I feel like I'm really doing it.

Madeline had finally found what she considered a true balance of work and mothering, but she also was forthcoming about the many challenges that she had faced and overcome as an Asian American working mother. Her earlier beliefs that she was not discriminated against as an Asian American woman changed dramatically when she became a mother and when she supported another Asian American woman at her company in a sexual harassment suit. She was glad that by scaling back on her career, she could focus more on her children, but she also acknowledged that she was "living on the edge" not only of model minority expectations but of even being able to afford the rent. Madeline had found work that she loved, but she also acknowledged that these changes had not been of her own choosing.

At first glance, Madeline's situation seemed very different from Amy's, who had been able to maintain a prestigious career as a surgeon. But under the surface, Amy also felt that her work-family choices had been limited, and although she did not experience outright discrimination at work, she too felt that the workplace served to other her in various interrelated ways stemming both from her being an Asian American woman and a mother.

Amy: They Can't Understand How a "Small Asian Woman" Is Their Surgeon

As a general surgeon at a busy and prestigious hospital, Amy felt that she was othered as a "small Asian woman" who constantly had to prove her credentials to her patients and to her co-workers. Even in a large West Coast city with many Asian American doctors, an Asian American woman surgeon was seen as an anomaly. She acknowledged the difficulties of managing her responsibilities as both a surgeon and a mother but resolved to meet these challenges, as the thought of leaving work entirely was unacceptable to her. While she spoke at length about the various challenges of being an Asian American woman in her field, she underscored that it was the specific responsibilities of motherhood that were making her, for the first time in her life, want to scale back from her demanding career.

> I could never live with myself if all I was was a stay-at-home mom. It would just be, to me, like all the years of struggling and years of working were for nothing. I made it to a surgeon, so I would never want to be some surgeon's wife, where that's all people think that I am. . . . I think that being a "small Asian woman" (because that's a thing, let me tell you), it's much harder to gain respect from patients. When people think that they're going to have surgery, they have an idea of who they're going to see, and they want to see some distinguished, professorial-looking, older White male with like a bow tie. People just have it in their mind, and then they see me and are like, "Is *that* the surgeon? That's *my* surgeon?" They can't understand how a small Asian woman is their surgeon. People will be happy with you as a pediatrician or maybe an internist, *but not a surgeon.*

Although Amy said that her life had been easier before her child, what she described was not only the difficulties of caring for her child but of doing so as a surgeon. At the same time, Amy also experienced being othered as a mother, for her decisions to delay having children, then to adopt a child, then to keep up her fast-paced career.

Amy longed for just slightly more time for a short period to give more attention to her recently adopted child, but even a minor reduction of her surgical schedule posed major challenges.

> I just started this trying to balance work and family thing. I was able to balance work and just having a husband and dog and a house, that

> was much easier than the child! Ideally, I would like to go to work four days a week, eight-hour days, come home by three, but as a surgeon that's just impossible! Because the operating room doesn't function that way; it's going to be ten-hour days. It'll be better once I get my reduced schedule, but it's not even *that* reduced. You're just talking about shaving off two hours here and there. But those two hours, if you're talking about getting home before bedtime, it is a big deal.

Amy was having to fight hard to "shave off" a few hours from her surgical schedule and she also wanted to reduce her administrative responsibilities. "I'm not interested in taking on more thankless work, to fight with people, so my goal is to have less responsibilities." But she recognized that just by asking to cut back on hours and administrative duties, she was foregoing consideration for promotions.

Amy's situation could be categorized under that amorphous, catch-all term *work-family conflict*. But this term does not fully capture the specificity of the challenges she faced as a second-generation Asian American woman and new mother, working in a highly demanding field. Amy emphasized that she loved her work as a surgeon; she also underscored that she had sacrificed much to achieve this position, and she did not want to lose her career or the status it conferred. Although she strongly identified as Asian American, she felt that her identity as a surgeon was equally or more important, and her strongest affinities were not necessarily with other Asian American women but with other women surgeons.

Contrary to stereotypes that depict Asian American women as a homogenous group, Amy felt that differences in their commitments to their careers and in their work-family responsibilities created stark divisions among them. Even with her own sister, despite their being close as children and sharing the same race, ethnicity, culture and even parents, she felt that they now had little in common simply by virtue of being Asian American mothers.

> I don't really feel like I get to call on my sister. I have an older sister who has two kids and stays home, but she's so overwhelmed by her life. It's useless talking to her. It's like talking to someone with no kids! She doesn't know [about my work] and she has no advice.

Amy felt that her sister could not relate to the strong pulls between professional and family responsibilities and thus could offer "no advice" that Amy found useful. Although they had been close as sisters growing up in an Asian American family in a predominantly White community, Amy felt that they now had little in common, as their work and mothering experiences had widely diverged.

Amy also felt removed from a group of Asian American stay-at-home mothers who were part of a mom's club to which her sister had tried to introduce her, but Amy had not been able to forge any meaningful or useful connections.

> So, my sister is in this mom's club. It's so annoying. They have play dates, they do this, they do that. When one of them has a baby, they have a schedule to bring her dinner and all this crap. Finally, I said, "Don't you have any working moms in mom's club?" She's like, "No, working moms don't have time for mom's club. We do all our activities during the week. Working moms, all they do is work and then on the weekends they go grocery shopping." And that's true, but there's still time for play dates, you know!

For Amy, the fact that the mothers in the mom's club either did not work or were not highly invested in their careers overrode whatever commonalities she might share with them simply as Asian Americans.

Amy also felt distanced from her own mother's working-class immigrant experience, and like her sister, she felt that her mother could offer little advice that was relevant to Amy's situation as a second-generation, college-educated Asian American working mother in a highly competitive profession. Contrary to stereotypes of Asian immigrant parents pushing their children to become doctors, Amy's parents had not pressured her to become one and had little understanding of what it demanded. Rather than being pressured by her parents, Amy attributed her motivation to become a doctor and her intense drive for high achievement more generally to the need to prove her worth and claim belonging in the mostly White, affluent community where she had been raised.

> We don't have a single doctor in the family. I didn't have any exposure, I didn't volunteer. Really the first time I ever stepped foot into a hospital was when I was a resident. When I decided to go to medical school, everyone started saying to me, "Oh, are your parents doctors?" I thought that was so funny because my parents were always struggling financially. It's not such a glamorous story, but one day I realized in high school that all these kids I thought were smarter than me all wanted to be doctors. I think that I just had this notion that that's what smart kids do, and I wanted to achieve it for that reason, mostly to prove myself to outside people.

Notably, Amy's desire to "prove" herself to "outside people" by becoming a doctor did not come from within her family but, rather, from how she and her family were perceived by others. Or, to put it another way, it was Amy's experience of being other in her community, due to both racial and class status, that motivated her to pursue a career in medicine.

While Amy credited these outside influences more than parental expectations as the driver of her career ambitions, she appreciated her parent's commitment to her and her sister's education and saw this as going against the cultural norms of other Korean immigrant families. Amy noted that her mother had strongly insisted that her daughters not work in their family business so they could prioritize their education. When asked the reason behind this, Amy explained that her mother's commitment to her daughters' education did not stem from Asian cultural values but was a response to discrimination in the United States.

> Korean culture is patriarchal, but [my parents] had all girls and they pushed us all to succeed. [My mom's] little motto was "If you're not White in this country, then you have to have a Ph.D. or M.D. next to your name." I kind of think she's right.

Following her mother's "little motto" that non-Whites needed the highest educational credentials to compete with Whites, Amy put her education and career first and regarded marriage and family as secondary pursuits. Given the extreme competitiveness of her field, especially for women and even more so for women of color, Amy understood that she would have to fully devote herself to her career if she wanted to be successful.

> I thought that it would be nice to be married, but I really thought that I never had the time or energy to put into it. It's also part of the territory with the work I do because I'm a female surgeon and half of them or more, historically, never married. It's changing now because the work hours are getting better, jobs are getting more understanding. But throughout my entire training, I think there were two or three female surgeons out of like fifty. That was my role model.

Amy had observed that few female surgeons were married, let alone had children, and although she had been willing to accept this possibility, she was happy that her life had followed a different path.

Amy had successfully fought and challenged gender and racial biases to become a surgeon, but she felt that her accomplishments as an individual Asian American woman were outweighed by negative perceptions of Asian women writ large. She articulated a "catch-22" for her and other Asian women: they had to challenge the stereotype of the meekly submissive Asian woman to earn credibility in a competitive field like medicine, but such assertiveness would be criticized for not fulfilling the stereotype of the meekly submissive Asian woman. These contradictory expectations were difficult to manage for Asian American women doctors in general and especially for surgeons, who were expected to constantly demonstrate their expertise and authority.

Amy constantly fought back against being othered as a "small Asian woman," but her efforts were primarily enacted individually rather than by joining in collective efforts to change her workplace or profession. In fact, she found it difficult to connect with other Asian and Asian American women, not just those who did not have as demanding a career but also those in the medical field. Having gone to great lengths to counter negative stereotypes, Amy criticized some of her Asian American women colleagues whom she felt conformed to stereotypical roles.

> I get very frustrated with Asian women who just constantly fit the role, who are quiet and meek or whatever. It just bugs me when they perpetuate the myth. I used to feel like I have to work to destroy that myth and be that one Asian woman that people are like, "Oh my god, where did she come from!" But I get a lot of criticism because of it. People are shocked, like, "Why are you talking like that? Why aren't you nice to me?" So, trust me, I've had a lot of misery at the hospital, because they don't want to see that.

Recognizing that Asian women often did not fit the model of what people expected in a surgeon, Amy struggled to be "that one Asian woman" who broke the mold. Although she had been able to successfully enter into a hypercompetitive profession, she found less success in her attempts to form supportive connections with other Asian American working mothers at her workplace. The othering that Amy experienced led her to distance herself from other Asian American women, as is often the case, as fears of being tokenized or lumped together undermined possibilities of joining together to challenge negative stereotypes, let alone create better shared working conditions.

Amy's awareness of how she and other Asian women were perceived as others influenced not only her work but also decisions in her personal life, especially those regarding starting a family. Amy's reproductive choices were strongly influenced by both her professional and personal commitments, particularly her decision to adopt a child after experiencing pregnancy complications.

> I'm a provider, that's my role in this world. I do not like being a patient. I was not interested in being some high-risk OB patient going for ultrasounds all the time. For what? Just to have a biological child? My husband would say, "What's so great about your genes anyway?" [*laughs*] . . . We see it all the time, people assume that everything is going to turn out fine, but we don't. There's a little unspoken rule in medicine: if you're going to operate on a physician or a physician's family, you're going to get a complication. So to us, it was a very simple, clear decision, but I gotta tell you, it was very hard for everyone to understand. They just kept thinking we're always trying to get pregnant on the sly. It's like, "No, we mean it. We can love and adopt a child, just like you can love any biological child!" All these people who were like, "What do you mean? You're still young, you should try again!" People gave me a lot of grief about "You need to have two kids. He is going to be lonely." He's not going to be lonely; there are plenty of only children in the world. He's everything we've ever wanted.

Although Amy and her husband were happy with their decision to adopt a child—and only one child, they experienced various negative reactions from their families, friends, and coworkers. For Amy, it was very clear that adopting one child was the best fit for her work and family situation, given her strong desire to continue to work full-time as a surgeon. "I would never go, 'Oh, I would really want to adopt three kids and then stop working.' I really would need to keep working, so we'll just adopt one."

Rather than respecting her reproductive choices, Amy was criticized not only by her family but by friends and colleagues at work who continued to pressure her to try for biological children or to adopt additional children. The various ways that people both at work and in her personal life gave Amy grief for her professional and personal choices reveal not only work-family conflict but various forms of othering. In the end, Amy faced criticism for her strong commitment to her work as a surgeon, but then she was also criticized at work for wanting to cut back to care for her child. The configuration of reproductive choices that Amy made set her apart not only from White men in her profession but from Asian American women who did not prioritize their careers in the same way. Further, Amy did not fit the normative model of mothering as she did not have a biological child and she had chosen to adopt just one child, even when others said this would subject that child to loneliness.

Despite her stellar professional credentials and her sense of fulfillment with her own work-family arrangements, Amy still encountered various messages that she was a mother/other. But as the following profile of Winnie illustrates, even when Asian American mothers prioritize normative family models and make sacrifices in their careers to do so, they are still subject to various forms of mother/othering.

Winnie: Taking Care of Everyone Else at Work

In her work as a forensic psychologist, Winnie conducted psychological evaluations for the courts and was highly respected for her expertise in handling high-stakes and confrontational cases. Although she prided herself on her skill in interacting with difficult clients, she felt that her co-workers often took this ability for granted, naturalizing it as an ingrained attribute of Asian women rather than recognizing it as a hard-earned professional competency. These dynamics became even more pronounced once she became a mother, as Winnie found herself increasingly called upon to play various kinds of maternal roles at work.

> It's possible that people try to push more onto me, but I don't know for sure whether it's because I'm Asian or because I've been in the system a long time and I know a lot of different players. I may be more willing to explore other options and to try to help people, to find some sort of resolution that everyone's happy with.

At the same time as she was often called upon to smooth over difficult interactions through her "people skills," Winnie recounted various incidents in which her professional credentials to provide evidence in court proceedings were often called into question. While she described these biases more in terms of race and gender and being an Asian American woman rather than specifically as an Asian American mother, they set up the larger context for the later challenges that she experienced related more directly to motherhood.

Despite her reputation and expertise, Winnie felt that she did not get the respect she deserved at work, as she was often asked to verify her expertise to testify in the courtroom, even by those who had interacted with her on numerous occasions. She shared the following example, framing it as revealing both gender and racial biases.

> I have been before some judges who I felt didn't give me the respect they should. Even though I have been before them several times before, they would be looking in the courtroom for the doctor. They would look right by me, then someone would say, "The doctor is sitting right there." They would say, "Oh" and would want me to introduce myself and go through all my credentials, stuff like that. Maybe it's because I'm a woman, but I am saying it's because I'm Asian. There are other female psychologists I work with and they have said, "They never treat me like that." When people talk about discrimination against women, I feel that it's pretty minor compared to discrimination against people based on race. I think being a woman is secondary to being Asian.

While Winnie initially ascribed this judge's questioning of her credentials to her being Asian, upon further reflection, she noted that this treatment was specific to being both Asian American and a woman. She observed that in her field, White women were rarely subject to the same kind of constant need to prove their expertise, nor were Asian American men. In fact, she noted how the visible presence of Asian American men in various fields produced a "halo effect" for them as a group, but Asian American women did not benefit from such positive associations. In addition, she felt that while many White women were mentored and encouraged to be "rising stars," Asian American women were often expected to accommodate others and mitigate conflicts.

Although Winnie had worked hard to develop various skills to be successful in this demanding position, she felt that these hard-won strengths were instead merely attributed to qualities that Asian women shared writ large, especially in dealing with challenging emotional dynamics. She elaborated:

> The court is a very combative place. It's very adversarial, so it is hard not to upset somebody in the job that I do. That has been one of the

> hardest parts of my job, like a family member gets really upset because someone is not getting help. But it also has been my strength in terms of my being able to navigate all the different systems I have to deal with: the lawyers, judges, the police officers and clerks, the hospital people, and the family—all that kind of stuff. So, I think I have been able to do all that well without offending people. They appreciate it when someone doesn't resort to being really authoritarian and arrogant . . . [but they associate this] with just being Asian and trying not to make waves.

In addition to attributing her ability to interact well with different kinds of people simply to her Asianness rather than her professional expertise as a psychologist, conversely, others imbued her with various qualities related to Asian culture that she in fact lacked. For instance, Winnie recounted that many people assumed that she possessed language proficiency and cultural familiarity to work with recent Asian immigrants, when in fact, she spoke only English and had grown up in mostly White suburban communities, not in immigrant enclaves.

> I am not bilingual. I don't know if I have enough understanding of Asian culture to work with the older Asians who just immigrated here and have different customs and moral views of how things should be done. You are straddling two worlds.

This sense of straddling different worlds became even more pronounced for Winnie when she became a mother, as others projected various qualities onto her not only as an Asian American woman but as an Asian American mother.

Winnie reflected that clients and co-workers had actually "respected my boundaries more when they thought I was young and single," but when she became a mother, they seemed to feel more at ease in asking her for advice or sharing problems with her. She noted that she found herself being asked to weigh in not only on work-related tasks but on matters as varied as "if their kid should learn Mandarin or study abroad." Winnie said she would defer on these inquiries, saying that she had not raised her children bilingually or sent them on return trips to Asia, as they preferred to hang out with their friends and do sports, which would prompt reactions of disbelief and even chagrin.

As she became more stretched by the demands of raising a family while continuing to work full-time, Winnie began to draw clearer boundaries around her work and was no longer as readily available to both personal inquiries and additional work requests. She described how becoming a mother produced a circular effect of hindering potential promotions and making her less interested in pursuing them.

> It was mostly having kids, you know, that made me less interested in promotion, which would have meant commuting, working longer hours, having less autonomy over my time, basically taking care of everyone else at work, and I sort of thought I had already had enough of that. It would have been a little bit more money, but in my mind, it wasn't worth it. There isn't much room for any real advancement unless I move into administration, which I thought about, but then decided I really didn't want the responsibility that came with it.

Like Amy, whose surgical career was made more challenging after motherhood, Winnie experienced heightened tensions between work and family that were specific to her identity as an Asian American mother in a demanding line of specialized work. As a psychologist, she prioritized mental health and healthy relationships over high achievement, but in contrast to her actual mothering approach which prioritized emotional attunement, many readily assumed that she possessed an authoritarian parenting style based on her Asian cultural background.

> I feel like people think I'm more strict with my kids because I'm Asian. If I'm having some kind of discussion of my parenting style, I feel like most people will then say, "Your kids are very well behaved, your kids are very smart. Maybe it is more from the Asian culture.". . . But the main thing for me to ask is not only how hard to push, but what is the sacrifice for working that hard? Are our kids going to be more harmed, or will they have more anxiety as a result of being pushed so hard—or depression? What about the parent-child relationship? What are you sacrificing in the relationship with your child if you push them too hard?

While Winnie struggled with these questions, she found that others had already made assumptions about her mothering priorities, based simply on her being Asian rather than taking into account her expertise as a psychologist. Specifically, she was often cast according to the script of the prevailing tiger mother stereotype, even when her parenting values strongly resisted this pressurized approach.

> Because people kept asking me if I were a tiger mom, I would usually say, "I'm a house-cat mother, actually." So, I felt like I needed to read it [Chua's book]. I was curious about what she said. . . . I thought it was very interesting. I also found it very funny too, but I don't think she intended to be funny! Some of the things she said seemed very outrageous to me. I agreed with her idea that kids do need to be directed in a certain way, and if they are left completely to their own devices, they'll choose things that aren't necessarily constructive or productive. But I disagreed with the extent that she went, how much she pushed them. She had this idea that happiness is not an important construct—that seemed irrelevant to her. Chua was saying, "Chinese kids always do all the extra credit," and I'm like, "Uh, I don't think my kids always do the extra credit."

Not only did Winnie challenge many of the tenets of tiger mothering, but she also called into question Chua's claim to speak for all Chinese mothers and children. Winnie took issue with Chua's broad generalizations by providing specific examples, such as challenging the ideas that all Chinese kids do the extra credit and that all Asian/Chinese mothers impelled them to do so.

Interestingly, while Winnie strongly disagreed with Chua's parenting style, she also respected the tremendous work and commitment that it required, especially given Chua's demanding job as a Yale Law School professor. Unlike many White mothers, Winnie could appreciate and identify with Chua's struggles as an Asian American working mother in a highly demanding field and refrained from turning her into either a caricature or threat.

> I couldn't believe anybody would say that or do that, but other times, I was admiring the fact that she was doing what was hard. Because there was an incredible amount of sacrifice and commitment on her part, and it was clearly not easy. I don't know how she managed to work full-time; she was publishing papers, presenting; her career was very demanding. It was a time when she was also going to all these lessons and auditions and concerts with her kids. I did admire her work ethic.

But even as she appreciated Chua's struggles and accomplishments not just in raising successful children but in achieving her own success as a working mother, Winnie was critical of the tiger mother approach and the ways that it fed into stereotypes and the resultant backlash against all Asian American mothers.

> People have been predominantly critical of her and her parenting style, so I would guess [that the tiger mother book] has produced

> more negative perceptions of Asian American mothers overall because it's so strong and the ideas are so different from mainstream American parenting right now, where there is so much more emphasis on letting your kids find themselves and their self-esteem and that kind of stuff. Although I think there are places like New York City and mainly the upper socioeconomic classes where there is much more of that feeling of having to push kids to succeed and compete.

Winnie noted that much of the criticism of tiger mothering stemmed from perceptions that it was "so different" from "mainstream American parenting." In other words, Winnie understood that Chua was seen as a mother/other. Further, she conjectured that those who did not have such adverse reactions to Chua were those who were similarly engaged in highly pressurized parenting approaches. Further, she attributed these approaches to their locales, such as New York City, and their class status, rather than solely a product of their race.

Supporting this observation, she shared that her White husband, a lawyer raised in the Northeast, was far more concerned than she was about their children's academic achievement.

> It was more my husband who wanted to push the kids harder, and I tried to talk him down. He is actually much more tiger mother than I am, way more. He feels like, in order for the kids to have a chance of succeeding as adults, they really need to work hard as teenagers, that they need to get into the best schools possible, to get the best grades possible. His idea is that the world is becoming more competitive, and in order to succeed, you just need to work very, very hard because he had to struggle and because he always worries about the worst-case scenario.

Winne recognized that her husband's desire to push their children stemmed from his fears that, unless they attended elite colleges and obtained the best educational credentials, they would be unable to secure a lifestyle comparable to that which she and her husband had provided them. Although she understood her husband's approach, Winnie often tried to "talk him down" from pressuring their children and was concerned that this pressure negatively impacted his relationship with them.

But more directly related to this chapter's focus on work and motherhood, Winnie's story highlights how her own personal and professional values as a psychologist came into tension with the intense competition for grades and, most intensely, college admissions. While Winnie strove for a relaxed parenting style in general and especially regarding academics, she confessed that when her children reached high school age, she too gave into pressures to direct them toward the most prestigious colleges. As with many Asian American mothers interviewed, she felt that the college admissions process put into bold relief the model minority standards that are imposed not only onto Asian American students but their parents, especially onto Asian American mothers as the ones responsible for getting them into these schools. Instead, drawing on her training as a psychologist, Winnie encouraged her children to focus on where they felt they would be happiest rather than on school prestige for its own sake. However, even with this encouragement, Winnie often felt unable to mitigate the generalized anxieties regarding the stakes of college admissions and the specific pressures on Asian American students and families.

> My son's grades were pretty good, but they weren't straight A's. He ended up getting into the three least competitive schools he applied to. He was rejected from the Ivy Leagues, the super-competitive schools. I think he was disappointed, I think he had higher expectations. But we talked about how the kids who did get into those schools had perfect SAT scores, perfect GPAs. Ultimately, he felt like he

> wouldn't have been happy if he had had to work that hard in high school, and he probably would not have been happy in the kind of environment in college where he had to work that hard.

Winnie was able to support her son to reevaluate his admissions results according to a different set of values based on his own fit with a specific college environment, and his own high school experiences. Additionally, Winnie was able to draw on the perspectives of her work associates, especially one colleague who had a much more relaxed attitude toward his child's college admission, which kept her from defaulting to the academic standards set by the model minority stereotype.

> I felt much better when I talked to somebody at work who is a physician, who is very well respected, accomplished, and really bright and not Asian—he's Caucasian. His son was going to a school that was not really that difficult to get into, and he seemed totally fine with it. I think I realized then, "Oh, this would be much easier if I weren't Asian! The White parents are able to be much more relaxed about it."

Thus, Winnie shifted her approach to her children's college admissions by drawing on her own work as a psychologist as well as the associates that she accessed through her professional networks. This enabled her to recognize the competitive college standards that she had internalized as tied to Asian American model minority standards and push back against them. However, she did not attribute the drive to gain admission into prestigious colleges wholly to Asian culture or her own socialization but, instead, to U.S. racial stereotypes that pressure Asian Americans to be high achievers. She explained:

> I think Asians have sort of identified themselves—or been identified—as excelling academically in this society. There's an expectation that they'll make the best grades and get into the best schools, you know,

> that they all get into Ivy League schools basically. I think that I still could be vulnerable to that. If I talk to somebody who says, "Oh yeah, my kid got into Harvard," then I would feel that maybe I hadn't pushed my son hard enough to get good grades or to study harder for the SATs or take them multiple times, that I had failed as a parent, based on this idea that Asian kids *all* get into Harvard, Princeton, and Yale.

Drawing on not just her professional knowledge but also the experiences of her colleagues, Winnie was able to gain some distance from these model minority standards and the adjoining pressures of tiger mothering. She reconfigured her expectations for her children's college admissions, as well as refusing to use them as the metric by which to judge herself and her mothering as a failure or success. Instead, Winnie made use of her expertise as a psychologist to focus on her children's well-being and the quality of the parent-child relationship. At the same time, even as she rewrote the script of her own mothering, she continued to experience various forms of othering that emerged in different social arenas but especially at the interface of work and family life.

In her workplace, like many Asian American mothers, Winnie felt the imposition of stereotypical expectations for Asian women to be accommodating caregivers, but her work also provided her with resources to clarify and assert her values as a mother. Unfortunately, not all Asian American mothers are so lucky, as many encounter barriers at work that fail to support their mothering priorities and even actively undermine them through various forms of discrimination.

Paid and Unpaid Maternal Labor and Mother/Othering in the Workplace

What can we learn from the experiences of Madeline, Amy, and Winnie and other Asian American mothers interviewed for this book?

What do they tell us about the specific challenges that Asian American mothers face at work, at home, and in the negotiation of work and family commitments? What do they reveal about the workplace as a site of various forms of discrimination and how they can coalesce into mother/othering? Their stories illuminate not only their own competing work and family responsibilities but show how the combination of being Asian American, a woman, and a mother coalesced into various forms of othering as mothers.

This chapter draws attention to the distinct challenges confronting Asian American working mothers and their similarities to and differences from White women, other women of color, and Asian American men. While processes of mother/othering presented differently for each Asian American mother, depending on professions and individual family circumstances, certain commonalities emerged that reflected community and cultural expectations, and the effects of these demands on their identities and their approaches to mothering. Their narratives show that while culture does play a role in shaping work and family decisions, other factors such as race, gender, sexuality, and class are also significant. Model minority standards dictated that even those mothers who attained high-status careers felt pressure to transfer their high achievement to the next generation.

In Madeline's case, she was not only unsupported but was actively undermined in both her career and mothering, culminating not only in racialized sexual harassment but her termination. Madeline's experiences of sexual harassment took on racialized forms targeted broadly at Asian women and women of color. But they also revealed factors particular to Asian American mothers, such as being held to different and higher standards of work performance and stronger repercussions for supposed failure to measure up, especially after returning from maternity leave. Her story at first reads as a model minority success narrative, seemingly the opposite of othering. But it quickly morphs into an illustration of how two main forces, in combination, can derail a woman's career: motherhood and sexual harassment. Madeline expressed pride in being an alternative role model to her children by fighting sexual harassment and leaving her high-paying corporate job. However, as with many women who supposedly opt out of work, Madeline was in fact "pushed out," to use Pamela Stone's term to counter the "opt-out" frame.[8]

Even more, Madeline's successful management career was destabilized not only by becoming a mother but by being sexually harassed and standing up against it. Sumi K. Cho, in her article "Racialized Sexual Harassment. Where the Model Minority Meets Suzie Wong," addresses how Asian American women are at particular risk for sexual harassment due to "the combustible and recombinant reaction of race with gender that produces sexualized racial stereotypes and racialized gender stereotypes."[9] However, while Cho's framework is incisive in many ways, it would be a mistake to merely append yet another stereotype to Madeline's story and reframe it as the model minority and Suzie Wong meeting the tiger mother. The kinds of mothering concerns that Madeline experienced were not those commonly associated with the high academic and professional achievement associated with tiger mothering. Rather, in addition to being put at risk for racialized sexual harassment as an Asian American woman, her status as a new mother and her support for another Asian American woman subjected her to retaliation and job termination. Even after she left this workplace, Madeline continued to encounter mother/othering in a different form due to her inability to fulfill model minority expectations following her termination, divorce, career change, and downsizing.

In Amy's case, she excelled in her career as a surgeon but encountered othering based on her perceived "failure" to meet the normative family model based on biological reproduction, as she felt judged by her choice to adopt a child, and only one child. Throughout her career, she had faced othering as a "small Asian woman," and while her active resistance to this stereotype had fueled her drive to succeed, it also caused distance between her and other Asian women colleagues. Her experiences reflect "token stress," a term developed to explain how Black elites often felt a sense of isolation and loss of identity while having to show greater competence in their workplaces.[10] In addition, Rosabeth Moss Kanter observed that women who feel they have to disprove gendered stereotypes often become "trapped in a more militant role than they might otherwise take."[11] Reflecting both racialized and gendered processes, Asian American women's negotiations of work and family responsibilities reflect their simultaneous locations in specific workplaces and professions, and their simultaneous identities.

Winnie similarly confronted matritropes about her as an Asian American working mother, but rather than being seen as a "small Asian woman," she was called on to play the role of "office mother." While she was not highly invested in her children attending prestigious colleges, she felt that others expected this and expected her to be the one to get them there. While professional mothers like Winnie felt pressure to push their children towards high achievement, mothers who did not meet standards of high professional achievement or perhaps had at one point in their lives but then experienced career disruptions or transitions often felt that their ability to raise high-achieving children was subject to question by their perceived failure to meet these standards themselves. Similar to Jill in the epigraph to this chapter, Winnie made a distinction between her identity as a woman and as an Asian, as well as the kind of discrimination she experienced due to each in her work as a psychologist. However, as she narrated her story, she drew a more nuanced picture of how gender and race combine to make Asian American women susceptible to specific forms of discrimination, particularly having their expertise constantly called into question while simultaneously being expected to smooth over difficult workplace relations.

Collectively, these profiles show that for many Asian American mothers, model minority expectations to excel at work often conflict with gendered expectations to prioritize motherhood and family. While much scholarship has explored how model minority standards are unattainable for many Asian Americans, this chapter has shone light on how these standards are particularly irreconcilable for Asian American mothers. Overshadowed by the model minority stereotype, little attention has been given to the lived experiences of second-generation Asian American women as they move into the workforce, become heads of households, and negotiate ties to ethnic communities and cultures. Much research on Asian American families has focused on a younger cohort and concentrated mainly on educational achievement and identity formation.[12] Current studies have also challenged the ideology of the model minority by revealing that while some segments of the U.S.-born-and-raised Asian American population have attained high levels of educational and socioeconomic achievement, they still encounter discrimination in their personal, professional, and public lives.[13] These profiles of Madeline, Amy, and Winnie trace the legacies of growing up in immigrant families into the next chapter, as second-generation Asian American women seek to define their work and family lives not as daughters but as mothers.

Many Asian American mothers interviewed experienced competing pressures to pursue high-status and high-paying careers while also facing equally strong pressures to devote themselves to childrearing. Many felt the need to constantly prove their credentials and assert authority at work but then were penalized for transgressing gender norms. Despite having some of the highest rates of education and representation in professional occupations, Asian American women's credentials are less likely to be rewarded with promotions to managerial and leadership positions and higher salaries.[14] Few resources are available to support Asian American women in the workplace, as Asian Americans are often not considered an underrepresented minority qualifying for diversity programs and, in fact, are seen by many as overrepresented not only in competitive colleges but in high-status professions.[15]

On top of the pressures that many women face in negotiating work and family, Asian American women also struggle with issues of racial belonging and perceived foreignness. As discussed in other chapters, model minority standards impose exceptionally high expectations for Asian American mothers' involvement not just in parenting within the home but at school and extracurricular activities. In addition, they must expend great effort in processing racial bias and instilling tools for their children to develop positive racial and ethnic identities. Thus, in addition to the general challenges of meeting work and family responsibilities, Asian American mothers confront racialized and gendered expectations to be both model minority professionals and devoted supermoms.

Conclusion

Many Asian American mothers find work fulfilling and are deeply invested in their careers, but it is one thing to be willingly invested in work, and it is another thing to have to perform to someone else's standards to prove racial worth. Many of the mothers interviewed were highly motivated at work, and some set their sights on breaking through the so-called bamboo ceiling. But many others came to regard these as futile efforts that fueled tokenism and did little to change the root problems of racial and gender inequality, while exacting a high price in their personal lives.

Previous studies have focused on how the model minority label shapes the educational and career aspirations of Asian American adolescents, but more research is needed on how this label affects adult Asian Americans, especially women, as they enter the workforce and start their own families. Work and family negotiations are often more intense and complicated for Asian American women because of pressures to demonstrate model minority qualities by working in high-status jobs while also meeting "supermom" standards to be highly involved parents.

Like all mothers and indeed all people, Asian American mothers should have the freedom to choose from a wide range of careers and degree of investment in careers and a wide range of family forms. However, Asian American mothers encounter a distinct set of challenges in realizing the fullest range of choices regarding work and family. Asian American mothers acknowledged multiple influences on their work and family arrangements but they noted certain commonalities and specific forms of discrimination and exclusion that derailed them from career pathways or limited their options to seek alternatives. Model minority racialization imposes strong pressures to pursue high-paying, high-status jobs not merely to realize personal ambitions but to prove racial belonging. Even when they succeed in meeting expectations, Asian American mothers are more likely to encounter resentment and suspicion than celebration of their accomplishments. But they do not merely acquiesce to these narrow terms of model minority inclusion as the final chapter shows. They strive to reinvent the meanings of work and family by "imagining motherwise."

Conclusion

From Mother/Othering to Imagining Motherwise

The radical potential of the word "mother" comes after the 'm.' It is the space that "other" takes in our mouths when we say it. We are something else.

ALEXIS PAULINE GUMBS, "m/other ourselves: a Black queer feminist genealogy for radical mothering" (2016)

I don't believe care work has to wreck us. This labor can be shared, social, collective—and transformative.

ANGELA GARBES, Essential Labor: Mothering as Social Change (2022)

It's hard to define what is an Asian American community, so what would a community of Asian American mothers even look like? It has to be about showing up for each other. It can't just be about being Korean, or Chinese, or whatever Asian country you came from. There are only a few mothers I would call my community, and they are from all kinds of backgrounds.

OLIVIA, interview, Korean American, activist

"It takes a village to raise a child," says the oft-cited adage.[1] But we are villageless. Rather than embracing each other as part of this proverbial village (which everyone seems to want to believe in, despite much evidence to the contrary), mothers have been pitted against each other in global mommy wars, manifesting in both figurative and actual war zones. But are mothers destined to be at war with each other? How can motherhood be imagined otherwise, not as a struggle for survival of the fittest but as collective caregiving?

In conversation with Alexis Pauline Gumbs and the editors and contributors to *Revolutionary Mothering: Love on the Front Lines*, what is the "something else" that can come after the "m" in *mother*, and how can *other* be reclaimed so as not to divide mothers but to recreate motherhood through relations of solidarity and care?[2] Further, as Angela Garbes asks, how can this work not wreck us and instead transform us?[3] Or in Olivia's succinct words above, what would it mean for mothers to show up for each other? And what transformations are necessary—as individuals and as societies—for mothers, Asian American and otherwise, to be able to stand with rather than against each other? Beyond analyzing the various dimensions of mother/othering, this final chapter explores some of the many small steps toward implementing change, as well as the barriers that stand in the way. Imagining motherwise requires new practices, policies, and priorities for motherhood, but in order to move forward, we have to acknowledge where we are, and how we got here. Rather than resuscitating the tired metaphor of the mommy wars or appropriating an oversimplified vision of a global village, what other ways of thinking about motherhood—and being mothers—can we imagine and enact?

I have invoked both the global mommy wars and the global village here as foils; they are oversimplifications that speak to the fears of living in an ever more hostile and competitive world and the fantasy of returning to simpler times. Yet we hold onto them for a reason. The global village refers to a well-known saying, which when grounded in the cultural contexts from which it emerged, can impart meaningful lessons to counter the rhetoric of a mother-eat-mother catfight. Unfortunately, it has instead been largely decontextualized and turned into a mere slogan and feel-good metaphor. Few people take the next step of asking what such a village would look like, what it would take to build it? Who would belong and who would be excluded?

The older edition of the mommy wars fed on the idea of an intractable divide between stay-at-home and working mothers; the current global version shifts from conflicts between home versus work to those across racial and national boundaries. While there are now many deeper lines drawn in these new global mommy wars, the old divisions have not disappeared; rather, they have been rearticulated, raising the stakes to not just which mothers are better or worse but who gets to claim the mantle of motherhood as a sanctified or suspect status. It is this larger context of global mommy wars on steroids that Asian American mothers have been cast not just as competitors but as others. Yet, what these old and new framings of the mommy wars have in common is that although they often play out between mothers, they are about much more than motherhood. At the same time, like previous iterations, the current discourse of global mommy wars (even when not named as such) can become self-fulfilling, as many mothers have too willingly joined the fray. Like many manifestations of mother/othering, these past and current iterations of the mommy wars are red herrings that misdirect attention away from the many social issues that make motherhood so challenging and instead, place blame on mothers themselves. But the many challenges defining contemporary motherhood are neither created solely by mothers nor can they be solved by mothers alone.

As with much of the language used to discuss motherhood that this book has critiqued, terms such as *the mommy wars* and *the global village* divide and flatten mothers into caricatures, both individually and as groups. This book has offered a range of new terms to more precisely name key fault lines between mothers and about motherhood. Thus far, I have developed various new concepts as components or subcategories of mother/othering, but in this final chapter, I strive not for synonyms but antonyms and, ideally, antidotes, which I conceive under the broad framework of imagining motherwise. The wide-ranging shifts from mother/othering to imagining motherwise can also be captured as moving from reproductive exclusion to reproductive justice. Building on these frameworks as tools and roadmaps for imagining motherwise, I revisit the terms developed earlier in the book with new questions and applications.

Rather than mapping out a concrete plan for policy, activism, and scholarship, this conclusion applies lessons from earlier chapters for thinking differently about motherhood, or imagining motherwise. Throughout this book, these ways of reimagining motherhood have emerged through in-depth conversations with Asian American mothers, drawing on their experiences and visions for alternative practices, beliefs, and conditions of motherhood. I bring in a few more of their voices here to not only picture alternatives to mother/othering but to illustrate different ways that Asian American mothers are putting these alternatives into practice. While foregrounding their voices, this chapter connects them to conceptual frameworks developed throughout this book and to the main social institutions that are the primary sites of mothering: families and communities, schools, and workplaces.

I also return to lessons from the earlier chapters related to reproductive exclusion and matritropes and apply their lessons to current debates about politics and representation related to Asian American mothers and the institution of motherhood itself. The larger aim is for this scholarship to speak not only to academic audiences but also to policymakers, journalists, educators, medical professionals, service providers, and most of all, to Asian American mothers and those who care about them. To provide a focal point, once again, I return to the tiger mother to illustrate not just mother/othering but resistance to it.

Reimagining the Tiger Mother and Other Matritropes

The Asian American women I know are a bunch of badasses. We joke about being failed tiger mothers. We're like slackers who drink wine in front of our kids, and if they don't want to brush their teeth one night that's OK. . . . It's more important that [my daughter] be a good social citizen. . . . It's not a big deal to me that she plays piano. . . . We're so counter, we might get a perverse pride if she didn't do well in school.

SUDHA, interview, Indian American–mixed race, professor

What would it mean to reimagine Asian American motherhood not merely against but beyond the confines of the tiger mother? Sudha joked about being a failed tiger mother but then went on to articulate a vision of motherhood with little concern for grades or piano, instead focusing on raising her daughter to be a "good social citizen." She articulated various dimensions of what this good social citizen would look like, not in terms of accomplishments but based on caring about and being cared for by a large community of extended kin, peers, and neighbors. Notably, Sudha did not define a citizen simply in terms of legal status but extended the meaning of citizenship to encompass mutual social ties and responsibilities. Her framing of the "good social citizen" directly counters the idea of "the other." Likewise, her description of herself and other Asian American mothers—those who were doing the maternal labor to raise these good social citizens—provides particularly evocative and economical language to counter mother/othering: "badasses."

Like Sudha, Asian American mothers have articulated new ways of imagining themselves as mothers and of reimagining the institution of motherhood, so as not to reproduce tiger mothering and not even be held to its metrics. But often, this effort requires naming the tiger mother as the standard to which they are being held. Throughout this book, the framework of mother/other has explored the many dimensions of the Asian American mother—as person, prototype, and projection—and how their multiple contradictions have coalesced around the figure of the tiger mother. But even more, it has centered how Asian American mothers have narrated their complex negotiations of the tiger mother matritrope. From annoyance, acquiescence, assimilation, and emulation to resistance, these negotiations of the tiger mother trope mirror negotiations of the broader model minority racial frame and of othering writ large, but they also require forms of mediation specific to Asian American motherhood.

To summarize earlier arguments, the tiger mother did more than uncover existing fears and stereotypes; it catalyzed new ones specifically related to motherhood and reproduction, reinscribing old racial and cultural subtexts while writing new ones. Tropes about motherhood gain traction precisely because they offer a convenient shorthand, whether the angel in the house or the maleficent monster mother; likewise, matritropes about "yellow motherhood"—whether prostitutes, mongrels, coolies, criminals, models, or tigers—name and encapsulate Asian America mothers as various forms of mother/others. The concept of matritropes has sought to provide a more precise language to disrupt these tried-and-true tropes and the divisions they foster.

Currently, Asian American mothers are most likely to be perceived as tiger mothers, but this matritrope masks and quickly devolves into much older and less flattering tropes. These range from being perceived as the "anti-Christmas mom" in Kyra's case to the ambiguous position of the model minority mother that Althea negotiated, simultaneously grouped together with "all those minorities" while being selectively exempted from this same grouping. While distinct in its particular content and emergence, the tiger mother is part of a long line of representations of certain groups of mothers as others.

The work of dismantling matritropes and creating new representations is an important dimension of imagining motherwise.

Fortunately, a broad range of representations are slowly emerging that expand maternal narrative plenitude specifically with regard to Asian American mothers. For example, in film, more complex and diverse representations of Asian American mothers have emerged across genres, from the Academy Award–winning performance by Michelle Yeoh in *Everything Everywhere All At Once* to the troubled but loving relationship between a widowed Indian American mother and her grieving daughter in the Netflix series *Never Have I Ever*, to the horror film *Umma* in which Sandra Oh plays a Korean American mother haunted by generational trauma, to (if we include North America) the animated portrayal of a Chinese Canadian mother who passes superpowers to her daughter in *Turning Red*. Novels such as Celeste Ng's *Our Missing Hearts* and Jessamine Chan's *The School for Good Mothers*, Lisa Ko's *The Leavers*, and Ocean Vuong's *On Earth We Are Briefly Gorgeous* (along with his poetry collection *Time is a Mother*)—to name just a few—are telling much more complex stories related to Asian American motherhood, although frequently grounded in dystopian visions and often still centering the immigrant mother.[4] None of these films, shows, and novels are perfect, nor should they have to be (although some come pretty close). Instead, they help to broaden the range of stories that are possible for Asian American mothers; the more films that are made, the more novels that are written, the more maternal narrative plentitude increases, the more possibilities can be imagined.

But in order to be seen and see ourselves differently, Asian American mothers must see how they have been denied other possibilities, especially but not solely by being rendered as tiger mothers. Like Sudha, Asian American mothers that I have interviewed have shared not only how the tiger mother has racially pigeonholed Asian American mothers but what is required of them to resist it. But no matter how much they and their families individually resist tiger mothering, the many social institutions that have called it forth—both celebrating and condemning it—must also change. These span the various sites of mothering and othering from cultural representation to laws, education, and employment that cooperatively define motherhood as a social institution and its parameters.

The persistence and prevalence of a wide range of matritropes speaks both to the power of motherhood as a social institution and the ways that it is shaped by a range of various other social institutions. In order to reimagine the tiger mother and other matritropes, it is necessary to not only talk and think differently about specific groups of mothers but to remake the institutions that constrain what we say and how we think about motherhood writ large, starting with the institution of the family itself and the meanings of culture and community that undergird it.

Reimagining Asian American Families, Communities, and Culture

I feel like my son has learned through seeing my interactions with the community and also how his dad and I talk about issues and how we work things out as a couple. . . . I started out doing work for some Filipina organizations who were working on community issues like immigration and workers' rights. I liked how they were to each other, their collective and nonhierarchical collaboration. . . . This work continues to be really important to me since I became a mother. I often just took my son to meetings. It was fine because other moms and other community organizers had their kids around, and they all just played together. . . . I feel like we're really thriving as a family.

REYNA, interview, Filipina American, community organizer

Reyna has been able to reimagine mothering by choosing to co-parent and forge a relationship with her partner outside a traditional marriage, raising her son collectively in a community of non-kin "aunties" and activists and integrating her work, family, and political commitments. Through this community of support, she has been able to challenge othering and to reimagine motherhood outside normative models of motherhood. By bringing her son to meetings at work and sharing work-related activities and discussions at home, Reyna challenged the very idea that work and family are separate spheres. Beyond striving for some ill-defined sense of work-family balance, she redefined the boundaries of both, redefining family, community, and culture for herself, her son, her partner, her colleagues, and those she hoped would benefit from her paid and unpaid labor as an Asian American mother and activist.

While addressing institutional and structural approaches to imagining motherwise, I also want to bring it closer to home, through examples like Reyna, for whom Asian American mothering was not about merely balancing but about thriving. What factors supported Reyna and her family to thrive? She outlined a number of key elements from a supportive partner to financial stability, to strong mentorship and community connections, to a close relationship with her child, to simply having a "whole package that works." While she attributed much of this to "luck," she also noted how much labor she had put in to make this whole package work and to keep it working.

Many Asian American mothers interviewed for this book expressed longing for the strong community of support that Reyna described, especially with other Asian American mothers. Like Olivia, quoted at the beginning of this chapter, they acknowledged their many differences, but they also felt that other Asian American mothers shared certain experiences and concerns, many of which revolved around their identities as Asian Americans. Many found that becoming mothers brought to the fore the need to define and assert not only their own identities but the very meanings of Asian American culture and community in new and challenging ways.

Asian American mothers are not destined to re-create their own families, whether the good or the bad, nor can they escape the influences of the families in which they grew up and the social worlds that they currently inhabit. They do not automatically channel their cultural heritage into their mothering; like all aspects of culture and family, they assert their personal approaches to mothering but within larger social and cultural conditions. While this book has taken a sociological rather than psychological approach to mothering and othering, it recognizes that these inner and outer worlds are always shaping each other; the individual and society, the micro and the macro are always interconnected. How mothers raise their children is not solely dictated by how they were raised nor is it completely disconnected. Those who are cast as others recast themselves, and in doing so, they redraw boundaries not only of self and other but of othering and belonging in larger social worlds.

As examined in chapter 3, from Leslie's choice of a name for her daughter to Annika's organizing of a culture camp, to Gina's efforts to raise her child bilingually in a multigenerational household, many Asian American mothers strive to mother with certain meanings of culture but against others. Misrepresentations of culture and cultural identity are at the core of othering, whether of mothers or broadly. Thus, a significant amount of Asian American maternal labor is invested in nurturing positive cultural identities in children but even more, in defining the very meaning of what constitutes Asian American culture and identity.

Efforts to transform motherhood and the intersectional maternal labor that it requires became significantly more fraught during and after the COVID-19 pandemic, which highlighted how visible expressions of Asian culture can attract not only prejudice but outright hostility and violence. This climate of heightened hostility was amplified by political leaders who openly deployed hateful rhetoric to blame the coronavirus pandemic on China—most notably, then-President Trump's references to the "Chinese virus" and the "kung flu"—which fueled and normalized an atmosphere of blame and hate against Asians and Asian Americans.[5]

This climate of increased racism and violence led many Asian American parents to keep their children close to home, even once schools and other public spaces reopened, as they feared that their children would be the targets of blame and discrimination.[6] But they also sought to build new forms of community. In one moving example of solidarity, the Auntie Sewing Squad countered the othering of Asian American women and families not only by making and donating masks when they were in short supply but even more, by using this simple activity to create a space for collective caregiving and mutual aid.[7] This example highlighted that imagining motherwise is not merely an individual exercise but a whole family and community project.

Many Asian American mothers have actively engaged their partners and extended families in these efforts. While being careful not to assume heterosexual partnerships or binary gender identities, more attention is needed to the role of Asian American fathers not only in feeding the tiger mother trope but in parenting broadly. As noted earlier, because the tendency has been to frame the mother psychologically as the other in relation to the child or the father, this book has intentionally shifted attention to how mothers are *socially* constructed as the other vis-à-vis each other and in relation to the dominant society and culture. But while Asian American motherhood is more centrally implicated in Asian American racialization, Asian American fathers are not exempt from these processes. It is difficult, if not impossible, to be a tiger mother without the backing of a tiger father or at least, a father who is on board with tiger mothering, even if he does not do the work himself. Likewise, resisting and reimagining the limiting trope of the tiger mother is not up to Asian American mothers alone.

The contested nature of the tiger mother has not only highlighted the many contradictions of model minority status but underscores that it is the reproduction of the model minority and the Asian

American mother as the agent of this reproduction that has positioned Asian Americans as a domestic and global threat. To the degree that it draws on any shared cultural roots or practices, tiger mothering needs to be understood less as an inheritance from Asia than as a product of an emerging Asian America. Like many cultural inheritances, it is something that most Asian Americans mothers did not choose for themselves but must constantly make choices about.

Mothering and othering are learned, people are socialized to be mothers, and people are taught who is other. Again, this learning happens on a very individual level but within institutional structures, especially families, schools, and workplaces. People have agency, and mothers have maternal agency: they both acquiesce and resist whatever social rules and roles are imposed on them. Mothers redefine what motherhood means to them, and in so doing, they change the social meanings of motherhood. But all of this requires work and substantial resources, both external and internal. Agency is not just based on individual thought and action; the ability of individuals to think and act beyond the limitations of their circumstances is still limited by their social conditions. Different social institutions, schools in particular, have the power to position certain mothers as others or to support imagining motherwise.

Rewriting the Hidden Maternal Curriculum in Schools

There were some really interesting, I think messed-up race dynamics in the school that we tried to point out to the administration, where the head teachers, were often the White teachers, and the secondary teachers were the Asian teachers, and they were paid a lot less. . . . My partner, Tess, and I are pretty activist, so we would be ready to tackle issues if they came up. We have a lot of training about how to do that, so we were willing to help the school.

MARLA, interview, Chinese American, non-profit director

What lessons can Asian American mothers impart about schools as a site of othering and resistance to othering? How do schools contribute to mother/othering, and what can they do to counter it and specifically, to better support Asian American mothers and families? Chapter 4 discussed that what mothers learn through the hidden maternal curriculum of schools extends far beyond their children's education to lessons about what kind of mothers and motherhood are valued. However, many mothers, such as Marla, above, and her partner, Tess (who is White), refused to follow narrow dictates about what their appropriate roles at the school should be. They were "willing to help the school" by challenging unfair labor practices in which White teachers were paid more than Asian teachers. They also found themselves called to tackle a range of issues from bilingual education to expanding the arts curriculum, to creating queer-friendly school policies. Thus, their intersectional maternal labor focused not only on their own children's educational needs but also on improving the school environment as a whole, including acts of solidarity such as organizing support for labor issues and pay raises for teachers at their children's school. But Marla underscored that she had a hard-won skillset based on her activist work to navigate these issues and the fraught interactions that they involved.

Marla and Tess's efforts resonate with the narratives of other mothers previously discussed. Not only do Asian American mothers have to perform additional intersectional maternal labor to make sure their children have positive experiences at school, but they often supplement this learning with language classes and cultural activities, while being hypervigilant to subtle forms of discrimination and outright bullying. From Althea's speaking up in playground conversations about disparaging comments about changing school demographics to Tae's advocating for gender-inclusive bathrooms and asserting their identity as a gender queer mother, all these efforts required a great deal of commitment and work. Many mothers felt like their efforts were mere drops in the bucket in the face of a tide of regressive school policies being unleashed across the country. But whether addressing censorship of books, respect for gender pronouns, or high-stakes testing, these everyday enactments of intersectional maternal labor are not separate from the big picture of government policies or cultural representations of motherhood.

A first step toward imagining motherwise in schools would be to recognize that Asian American mothers need support, because many interview participants noted that schools rarely reached out to them and assumed that they were already involved—if not overinvolved—in their children's schooling. School leaders and staff can recognize that there is in fact a hidden maternal curriculum that often others Asian American mothers. Rather than dismissing them as tiger mothers, schools can take them seriously and even welcome Asian American mothers' involvement in activities ranging from tutoring, to fundraising, to organizing cultural events.

A seemingly simple suggestion to counter mother/othering would be to create more space and opportunities for mothers from all backgrounds to be more active in their children's schools, but even these kinds of efforts are not straightforward. On the one hand, greater participation and dialogue among mothers and with school officials and teachers could encourage mothers whose voices are often marginalized to offer meaningful feedback about school programming, curriculum and climate. Like Kyra's efforts to broaden school-sponsored holiday celebrations beyond a Christmas shopping day, these conversations could begin with recognizing and learning about more diverse cultural holidays and integrating them into school programs. This would be an important first step that would hopefully move beyond hosting intermittent multicultural events to fostering greater diversity in the core mission and atmosphere of the school.

On the other hand, without clear goals and parameters, merely talking about issues runs the risk of increasing divisions, undermining the authority and expertise of teachers and administrators, and opening the door for even more contentious and volatile school board meetings, not to mention sports events and playground conversations. As Althea described, unfiltered discussions among mothers often place Asian American mothers in the awkward position of hearing racist comments about "minorities" and having either to counter or absorb them. Giving parents more authority to shape curriculum and programming could fuel more intense organizing by parent's rights groups on issues ranging from trans inclusivity to banning books, thus making it even more difficult for mothers who are not part of organized groups to express concerns. Althea's experiences show that it is a tall order to expect mothers on their own, to initiate discussions about race, let alone to institute concrete initiatives or work together in implementing them. In a moment when such programs are being banned at local and state levels, when even just saying "DEI" has become a flashpoint, stories such as Althea's show how important it is to implement these discussions and programs systematically rather than having individual mothers take on the responsibility of transforming entire schools or communities.

Further, Asian American mothers, like all mothers, have taken all different sides on these issues; they can be seen powerfully resisting othering and also contributing to it, whether through acts of omission or commission. This is especially true around issues related to education. Take the case of affirmative action. A study by Pew Research Center found that while Asian Americans hold mixed views toward affirmative action, the majority support it.[8] Yet, a small group of Asian American mothers have played an instrumental role in dismantling affirmative action programs locally and nationally.[9] The struggles in New York City public schools are also instructive, as Asian American mothers have vocally advocated for and against efforts to place less emphasis on a single entrance for magnet or other competitive public schools.[10] Jackie, an Asian American mother whose daughter attended New York City public schools and was directly impacted by these debates, shared in an interview, "If you talk to five different Asian American moms in New York, you will get five different positions [on the testing issue]. It doesn't even break down by new immigrants versus Asian Americans who were born and raised here."

Rather than recognizing these diverse positions among Asian Americans with regard to a competitive testing and selective admissions let alone to educational approaches broadly, the figure of the self-serving anti-affirmative action mother has emerged as yet another matritrope with which Asian American mothers must now contend.[11] As with the well-worn tiger mother trope, these mothers are not seen as individuals with complex motivations and histories but as representatives of all Asian American mothers, often obscuring their complex positions in these debates. Those who have argued against high-stakes testing have done so for a range of reasons, arguing that it is unfair to students who cannot afford specialized test-preparation courses. On the other hand, Asian American mothers who have defended selective admissions and testing argue that Asian Americans have one of the highest poverty rates in the city and should not be penalized for investing their family resources to help their children succeed academically. They also argue that admissions systems that use more holistic measurements are likely to discriminate against Asian American candidates, often citing beliefs that admission processes give low scores to Asian American applicants based on subjective personal qualities.[12] More generally, many progressive Asian Americans argue that the testing debates are yet another instance in which discourses of Asian Americans as the model minority have pitted them against disadvantaged Black, Latinx, and Indigenous communities.[13] These diverse concerns deserve full consideration rather than being reduced to assumptions of tiger mothering or other matritropes and then used to fuel divisions among mothers and the different communities they represent.

The tiger mother trope simultaneously gives the mother too much credit if their children do well and too much blame if they don't. In addition, encapsulating Asian American mothers' concerns about education to tiger mothering does them a disservice and detracts from larger structural inequalities shaping schools. In a parallel example, the attribution of a "culture of poverty" to Black and Latinx mothers not only pathologizes them but draws attention away from the structural conditions that are far more salient in determining their children's educational outcomes, ranging from underfunded schools to racial and other forms of bias.

Likewise, the attribution of Asian American students' academic success to having tiger mothers also distracts from the structural factors that contribute to some but not all of them doing well. It is true that a certain population of Asian American students excel, but they do so for a broad range of reasons from having parents who were hyper-selected through an immigration system that privileges those who already possess substantial resources to offer their children to the "stereotype promise" that biases teachers in their favor, especially in subjects such as science and math.[14] These all contribute to a hidden maternal curriculum that both schools mothers into their expected roles while creating presumptions that they will be difficult and demanding tiger mothers.

Mothers cut their political teeth by speaking up at school board meetings, and depending on the response they get, they run leadership positions on these boards or their voices are further shut down. These interactions unfold between mothers, but schools themselves play a significant role in how they play out. Through the mundane negotiation of field trips, fundraisers, and a wide array of activities that take place in or around schools, mothers are schooled in a hidden curriculum that is about much more than schooling. Mother/othering is a central part of this hidden maternal curriculum, as schools not only educate mothers as to how they are expected to educate their children but about which mothers and which children are most valued at school and beyond. The micro-interactions among mothers in schools reflect macro-level social structures but can also accumulate into significant steps toward changing these structures. Likewise, small measures can have significant impacts in reimagining the workplace as an institution that supports rather than others mothers.

Countering Mother/Othering at Work

I was actually shocked when my boss asked me if I wanted to take the day off for the Lunar New Year. Most of the other places that I have worked, I felt like they expected me to bring in Chinese food for them or hand out those little red envelopes. . . . My boss actually understood that it was a day for me to be with my family.

SARAH, interview, Chinese American, human resources manager

What kind of policies are necessary to support Asian American mothers at work and to recognize and disrupt broader patterns of mother/othering that emerge in workplaces? There are many kinds of workplace policies that have been shown to benefit parents in general—such as more generous parental leave, paid sick days, on-site childcare, and flexibility to work remotely.[15] In addition, Asian American mothers would benefit not only from specific policies that address their needs but from changes in overall workplace cultures. Other measures range from flexibility and support not only for childcare but for eldercare, mentoring and support groups, workplace trainings to counter the kinds of implicit biases that they are most likely to encounter, clearer criteria for raises and promotions, and documentation of patterns of inequality in raises and promotions.[16] While these structural changes and policies are crucial, Sarah's example above shows that simple gestures can also make a huge difference, such as a boss recognizing culturally specific holidays and providing support to celebrate these with families and communities, rather than making them into extra unpaid labor to promote a multicultural workplace.

Motherhood has become a high-wire balancing act—not just between the responsibilities of work and family but across the chasms of belonging and othering—and Asian American mothers must walk a particularly precarious tightrope. Managing the contradictory demands imposed by employers and families is not a unique challenge to Asian American working mothers, but it has specific dimensions. Hays demonstrated the sharp "cultural contradictions of motherhood" between work and family that have raised standards for "intensive mothering" not in spite of mothers working full-time jobs but because they pursue careers, they have to prove that they are even more devoted as mothers.[17] In addition to these generalized cultural contradictions, Asian American mothers contend with racialized forms of intensive mothering that require them to be both high-achieving model minority producers at the office and devoted reproducers of high-achieving children at home.

But Asian American mothers should not be expected to continuously climb the career ladder nor to automatically put family first; like all mothers, they have a range of different priorities, that shift from day to day and from person to person. As chapter 5 demonstrated, while many Asian American mothers are highly motivated for various reasons to stay in the labor force and advance their careers, many others would like to cut back or stay at home with children full time. These are very personal choices, but they are often structured by social conditions that shape specific forms of work-family conflict for Asian American mothers. Not only are many simultaneously negotiating childcare and eldercare, but these responsibilities make it financially difficult for them to "opt out" from the labor market or even to scale back for short periods of time. In addition to their own family obligations, societal expectations for them to fulfill model minority standards of achievement often impose significant pressure to seek out and stay employed in high-status jobs.

Like many working parents, Asian American mothers have highly personal reasons for the decisions they make regarding their investments in careers and families. But rather than being seen as individuals, many Asian American mothers reported feeling that their needs and commitment to work were often assumed based on their race. This sense of having to represent Asian American women as a group is especially heightened for those employed in workplaces or professions in which they were the only Asian American woman or one of only a few, such as Amy, the surgeon in chapter 5. Further, as Amy reported, especially in leadership roles, Asian American women encounter specific racial and gender tropes, such as that of the "small Asian woman," which undermine their authority but then result in them being labeled as too loud or pushy when they assert themselves. While Black women often have to battle the "angry Black woman" stereotype, Asian American women often have to dispel assumptions that they are passive pushovers, but they then pay a price for failing to conform to type.[18]

Many Asian American mothers interviewed mentioned some version of the "quiet Asian woman" stereotype and the accompanying expectations for them to be hard working, uncomplaining, and good team players. These expectations created a workplace culture in which others seemed to take for granted that they would pick up extra work related to their actual job descriptions but also informal tasks outside their official duties, ranging from ordering food to arranging meetings, to smoothing over conflicts. Further, while they were more susceptible to requests for unrecognized and unpaid labor, they were also more likely to be penalized if they refused. Similar to Winnie in chapter 5, several Asian American mothers recounted co-workers who assumed that they had proficiency in Asian languages and asking them for help not only related to work but regarding travel or activities for their children. If these requests came from a person with whom they had a cordial relationship or who openly acknowledged that they were asking a favor, they were not necessarily regarded as impositions. But it was often a slippery slope between accommodating personal requests and becoming vulnerable to inappropriate demands, which in some cases, crossed the line into sexual harassment.

As described by Madeline, racialized sexual harassment can compound the effects of the motherhood penalty at work, leading to negative performance reviews and other forms of retribution. Thus, Asian American mothers can be more susceptible both to unwanted advances and to negative repercussions for refusing them. Matritropes of Asian women as "prostitutes" and "war brides" are deeply entrenched and continue to frame Asian American women as sexually available; these perceptions carry over to workplace settings and do not disappear simply because they become mothers. Workplaces need to be aware of these overlapping forms of racial and sexual othering and to take them seriously, rather than pushing out those who are their targets.

In sum, Asian American mothers should not feel bound to pursue high-status jobs, nor should they be excluded or derailed from doing so, and especially not by steeper motherhood penalties combined with racialized sexual harassment, such as that encountered by Madeline. They should not encounter either automatic suspicion or celebration for their accomplishments. They should have the freedom to choose from a wide range of careers and investments in careers and a wide range of family forms and commitments. Awareness of how mother/othering operates in the workplace could help identify the specific challenges that Asian American mothers face but also help to implement broader employment policies and shifts in unofficial workplace cultures.

Reimagining Laws, Policies, and Politics

What the framework of mother/othering and its related concepts can offer is less about the pros and cons of specific policy initiatives; rather, its main contribution is to understand the reasons why it is so hard to pass policies that would support mothers and why there is so little political will and instead, such strong pushback against what are seen as basic entitlements in many other developed countries.

Spotlighting the history of reproductive exclusion for Asian Americans shows that the policies that are normally associated with supporting mothers, such as paid parental leave and childcare supports, while necessary and important, are only a small slice of the legal and legislative powers that shape motherhood. The lens of mother/othering zooms out from the narrow policies that are usually considered as relevant for mothers and families to encompass issues ranging from border control to military actions, to criminalization and control of reproduction.

However, in addressing these issues, Asian American mothers, just like mothers overall, are as likely to face off against one another as they are to stand together. But shouldn't they—and mothers in general—know better? At least according to the prevailing mythology, mothers should be the first to put the needs of others first, even to embrace others' needs as their own, and to join together with other mothers in doing the same. Recent years, however, have shown that mothers cannot be assumed to be allies simply by virtue of being mothers. Some have led struggles for greater diversity, equity, and inclusion in education, employment, cultural representation, and laws; others have opposed these efforts and have actively participated in turning *DEI* into an epithet. Mothers are as likely to be seen forming exclusive playdate pods and buying their children's way into exclusive colleges as they are to be joining hands on the frontlines of struggles for gun safety, universal healthcare, or environmental sustainability.

Likewise, Asian American mothers can be found on all sides of every issue across the political spectrum. This should come as no surprise, and yet, it strikes many as surprising, because the ready assumption is that Asian Americans are all the same, and that they stick together. This assumption has turned out to be glaringly wrong, as Asian American mothers have found themselves at loggerheads around a range of issues. But because of the still strong tendency to lump them together, the positions of a few Asian American mothers have come to define them as a group.

Current conflicts among mothers are both something new and someplace we have been before, many times over. Mother/othering, however, is not simply about how mothers dislike or antagonize other each other, but about how the social conditions in which they live often turn them against each other, at great costs. These costs range from increased stress, conflicted relationships, and heightened competition for jobs and economic resources to deeper and more intense political polarization. Mothers in general must find the right balance of being involved with their children, neither too involved nor not involved enough. But for Asian American mothers, they must negotiate not merely the right amount of involvement for themselves as individuals but how their involvement will be perceived based on the prevailing perceptions of them as a group that is widely viewed as other.

Mother/othering—its mechanisms and consequences—are systemic and not of mothers' own making. But mothers are accountable for choices they make to fuel othering, and they are capable of making different choices. Notions of belonging and non-belonging are defined not only by national borders but by the invisible lines drawn among neighbors, co-workers, friends, and families—and mothers can enforce these lines or redraw them. This requires both a reimagining of motherhood and concerted maternal labor to enact new visions. The work of creating a new kind of motherland will require changes in every social institution and in all human relationships, not to mention hearts and minds.

Asian American Mothers Imagining Motherwise

Asian American mothers can be a powerful force in resisting and reshaping processes of mother/othering, but this is a possibility, not a given. While I have purposely focused on the social rather than the psychological dimensions of mothering and othering, I do not want to underplay the emotional fortitude and internal resources that imagining motherwise requires. In addition, a broad network of external support is needed—from therapists, doctors, teachers, school counselors, friends, and family—to understand and address the tremendous pressures that the standards of tiger mothering impose and their wide-ranging costs to all mothers and to society as a whole. In fields ranging from mental health to education, to human resources, to government, the framework of mother/othering and its associated concepts can hopefully move institutions and the people who staff them to focus less on meeting rubrics and deliverables and more on listening to and building relationships with actual mothers, families, and communities.

This is not work that mothers—Asian American or otherwise—can do alone. But they can move the needle. In fact, they are part of a long motherline that has done precisely this, from learning about their histories, to rewriting narratives that have misrepresented them, to protesting against multiple forms of reproductive exclusion. Asian American mothers have chosen to pass on parts of their cultures that they value, while refusing to pass on other parts that have devalued them. They have marched in the streets and kept their children and elders safe at home. Asian American mothers are a work in progress; they are not one thing, but in combination, they can be a force to be reckoned with.

Mothers can be powerful change agents, but the changes for which they advocate are as varied as mothers themselves. Mothers—including Asian American mothers—do not merely reflect the heightened state of current political divisions but have actively contributed to shaping them, for better and for worse. The stakes of motherhood and of reimagining motherhood are high; so are the potential rewards. The consequences of which mothers and which versions of motherhood come out on top are far-reaching, influencing which mothers and children are included or excluded, thrive or flounder, are regarded as fully human or as *other*.

Epilogue: In (M)otherwords

Motherhood does not always bring out the best in us. In fact, it increasingly seems to bring out the worst. The current competition among mothers to secure the best schools, houses, neighborhoods, jobs, and other prizes for their own children can drive us to ignore the basic needs of other children and other mothers, whether across the street or across the world. But mothers are not destined to be each other's worst enemies, although they are increasingly pitted against each other as such by a wide range of social institutions from the school to the state. In other words, the categories of "mother" and "other" are felt very personally but are not just personal, they are structural.

In exploring these concerns, I started off with grand ambitions for this book: to set the record straight on Asian American motherhood, give voice to a new generation of Asian American mothers, take back the narrative about us, and rewrite our own stories. I end up writing from a much humbler place, with the simple hope that this book will offer some clarity, insight, or sense of connection, especially but not solely to those who self-identify as Asian American mothers.

In the spring of 2020, I was on a research leave and in the middle of a deep dive into the histories, politics, and experiences of Asian

American mothers, when the world went into lockdown. A global pandemic. A domestic insurrection. The development of vaccines, the rise of anti-vaccine movements. A racial reckoning, and yet another refusal to reckon with race. One crisis, another, and yet another. Days stood at a standstill, the before-times receding, the future on hold. As with many Asian Americans, these crises and the accompanying rise in anti-Asian violence hit close to home, most painfully, in the 2021 mass shooting in Atlanta massage spas in which a White man with a supposed "sex addiction" killed eight people, six of them Asian women. As with many Asian American scholars, I put my research on hold as I tried to respond publicly and privately to these multiple crises.[1]

In the wake of these tragedies, the earlier iteration of the book—which focused on negotiations of work and family by Asian American mothers in the shadow of the tiger mother trope—seemed glaringly out of touch with the urgency of the current moment. The news headlines had shifted from concerns about Asian American tiger mothers pushing their children too hard to Asian American women being pushed onto sidewalks or in front of subway trains with no one stepping forward to help. Discussions about Asian Americans and schooling refocused from perfect SAT scores to the perfect storm of the COVID-19 pandemic, the scapegoating of Asian Americans, and the coinciding rise in anti-Asian violence. Mental health concerns for Asian Americans were no longer about letting down parents with an "Asian F" (i.e., an A-) but about not being able to let down their guard against racist remarks uttered by the president or by close friends and colleagues.

In the midst of all this, Asian Americans rallied in support of Black Lives Matter but also against affirmative action. Some marched to protest the overturning of *Roe v. Wade*, others celebrated its demise. The fissures and cracks within Asian American communities emerged starkly, just as they were being cast in a singular mold, this time not as tiger mothers but as carriers of the "China virus" and the "kung flu." On the one hand, the COVID-19 pandemic and its ongoing impacts on Asian American communities have been unprecedented. On the other hand, the current moment has been centuries in the making.

In this newly unfolding but historically contiguous context, I revisited many of the book's earlier concerns, as questions about how Asian American mothers negotiate their careers and family responsibilities while resisting the tiger mother stereotype now seemed parochial, even tone-deaf. But as I went back through the interview data, I was struck by how conversations that began in the before-times foreshadowed the after-times. I recognized how the interviews I had conducted before, during, and after the pandemic raised consistent themes that challenged the false narrative that the rise in anti-Asian hate was merely a product of COVID-19 and hence, would wane once the virus was contained. Instead, the stories that I had collected from Asian American mothers in the years leading up to the pandemic seemed prescient. Some of them, articulating their worst fears, predicted what was to come. Others asserted more optimistic visions, only to have that optimism shattered.

So, it is a both/and situation in which Asian Americans continually find ourselves, something unprecedented and someplace we have been many times before: simultaneously model and peril, both idealized and othered. This contradictory state is captured in the varying reactions I have received when I told people the topic of this book. When I started this research over a decade ago and would try to explain its main premise—that Asian American mothers are regarded as others and that the othering of mothers is central to the othering of Asian Americans as a racial group—I would often get quizzical looks, mostly from non-Asians but also from some Asian Americans. *But aren't Asian American mothers widely admired? Aren't their kids amazingly successful? Isn't it a compliment to be called a tiger mother? How does this constitute othering?*

In the before-times, I was often pressed to justify the book's central premise and would attempt to condense its main arguments to prove that mother/othering is indeed a thing—and that it often revolves around Asian American mothers. That beginning with the Page Act of 1875, virtually all single Asian women seeking to immigrate to the United States were marked as prostitutes and became the first group, along with Asian "coolie" laborers, to be legally excluded. That the desire to control Asian women's sexuality and reproduction further fueled the passage of the Chinese Exclusion Act of 1882, and over half a century of Asian exclusion. *But isn't that old history? Aren't Asian Americans now fully accepted, and in fact, doing better than Whites?* To which I would respond by shifting attention to more contemporary examples, some of which I have written about here. How from 2011 to 2013, two Asian American women, Bei Bei Shuai and Purvi Patel, became the first to be charged under feticide laws that were meant to protect pregnant women from violent crimes but were used instead to indict the mothers themselves. How, despite these complex histories and concerns, contemporary Asian American mothers have been caricatured as a monolithic group of cutthroat, Ivy-League-obsessed tiger mothers.

But the assertion that Asian American mothers are othered no longer seems to cause cognitive dissonance, not because people's knowledge of history has changed but because the world we live in has. Now, when I talk about Asian American mothers as others, for better and worse, it does not elicit disagreement so much as discomfort. Something seems to have shifted, at least momentarily. There is a growing recognition that Asian Americans are not the model minority, not honorary Whites nor White adjacent, not proof of the American dream—or at least, not *all* Asian Americans. Yet, while many may feel unaccepted and even unsafe, Asian Americans as a racial group have not been subject to the same levels of surveillance as Black, Latinx, Native, and Indigenous peoples or to the same hypervigilance of having to protect our children from being taken from us, although individuals and segments of the Asian American population have and continue to experience multiple forms of violence.

There are still many concerns that this book has not addressed. The more I have tried to nail down the figure of the Asian American mother, the more she morphs into new figurations. The more I try to recuperate her from historical erasure, the more I realize how much still needs to be recuperated. The more I try to tell more diverse stories about Asian American motherhood, the more stories demand to be told. Many emerging scholars, writers, and artists are writing these new stories; I have learned from many of them, and I look forward to learning from many more to come.

My hope is that this book will find its way into the hands of those mothers who need it most, those who find themselves pacing the floor at 2 a.m. wondering how they got there and how they can possibly keep up with all that is asked or expected of them. I want this book to speak not only *about* but *to* and *with* mothers, especially but not only those who identify as Asian American mothers, and those who wish to understand and support them. By naming and exploring the contours of mother/othering, my hope is that mothers will be less susceptible to it, whether as its targets or its agents. It is a tall order and not one that any individual, or mother, can fill alone. But together, we might get somewhere better. My dream is that by collectively imagining motherwise, we can not only remake motherhood but repair the world.

Acknowledgments

First and foremost, this book is indebted to and dedicated to the Asian American mothers who shared their stories and lives with me toward the shared goal of contributing greater knowledge and support for Asian American mothers and families.

I could not have written this book without the support of many individuals and institutions. I am deeply indebted to all of them, but any mistakes or misinterpretations are my own. I apologize in advance for omissions as I know I cannot mention everyone by name that I want to thank, but just want them to know that all the forms of support—from café writing dates, to airport pickups, to dog sitting, to book club potlucks, to kimchi making, to late-night phone calls, to offering their homes for writing retreats, to just being amazing and inspiring people—have been invaluable.

I have had the opportunity to develop arguments for this book through several other publications. I have reprinted sections of Miliann Kang, "Reproducing Asian American Studies: Rethinking Asian Exclusion as Reproductive Exclusion," *Amerasia Journal*, 46(2): 136–146, copyright © 2020 The Regents of the University of California, with permission of Informa UK Limited, trading as Taylor & Francis Group, www.tandfonline.com on behalf of The Regents of the

University of California. I am grateful to the guest editors, Genevieve Clutario and Rana Jaleel for including me in the special issue on "Rethinking Gendered Citizenship," and to Victor Bascara, Arnold Pan, Karen Umemoto and other members of the Amerasia board and community that I have been fortunate to be part of. Several other previous publications are not directly reprinted but parts have been revised and adapted according to fair use and are cited in the notes and references, and I am grateful to all those who shepherded these important journals and edited volumes and included me.

I am fortunate to have wonderful colleagues at UMass Amherst in the Women, Gender, Sexuality Studies Department—Kiran Asher, Cameron Awkward-Rich, Laura Briggs, Laura Ciolkowski, Kirsten Leng, Beaudelaine Pierre, Svati Shah, Banu Subramaniam, and Angela Willey, and many others who are part of our larger WGSS community—who have fostered a vibrant sense of intellectual community and have pushed me to be a better scholar, teacher, and colleague. By breaking the mold and showing what interdisciplinary feminist scholarship can look like, they have created space for me to explore my own writing voice and form. I especially want to thank Banu Subramaniam, who as chair, sustained my belief in this book and encouraged me to teach courses that would keep me engaged and chipping away at it. I am also grateful to my current chair, Svati Shah, and the College of Humanities and Fine Arts Dean Lupe Davidson for various forms of support, especially for the ongoing Asian American Feminisms speaker series (also supported by the Mellon Foundation) and to all the speakers, students and attendees of the series who have fostered many conversations that have fed this book. Past Dean Julie Hayes and Associate Dean Joye Bowman also provided crucial support including a mid-career research leave and constant encouragement.

Additional funding included an American Association of University Women fellowship, a UMass Amherst Healey faculty research grant, and a UMass Boston Institute for Asian American Studies fellowship. I was also part of a year-long Smith College Kahn Research Institute Fellowship (organized by Ginetta Candelario and Daphne Lamothe) that brought me into a community of scholars around the theme of "mothers and others." I received Fulbright and Korea Society grants which funded separate but related research project related to gender, work and family issues in South Korea (through the sponsorship and collegiality of Eun Mee Kim at Ewha University and Hye Jun Park at Seoul National University) and provided time and a transnational context and network of scholars to frame this research.

In addition, many colleagues in other departments and programs, especially Sociology, the UMass Asian & Asian American Studies Certificate, and the Five College Asian Pacific American Studies Certificate program, have provided incisive feedback. I have had the opportunity to present and receive valuable feedback through conference presentations at the annual meetings of the American Sociological Association, Association for Asian American Studies, and National Women's Studies Association. I also benefitted greatly from giving invited talks on various parts of this book and want to thank all those who helped to host me, including: Jerry Jacobs, Annette Lareau and Guobin Yang (University of Pennsylvania); Pawan Dhingra (Tufts University); Cassaundra Rodriguez (University of Nevada, Las Vegas); Kate Mason (Wheaton College); Kyung-Sook Boo and Jae H. Lee (Sogang University); Pei-Chia Lan (National Taiwan University); and Jae Won Lee and Alvin Wong (Yonsei University).

I cannot seem to write alone, so participation in several formal and informal writing and feedback groups have sustained me. These include: the Third Spaces writing group (sponsored by the UMass Office of Equity and Inclusion); the Five College APA Studies Works-in-Progress group (organized by Iyko Day, Asha Nadkarni, Nozomi Saito and others); Scholars Writing with Attitude Group (or SWWAG, organized by Kristen Luschen); the ethnography writing group (organized by Amy Schalet); the Office for Faculty Development

Scholars program (organized by Rebecca Dingo); the Carework Working Group (organized by Joya Misra); and last but probably most important, the weekly magic writing circle (led by Arlene Avakian).

I owe a particular debt to many people who have generously given detailed feedback, critical insights and moral and material support over many years, including: Riché J. Daniel Barnes, Karen Cardozo, Kim Chang, Floyd Cheung, Michael Chwe, Jacklyn Cleofas, Pawan Dhingra, Dawn M. Dow, Nancy Folbre, Charu Gupta, Nadia Kim, Kim Kono, Robert Ku, James Kyung-Jin Lee, Namhee Lee, Karen Leong, Pamila Lew, Joya Misra, Aida Villanueva Montalvo, Kelly Moore, Asha Nadkarni, erin Khuê Ninh, Franklin Odo, Lisa Sun-Hee Park, Megan Saltzman, Ken Chih-Yan Sun, Susan Walzer, Judy Tzu-Chun Wu, Caroline Yang, and many others.

In addition, I had two writing coaches/developmental editors who did yeoman's work to help me get this book out the door. Cathy Luna provided regular accountability, structure, and support to keep writing through times when everything seemed to conspire against writing (from the pandemic to parental care crises). Rhys Williams read the entire manuscript and offered conceptual clarity, line-by-line copy editing and good humor.

I have been very fortunate to work with talented, meticulous, and committed graduate and undergraduate research assistants, especially Angela Kim, Julia Kim, Nahee Kwak, Eunbi Lee, Sonny Nordmarken, Juyeon Park, Monroe Randall, Mahala Stewart, Esther Suh, Gillian Teng, Porntip Twishime, and Sandy Yu. They helped conduct, transcribe, and code interviews, dove into archival and scholarly research, asked great questions, and shared their own work and critical insights.

This is the second book that I have published with the University of California Press, and like my first "baby," they treated my second book "child" with great care and patience. I am especially grateful to my editor, Naomi Schneider, for her vision for this book, to the press board and reviewers for helping to improve it, to Barbara Armentrout for copy editing, and to Aline Dolinh, Emily Park, and the production team for turning it into a reality.

In the course of writing this book, I experienced several major health challenges and I am grateful to my university for supporting a disability accommodation without which I could not have been able to continue to write and teach. I am especially indebted to our faculty union, the Massachusetts Society of Professors, and the leadership of Eve Weinbaum, Lori Reardon, Jacquie Kurland, Max Page, Sigrid Schmalzer, Ferd Wulkan, and many others who have advocated for better conditions for faculty to do our work. I am also grateful to all those who have engaged in the work of diversity, equity, and inclusion to foster a sense of belonging on our campus and beyond, including Benita Barnes, Nikia Burdick, Mari Castañeda, Kathy Forde, Nefertiti Walker, Wilmore Webley, Linda Ziegenbein, and many others. And I want to thank The Sphere, a beautiful co-working space for women and nonbinary folks that provides not only a room of one's own but a room filled with shared creative energy.

Most of all, this book would not have been possible without the unfailing support of my family. C. N. Le, my husband and colleague extraordinaire, has ridden every wave of this book with me. He has read and discussed every page, kept me from getting lost on subways and side streets on the way to interviews, picked up more than his share of caregiving and domestic work, formatted citations, and cheered me on through the long years that this book took to complete. My mother, Liann Soon Lavrence, has taught me what it means to love and be loved by our mothers. My daughter, Sangha, has kept me grounded and served as the constant living reminder of why motherhood is so important to me. Zendo, our dearly departed lap dog, sat next to me and provided body warmth for hours on end, and Mandu and Bingsu, three-month-old puppies from Texas, arrived just in time to provide the constant dopamine hits to get this book done and out into the world.

Notes

Prologue

1. As with all interview participants, "Eunhee" is a pseudonym, and personal details have been removed or obscured to protect confidentiality.

2. Chua 2011a.

3. Chuh 2003, 9.

Introduction

1. See Napierski-Prancl 2019; Peskowitz 2005; Steiner 2006.

2. Tatjana Takševa (2019) asserts that de Beauvoir herself and much of feminist discourse, while challenging the notion of "woman" as a biological given, still often adhere to "universalist and essentialist accounts of motherhood and versions of the maternal" (29).

3. Chua 2011a.

4. Cited in Kang 2015a.

5. Martha Fineman (1995) has argued that replacing *mothering* with *parenting* in family law in the name of gender neutrality has "neutered" and harmed the most vulnerable mothers and reinforced patriarchal norms.

6. Key texts that have contributed to rethinking motherhood through frameworks such as reproductive labor, matricentric feminism, maternal theory, and the growing field of motherhood studies include Nakano Glenn 1993; Rich 1995; Gumbs, Martens, and Williams 2016; Kawash 2011; Kinser 2008; O'Reilly 2021, 2023.

7. Paris 2020.

8. For background on the politicization of motherhood, see Bracewell and Daily 2024; Briggs 2017; O'Reilly 2023.

9. For example, see Gambol 2023; Min and Chung 2016; Raza and Sakamoto 2024; Sakamoto and Hsu 2020.

10. Some well-known texts focusing on Asian American mother-daughter relations include Kingston 1989; Ng 2014; Tan 1990. Important scholarly critiques of Asian American mother-daughter themes include Ho 1999; Ninh 2011b. Recent scholarship, memoirs, and essays offering more nuanced explorations of Asian American mother-daughter relations across different generations include Cheng 2024; Cho 2021; Hong 2020; Khúc 2024.

11. Scholars who have complicated and expanded the frameworks for studying Asian American mothers, families, and reproduction to address structural and historical conditions and variation across generation, region, national origin, class, and other factors include: Chung 2016; Fujiwara 2008; Lan 2018; Nguyen 2024; Sugino 2024.

12. Collins 1999. Other scholars have also used "mother" and "other "in connection to each other in various ways; see Anatol 2002; Gumbs 2016; Letherby 1999; Lydall 1998; Maddox 2024; Rock 2007.

13. Said 1979.

14. Kang 2020b; Kang 2023. In these previously published texts, I have discussed how "reproductive exclusion" aims to integrate "reproduction," one of the core concepts in studies of gender and sexuality, with "exclusion," one of the foundational concerns in the field of Asian American studies.

15. Sister Song 2026.

16. See Fried and Ross 2025; Ross and Solinger 2017; Silliman et al. 2016.

17. See O'Reilly 2021 and 2023.

18. Okihiro 1994, 141.

19. For discussion of the various ways of writing and categorizing *Asian American*, see Fujiwara and Roshanravan 2018; Hall 2015; Lee 2015; Palumbo-Liu 1999.

20. Davis and Craven 2011; Visweswaran 1997.

21. I follow the practice of using *second generation* to include members of the 1.5 generation who came to the United States as children (Rumbaut 2008; Danico 2004).

22. Kang 2002.

23. Chuh 2003.

24. Lee and Ramakrishnan 2021; Nguyen 2018; Yee 2023.

25. Geertz 1973, 3.

26. Hartman 2020.

27. Burawoy et al. 1991, 281. I have also discussed my use of extended case method in Kang 2015b.

28. Small 2009, 24.

29. Small 2009, 22.

30. Du Bois 1903.

31. Spillers 1987.

32. Spillers 1987.

33. Dhingra 2020.

34. Deomampo 2016; Rudrappa 2015; Shimizu 2007.

35. Chen 2002; Dill 1994; Lee and Yung 2010.

36. Cheng 2014; Hing 2004; Hsu 2017; Park 2004; Wang 1998; Wu 2014.

37. Glenn 1992.

38. Choy 2003; Espiritu 2003; Guevarra 2009; Parreñas 2015; Rodriguez 2010.

39. Chuh 2003.

Chapter One

1. Natalie herself used "other" as a term; other interviews implied this meaning.

2. Julia Lee 2016, 63.

3. Chua 2011b.

4. Couric 2011.

5. Senior 2015, 93.

6. Eagan 2018.

7. This interview with Cara was previously quoted in Kang 2020a.

8. Koshy 2013; Nguyen 2002; Ninh 2011a; Ninh 2011b.

9. For example, see Cheah, Leung, and Zhou 2013; Choi et al. 2013; Guo 2013; Hoshino 2018; Kim et al. 2013; Lui and Rollock 2013; Nguyen, Chang, and Loh 2014; Suissa 2013.

10. Rhee 2013.

11. See Eagan 2018; Kang 2015, 2020a; Khuê Ninh 2011a; Loh 2011; Manjikian 2011; Poon 2011.

12. Briggs 2017.

Chapter Two

1. Cheng 2019, ix.

2. Mayer 2013; Tchen and Yeats 2014.

3. Bow 2022; Curington, Lin, and Lundquist 2021; Lundquist and Lin 2015; Lundquist, Lin, and Curington 2024; Ly 2025; Williams 2024; Zheng 2016.

4. Lye 2004, 4.

5. Ngai 2014.

6. Collins 1991, 76–106; Roberts 1997.

7. Tropes of yellow mothers are rarely named as such but can be traced in various archives of testimonies by Chinese immigrants and government officials during the exclusion era. Various scholars and organization have conducted meticulous work to preserve and examine these records, especially those in the National Archives and Records Administration (NARA) (National Archives 2023).

8. A small sample includes Lee 2015; Wu 2013; Wu and Mink 2022; Yuh 2002; Yung 1995, 1999. These scholars are among many Asian American feminist historians who are cited throughout this book in reference to specific cases and historical periods. For further resources, see Fujiwara and Roshanravan 2018; Hune and Nomura 2020.

9. Robinson 2015, 68.

10. Briggs 2017; Ross and Solinger 2017; Waggoner 2017.

11. Cabaniss and Cameron 2017; Jin 2022; Catherine Lee 2010; Mabute-Louie 2025; Ngai 2007.

12. Choy 2022; Foner and Rosenberg 1993; Tchen and Yeats 2014.

13. Abrams 2005a, 641.

14. Abrams 2005a.

15. Interviewed and cited in Kang and Le 2022.

16. Chan 1991.

17. Cott 2002; D'Emilio and Freedman 2012; Freedman 1982.

18. *Chy Lung v. Freeman*, 92 U.S. 275 (1876), record at 6–7 (testimony of Rudolph Norwin Piotrowski), cited in Abrams 2005a.

19. Peffer 1999, 47.

20. Peffer 1999. In addition, through comparisons of Chinese women's immigration to other countries, Peffer shows the widespread impact of the Page Act as Chinese women's immigration to the United States virtually ground to a halt, but their immigration continued to other destinations that did not impose restrictions, such as Singapore, Malacca, and Hawaii.

21. Chan 1991; Peffer 1999.

22. Pixley provided this testimony for the 1876 Joint Committee report, arguing that the suspect nature of even married Chinese women served as grounds for exclusion.

23. Smearman 2009, 382.

24. Cott 2002, 139.

25. Osburg 2008; Shen 2005; Tam 1996, 2005.

26. Merriam-Webster 2023.

27. Cited in Robert Lee 1999, 16, with permission of the Beinecke Library, Yale University.

28. Jung 2008, 4–5.

29. Phelan 1901, 674.

30. Higginbotham Jr. and Kopytoff 2003, 2003; Moran 2001; Sohoni 2007.

31. Peggy Pascoe 1996.

32. Haney López 1996; Koshy 2005; Marchetti 1993; Sohoni 2007.

33. Watson 2016.

34. *Naim v. Naim* 197 Va. 80 (1955), quoted in Sohoni 2007, 611–12.

35. Hinnershitz 2020.

36. Cited in Okihiro 1994, 169.

37. Memorandum from Commanding General John L. DeWitt to Secretary of War Henry L. Stimson on "'Evacuation of Japanese and Other Subversive Persons From the Pacific Coast,'" February 1942, cited in Hersey 1988; full document at http://www.sfmuseum.org/war/dewitt4.html.

38. Quoted in Reeves 2016, 48.

39. Burton et al. 2000.

40. Reported in the *New Leader*, a labor weekly, cited in Ordover 2003, 160.

41. Ordover 2003, 161, citing Leong et al. 1981.

42. Lyon 2020.

43. "Statement from Mothers of Topaz, W.R.A. Center," March 11, 1944, cited in Wallace 2021.

44. "Mothers' Petition Answered," *Topaz Times*, April 12, 1944; and "Three Answers to Mothers' Petition Here," *Topaz Times*, April 18, 1944, cited in Lyon 2020.

45. Dillon Myer to Adachi, March 27, 1944, reprinted in "Mothers' Petition Answered," *Topaz Times*, April 12, 1944, cited in Lyon 2020.

46. See Takei 2019.

47. Takei 2012.

48. Donald Collins 1985.

49. Ngai 2014, 311, citing letter from Wayne Collins to K.Y., January 5, 1955, *Collins Papers* 3/70.

50. *Los Angeles Times* 2016 (letter written by Steve Hawes).

51. Lipschutz, Rosenblatt, and Wang 2019, time stamp 43:26–44:04.

52. Pollitt 2012.

53. In Lipschutz, Rosenblatt, and Wang 2019, Indiana State Senator Murphy questioned whether the public prosecutor, Terry Curry, was politically motivated in using the Shuai case to seek re-election as a Democrat in a strongly Republican and anti-abortion state.

54. Jorawar 2015.

55. Brown 2014; Turner 2013.

56. Pilkington 2012.

57. Quoted in Lipschutz, Rosenblatt, and Wang 2019.

58. Gastelum 2015.

59. Chowdhury 2015.

60. "National Asian Pacific American Women's Forum Denounces Attack on Pregnant Women's Rights" 2016.

61. DasGupta 2015.

62. Citro et al. 2014.

63. Sohoni 2007, 608.

64. Saito 1997.

65. Ngai 2014, 200.

66. See Aptheker 1983; Battisti 2012; Dass 2010; Iacovetta 2006; Roberts 2005; Rogin 1984; Yellowhorn and Lowinger 2019.

67. Kandaswamy 2018, 232.

68. Although the stated intent of feticide laws was to recognize a fetus in utero as a legal victim in crimes of violence, critics argue that in practice, it has been used to undermine abortion rights and prosecute mothers, especially mothers of color, for violating the rights of "fetal personhood." The paradigmatic case is that of Laci Peterson, a White woman who was murdered by her husband, Scott, while eight months pregnant, spurring the passage of the Unborn Victims of Violence Act in 2004 (often referred to as Laci and Conner's law). See Bumiller 2008; Flavin 2010.

69. Cohen 2001; Kim 2021; Lubiano 1992.

70. Gumbs 2016; Roberts 1997.

Chapter Three

1. Abu-Lughod 1991, 143.

2. Swidler 1986, 273.

3. Abu-Lughod 1991, 139.

4. Hays 1998.

5. Le 2007; Sharon Lee and Boyd 2008; Min and Kim 2009; Mishra 2018; Okamoto 2007; Qian and Qian 2020.

6. Alba 1990; Bogardus 1967; Gordon 1964; Waters 1990.

7. Chang 2015; Lorenzo-Blanco, Bares, and Delva 2013; Washington 2019.

8. Subramaniam 2019, xii.

9. See Fussell 2014; Luthra, Soehl, and Waldinger 2018; Massey and Sanchez 2012; Portes and Rumbaut 2006; and Rumbaut 2008 for discussions about factors that affect the assimilation and integration outcomes of immigrants that include government policy, demographic composition of resettlement neighborhood, and the state of the national economy at time of arrival.

10. See Chen and Park 2019; Jeung, Chen, and Park 2012; Park and Ecklund 2007. Attesting to diverse religious practices among Asian Americans, Iwamura et al. (2014) point out that Asian American Christians (of all generations) tend to be more "devout" than the general U.S. Christian population and 27 percent of Asian American Buddhists said that religion is very important in their lives.

11. It is difficult to find definitive statistics on the prevalence and process of keeping ethnic last names after marriage among Asian Americans, or choosing ethnic first names for children, but the significance of this issue emerged in this study's interview data along with other public writing. For instance, see Jami Nakamura Lin's discussion of naming her daughter to reflect her mixed-race and pan-Asian identity (Lin 2020).

12. Bertrand and Mullainathan 2004; Derous and Ryan 2019; Quillian, Lee, and Oliver 2020.

13. Gee and Wong 2016; Kim and Lewis 1994.

14. Banerjee, Reitz, and Oreopoulos 2018; Oreopoulos 2011; Thanasombat and Trasviña 2005; Zhao and Biernat 2017.

15. Jennifer Lee 2016.

16. Chang 2015.

17. Scholarship on race, disability, and mothering is giving fuller attention to Asian American mothers and the specific challenges and concerns they face in parenting special-needs children (see Chang 2017; He 2017; Jegatheesan 2009; Wong and Tsang 2004). This scholarship builds on research showing how Black mothers have been pathologized as unfit, based on racist constructions of physical and mental inferiorities (Brown Barkley, King, and Ransby 2014; Cheatham 2015; Childs, Laudone, and Tavernier 2009; Collins 1991, 1999; Roberts 1997).

18. Hsiao et al. 2006.

19. Ma 1999, 422.

20. Briggs 2020; Jacobs 2011; Lopez 2019; Wallace and Zepeda-Millán 2020; Williams 2016.

21. The "culture of poverty" theory and ideology was first coined by anthropologist Oscar Lewis in his research about low-income families in Mexico (1959), but it gained wide notoriety through New York Senator Daniel P. Moynihan's report about Black Americans that attributed the poverty of Black families in urban areas to a cultural "tangle of pathology." (Moynihan and Office of Policy Planning and Research, Department of Labor 1965). The report sought to make a moral case for increased federal intervention to break this cycle of poverty (and influenced President Johnson's launching of the "war on poverty"), but critics charged that it ultimately blamed Black people themselves for their low socioeconomic status rather than addressing social inequalities (Bobo, Kluegal, and Smith 1997; Bonilla-Silva 2003; Fischer et al. 1996; Massey and Denton 1993; Ryan 1971).

22. Barnes 2015; Collins 1998; Dow 2019; Hill and Sprague 1999; Jones 1982; Williams 2016.

23. *Enculturation* is most often understood as a process that shapes "the maintenance of, adherence to, and preference for the values and practices of one's native culture" (Berry 2002, 4). It has most often been studied at the individual-level and is more used by psychologists. In contrast, "acculturation" is the term more often used by sociologists to refer to social patterns in which groups of people adapt to a different culture or society, which included acquiring values, customs, and behaviors of the host society (Gans 2007; Hirschman 2013; Hou, Schellenberg, and Berry 2018; Lee and Kye 2016; Nguyen 2011; Rumbaut 2008; Waters et al. 2010).

Chapter Four

1. In developing the concept of the "hidden curriculum," Giroux and Penna (1979) argued that two different kinds of curriculum exist in schools: "the official curriculum, namely the explicit cognitive and affective goals of formal instruction, and the 'hidden curriculum,' namely the unstated norms, values, and beliefs that are transmitted to students through the underlying structure of meaning in both the formal content as well as the social relations of school and classroom life" (23). Philip Jackson ([1968] 1990) is often credited with first coining the term *hidden curriculum* in his book *Life in Classrooms*.

2. Vallence (1983, 4) further contributed to understandings of the hidden curriculum as "the inculcation of values, political socialization, training obedience

and docility, the perpetuation of traditional class structure—functions that may be characterized generally as social control."

3. Abroampa 2020; Gunio 2021.

4. Bowles and Gintis (1976) developed a Marxist approach to understanding the hidden curriculum as institutional mechanisms that socialize students into workers and sort them into different rungs in the capitalist system.

5. Paul Willis (1981), in *Learning to Labor: How Working Class Kids Get Working Class Jobs*, further suggested that the poor performance and behavior of working-class "lads" was encouraged by schools, or at least fostered in school environments, in ways that reproduced class inequalities by channeling working-class students into working-class jobs.

6. Ferguson 2001; Morris, Conteh, and Harris-Perry 2018.

7. Carter 2007, 47.

8. Barnes 2015; Dow 2019.

9. Hartlep and Scott 2016; Lee and Weis 2005; Pang 2006.

10. Dhingra 2020.

11. Lee and Zhou 2015.

12. Bettie 2003.

13. Foucault 1979.

14. Epstein 1995, 57.

15. Thorne 1993, 157.

16. Duncan and Magnuson 2005; Gadsden, Ford, and Breiner 2016; Gissmer and Eiseman 2008.

17. Cucchiara, Cassar, and Clark 2019, 326.

18. School policies that punish parents for their kids' absenteeism or truancy often have long-term unintended consequences and often disproportionately affect low-income families and families of color (Goldstein 2015; Mason and Finnegan 2019; Mireles-Rios, Rios, and Reyes 2020; Mowen 2017; Peters 2012; Varnham 2014).

19. Molz 2017.

20. Arnado 2021; Bolton 2023; Chu 2022; Clutario 2017; McKenna 2017; Ocampo 2016.

21. Scholars, educators, and journalists have discussed efforts to broaden how cultural holidays, including Christmas, are celebrated in schools to make them more inclusive (see Chen 2020; Gelb 2013; Minero 2020; Myers and Myers 2001; Purinton and Gunther 2011), along with the conservative backlash against such efforts (Bowler 2016; Schweitzer 2015).

22. In addition to addressing how schools socialize children to become consumers, scholarship on the commercialization of education has shown the encroachment of corporate and capitalist elements into schools through product sponsorships, for-profit schools, and taxpayer-financed vouchers for private schools (Gidney 2019; Molnar 1996; Robelen 1998; Schrum 2002).

23. Cucchiara, Cassar, and Clark 2019, 326. Parental education programs often are premised on beliefs that early interventions are needed to educate low-income mothers to improve their children's learning outcomes (Duncan and Magnuson 2005; Gadsden, Ford, and Breiner 2016; Gissmer and Eiseman 2008; Rothstein 2004).

24. Delgado-Gaitan 2001; Dika and Singh 2002; Horvat, Weininger, and Lareau 2003; Lareau 2000; McNeal 1999.

25. Pascoe (2007) described how masculinity is used to enforce heteronormativity and discipline those who transgress its norms. Moreover, scholars have also written about how heterosexual norms are implicitly and explicitly enforced within school environments (Duckworth and Trautner 2019; Renold 2005; Szirom 2018; Thorne 1993). In addition, many studies discuss sexuality education and how such programs encounter resistance from parents, especially mothers (Eisenberg et al. 2008; Geasler, Dannison, and Edlund 1995; Goldman 2008; Walker 2004).

Chapter Five

1. Williams, Phillips, and Hall 2014, 18.

2. Arora and Kumari 2022; Budig, Misra, and Boeckmann 2012; Collins 2019; England et al. 2016; Hochschild 1989; Stone 2007; Williams 2004.

3. Hays 1998.

4. Espinosa et al. 2019. In this 2019 report using census data from 2017, the American Council on Education notes that Asian American women had the highest college degree attainment rate (32.2%) among all racial and gender groups, followed by Asian American men (28.9%), White women (23.9%), White men (23.6%), mixed-race women (21.7%), mixed-race men (19.9%), Native Hawaiian/Pacific Islander men (19.8%), Native Hawaiian/Pacific Islander women (17.4%), Black women (15.4%), Black men (15.2%), American Indian/Alaskan Native women (14.4%), Hispanic women (12.9%), American Indian/Alaskan Native men (12.4%), and Hispanic men (11.4%).

5. Kramer 2020.

6. Catalyst 2003, 2.

7. Bachman 2017; Chin 2016, 2020; Tso 2018.

8. Stone 2007.

9. Cho 1997, 182.

10. Jackson, Thoits, and Taylor 1995.

11. Kanter 1977, 236.

12. Garbes 2022; Hong and Min 1999; Portes and Rumbaut 2001; Pyke and Dang 2003.

13. De Jong and Madamba 2001; Waters 1999; Woo 2002.

14. Chin 2020; Chinn 2002; Kramer 2020; Valverde and Dariotis 2019; Wu 1997.

15. McGirt 2018; Williams, Multhaup, and Korn 2018.

Conclusion

1. This phrase is frequently referred to as an African proverb, but its exact roots are difficult to determine (see Goldberg 2016). It is often associated with Hillary Clinton's book *It Takes a Village* (1996).

2. Gumbs 2016, 21. See also Gumbs, Martens, and Williams 2016.

3. Garbes 2022, 80.

4. Chan 2022; Ko 2018; Ng 2022; Vuong 2019, 2023.

5. Gover, Harper, and Langton 2020; Le, Arora, and Stout 2020; Li and Nicholson 2021; Reny and Barreto 2020.

6. Hanson 2021; Healy 2021.

7. Wong and Solnit 2021.

8. Ruiz, Tian, and Krogstad 2023.

9. Eligon 2018; Jennifer Lee 2021; Museus et al. 2019; Poon et al. 2019; Yi and Todd 2021.

10. As the *New York Times* summarized in 2019, Asian American students were significantly overrepresented in specialized high schools; while they comprise 16 percent of the total student population in New York City, they were 62 percent of students in the eight specialized high schools. Shapiro and Lai 2019.

11. Kosman 2023.

12. Chin and Syed 2018; Shapiro 2019; Veiga 2018.

13. Litam and Chan 2021; Moon 2021; Saavedra and Yoo 2023; Wang and Santos 2023; Xu and Nguyen-Okwu 2022.

14. Lee and Zhou 2015; Okura 2022.

15. Budig, Misra, and Boeckmann 2012; Garbes 2022; Lee, Misra, and Murray-Close 2019

16. Chin 2020.
17. Hays 1998.
18. Collins 1999; Wingfield 2010; Zambrana et al. 2016.

Epilogue

1. Kang 2021; Kang and Le 2022.

References

Abrams, Kerry. 2005a "Polygamy, Prostitution, and the Federalization of Immigration Law." *Columbia Law Review* 105(3): 641–716.

Abroampa, Winston Kwame. 2020. "The Hidden Curriculum and the Development of Latent Skills: The Praxis." *Journal of Curriculum and Teaching* 9(2): 70–77.

Abu-Lughod, Lila. 1991. "Writing Against Culture." In *Recapturing Anthropology: Working in the Present*, edited by R. G. Fox. Santa Fe: School of American Research Press.

Alba, Richard. 1990. *Ethnic Identity: The Transformation of White America*. New Haven: Yale University Press.

Anatol, Giselle Liza. 2002. "Speaking in (M)Other Tongues: The Role of Language in Jamaica Kincaid's The Autobiography of My Mother." *Callaloo* 25(3): 938–53.

Aptheker, Herbert. 1983. *American Negro Slave Revolts*. 5th ed. New York: International Publishers.

Arnado, Janet M. 2021. "Cultural Whitening, Mobility and Differentiation: Lived Experiences of Filipina Wives to White Men." *Journal of Ethnic and Migration Studies* 47(9): 1994–2010.

Arora, Sunaina, and Neeraj Kumari. 2022. "Diverging Women on the Mommy Track to the Career Track." *Journal of International Women's Studies* 23(5): 142–154.

Bachman, Eric. 2017. "Silicon Valley Lack of Asian American Executives." *National Law Review*, October 31. https://www.natlawreview.com/article/bamboo-ceiling-and-lack-asian-american-executives-silicon-valley.

Banerjee, Rupa, Jeffrey G. Reitz, and Phil Oreopoulos. 2018. "Do Large Employers Treat Racial Minorities More Fairly?: An Analysis of Canadian Field Experiment Data." *Canadian Public Policy* 44(1): 1–20.

Barnes, Riché J. Daniel. 2015. *Raising the Race: Black Career Women Redefine Marriage, Motherhood, and Community*. New Brunswick, NJ: Rutgers University Press.

Battisti, Danielle. 2012. "The American Committee on Italian Migration, Anti-Communism, and Immigration Reform." *Journal of American Ethnic History* 31(2): 11–40.

Beauvoir, Simone de. 2011. *The Second Sex*. New York: Vintage.

Berry, John W. 2002. "Conceptual Approaches to Acculturation." In *Acculturation: Advances in Theory, Measurement, and Applied Research*, edited by K.M. Chun, P.B. Organista, and G. Marin. Washington, DC: American Psychological Association.

Bertrand, Marianne, and Sendhil Mullainathan. 2004. "Are Emily and Greg More Employable Than Lakisha and Jamal? A Field Experiment on Labor Market Discrimination." *American Economic Review* 94(4): 991–1013.

Bettie, Julie. 2003. *Women Without Class: Girls, Race, and Identity*. Berkeley: University of California Press.

Bobo, Lawrence D., James R. Kluegal, and Ryan A. Smith. 1997. "Laissez-Faire Racism: The Crystallization of a Kinder, Gentler, Antiblack Ideology." In *Racial Attitudes in the 1990s: Continuity and Change*, edited by S.A. Tuch and J.K. Martin. Westport, CT: Praeger.

Bogardus, Emory. 1967. *A Forty-Year Racial Distance Study*. Los Angeles: University of Southern California.

Bolton, Sony Coráñez. 2023. *Crip Colony: Mestizaje, US Imperialism, and the Queer Politics of Disability in the Philippines*. Durham, NC: Duke University Press Books.

Bonilla-Silva, Eduardo. 2003. *Racism Without Racists: Color-Blind Racism and the Persistence of Racial Inequality in the United States*. Austin: University of Texas Press.

Bow, Leslie. 2022. *Racist Love: Asian Abstraction and the Pleasures of Fantasy*. Durham, NC: Duke University Press Books.

Bowler, Gerry. 2016. *Christmas in the Crosshairs: Two Thousand Years of Denouncing and Defending the World's Most Celebrated Holiday*. New York: Oxford University Press.

Bowles, Samuel, and Herbert Gintis. 1976. *Schooling in Capitalist America: Educational Reform and the Contradictions of Economic Life*. Chicago: Haymarket Books.

Bracewell, Lorna, and Anna Daily. 2024. "'This Is a Work for the Mothers': Strategic Maternalism against the Far Right." *Signs: Journal of Women in Culture and Society* 50(1): 93–118.

Briggs, Laura. 2017. *How All Politics Became Reproductive Politics: From Welfare Reform to Foreclosure to Trump*. Berkeley: University of California Press.

Briggs, Laura. 2020. *Taking Children: A History of American Terror*. Oakland: University of California Press.

Brown Barkley, Elsa, Deborah K. King, and Barbara Ransby. 2014. "African American Women in Defense of Ourselves." In *Ain't Gonna Let Nobody Turn Me Around: Forty Years of Movement Building with Barbara Smith*, edited by A. Jones, V. Eubanks, and B. Smith. Albany: State University of New York Press.

Brown, Geneva. 2014. "Bei Bei Shuai: Pregnancy, Murder, and Mayhem in Indiana." *Journal of Gender, Race and Justice* 17: 221.

Budig, Michelle J., Joya Misra, and Irene Boeckmann. 2012. "The Motherhood Penalty in Cross-National Perspective: The Importance of Work–Family Policies and Cultural Attitudes." *Social Politics: International Studies in Gender, State & Society* 19(2): 163–93.

Bumiller, Kristin. 2008. *In an Abusive State: How Neoliberalism Appropriated the Feminist Movement against Sexual Violence*. Durham, NC: Duke University Press Books.

Burawoy, Michael, Alice Burton, Ann Arnett Ferguson, et al. 1991. *Ethnography Unbound: Power and Resistance in the Modern Metropolis*. Berkeley: University of California Press.

Burton, Jeffrey F., Mary M. Farrell, Florence B. Lord, and Richard W. Lord. 2000. "A Brief History of Japanese American Relocation During World War II" (excerpts from *Confinement and Ethnicity: An Overview of World War II Japanese American Relocation Sites*). National Park Service (unnamed blog). https://www.nps.gov/articles/historyinternment.htm.

Cabaniss, Emily R., and Abigail E. Cameron. 2017. "'Unassimilable and Undesirable': News Elites? Discursive Construction of the American Immigrant during the Ellis Island Years." *Discourse & Society* 28(6): 614–34.

Carter, Prudence L. 2007. *Keepin' It Real: School Success Beyond Black and White*. New York: Oxford University Press.

Catalyst. 2003. *Advancing Asian Women in the Workplace: What Managers Need to Know*. https://www.catalyst.org/wp-content/uploads/2019/01/Advancing_Asian_Women_in_the_Workplace_What_Managers_Need_to_Know.pdf.
Chan, Jessamine. 2022. *The School for Good Mothers: A Novel*. 37 Ink.
Chan, Sucheng. 1991. "The Exclusion of Chinese Women, 1870–1943." In *Entry Denied: Exclusion and the Chinese Community in America, 1882–1943*, edited by S. Chan. Philadelphia: Temple University Press.
Chang, Clio. 2017. "The Forgotten History of America's Radical Asian Activists." *Splinter* (blog), December 6. https://splinternews.com/the-forgotten-history-of-america-s-radical-asian-activi-1821046399.
Chang, Sharon. 2015. *Raising Mixed Race: Multiracial Asian Children in a Post-Racial World*. New York: Routledge.
Cheah, Clarissa S., Christy Y. Leung, and Nan Zhou. 2013. "Understanding 'Tiger Parenting' through the Perceptions of Chinese Immigrant Mothers: Can Chinese and U.S. Parenting Coexist?" *Asian American Journal of Psychology* 4(1): 30–40.
Cheatham, Dionna. 2015. "Unpacking the Social and Economic Disparities Among Disabled Black Mothers." *McNair Scholars Journal* 19(1): 18–25. http://scholarworks.gvsu.edu/mcnair/vol19/iss1/6.
Chee, Alexander. 2019. "Alexander Chee on How to Unlearn Everything." *Vulture* (blog), October 30. https://www.vulture.com/2019/10/author-alexander-chee-on-his-advice-to-writers.html.
Chen, Carolyn, and Jerry Z. Park. 2019. "Pathways of Religious Assimilation: Second-Generation Asian Americans' Religious Retention and Religiosity." *Journal for the Scientific Study of Religion* 58(3): 666–88.
Chen, Grace. 2020. "Public School Holiday Celebrations: Christmas-centric or Multicultural?" *Public School Review* (blog). https://www.publicschoolreview.com/blog/public-school-holiday-celebrations-christmas-centric-or-multicultural.
Chen, Yong. 2002. *Chinese San Francisco, 1850–1943: A Trans-Pacific Community*. Palo Alto: Stanford University Press.
Cheng, Anne Anlin. 2019. *Ornamentalism*. New York: Oxford University Press.
Cheng, Anne Anlin. 2024. *Ordinary Disasters: How I Stopped Being a Model Minority*. New York: Pantheon.
Cheng, Cindy I.-Fen. 2014. *Citizens of Asian America: Democracy and Race during the Cold War*. New York: NYU Press.
Childs, Erica Chito, Stephanie Laudone, and LaToya Tavernier. 2009. "Revisiting Black Sexualities in Families: Problems, Puzzles, and Prospects." In *Black*

Sexualities: Probing Powers, Passions, Practices, and Policies, edited by J. Battle and S. L. Barnes. New Brunswick, NJ: Rutgers University Press.

Chin, Margaret M. 2016. "Asian Americans, Bamboo Ceilings, and Affirmative Action." *Contexts* 15(1): 70–73.

Chin, Margaret M. 2020. *Stuck: Why Asian Americans Don't Reach the Top of the Corporate Ladder*. New York: NYU Press.

Chin, Margaret M., and Ali Syed. 2018. "What's Going On With New York's Elite Public High Schools?" http://www.theatlantic.com/education/archive/2018/06/new-york-high-schools-stuyvesant-brooklyn-bronx/562772/.

Chinn, Pauline W. U. 2002. "Asian and Pacific Islander Women Scientists and Engineers: A Narrative Exploration of Model Minority, Gender, and Racial Stereotypes." *Journal of Research in Science Teaching* 39(4): 302–23.

Cho, Grace M. 2021. *Tastes Like War: A Memoir*. New York: Feminist Press at CUNY.

Cho, Sumi K. 1997. "Converging Stereotypes in Racialized Sexual Harassment: Where the Model Minority Meets Suzie Wong." *Journal of Gender, Race and Justice* 1: 177–211.

Choi, Yoonsun, You Seung Kim, Su Yeong Kim, and Irene J. K. Park. 2013. "Is Asian American Parenting Controlling and Harsh? Empirical Testing of Relationships between Korean American and Western Parenting Measures." *Asian American Journal of Psychology* 4(1): 19–29.

Chowdhury, Jennifer. 2015. "Indiana Sentences Purvi Patel to 20 Years for Feticide." NBC News, March 31. https://www.nbcnews.com/news/asian-america/indiana-has-now-charged-two-asian-american-women-feticide-n332761.

Choy, Catherine Ceniza. 2003. *Empire of Care: Nursing and Migration in Filipino Nursing History*. Durham, NC: Duke University Press.

Choy, Catherine Ceniza. 2022. *Asian American Histories of the United States*. Boston: Beacon Press.

Chu, Richard. 2022. "Including the Excluded: The 'Chinese' in the Philippines and the Study of 'Migration' in Filipinx American Studies." In *Filipinx American Studies: Reckoning, Reclamation, Transformation*, edited by R. Bonus and A. Tiongson Jr. New York: Fordham University Press.

Chua, Amy. 2011a. *Battle Hymn of the Tiger Mother*. New York: Penguin Press.

Chua, Amy. 2011b. "Why Chinese Mothers Are Superior." *Wall Street Journal*, January 8. https://www.wsj.com/articles/SB10001424052748704111504576059713528698754.

Chuh, Kandice. 2003. *Imagine Otherwise: On Asian Americanist Critique*. Durham, NC: Duke University Press Books.

Chung, Angie Y. 2016. *Saving Face: The Emotional Costs of the Asian Immigrant Family Myth*. New Brunswick: Rutgers University Press.

Citro, Brian, Jeff Gilson, Sital Kalantry, Kelsey Stricker, University of Chicago Law School. International Human Rights Clinic, National Asian Pacific American Women's Forum (U.S.), and Advancing New Standards in Reproductive Health (Organization). 2014. "Replacing Myths with Facts: Sex-Selective Abortion Laws in the United States." *Cornell Law Faculty Publications* (1399). https://scholarship.law.cornell.edu/facpub/1399.

Clutario, Genevieve. 2017. "Metroimperial Intimacies: Fantasy, Racial-Sexual Governance, and the Philippines in U.S. Imperialism, 1899–1913." *Journal of American History* 104(1): 220–21.

Cohen, Cathy J. 2001. "Punks, Bulldaggers, and Welfare Queens: The Radical Potential of Queer Politics." *Feminist Studies* (December): 322–31.

Collins, Caitlyn. 2019. *Making Motherhood Work: How Women Manage Careers and Caregiving*. Princeton, NJ: Princeton University Press.

Collins, Donald E. 1985. *Native American Aliens: Disloyalty and the Renunciation of Citizenship by Japanese Americans During World War II*. Westport, CT: Praeger.

Collins, Patricia Hill. 1991. *Black Feminist Thought: Knowledge, Consciousness, and the Politics of Empowerment*. New York: Routledge Press.

Collins, Patricia Hill. 1998. "It's All In the Family: Intersections of Gender, Race, and Nation." *Hypatia* 13(3): 62–82.

Collins, Patricia Hill. 1999. *Fighting Words: Black Women and the Search for Justice*. Minneapolis: University of Minnesota Press.

Cott, Nancy F. 2002. *Public Vows: A History of Marriage and the Nation*. Cambridge: Harvard University Press.

Couric, Katie. 2011. "Did Amy Chua, the Tiger Mother, Have a Point?" Interview with Liz Gumbinner. CBS News, February 7.

Cucchiara, Maia, Erin Cassar, and Monica Clark. 2019. "'I Just Need a Job!' Behavioral Solutions, Structural Problems, and the Hidden Curriculum of Parenting Education." *Sociology of Education* 92(4): 326–45.

Curington, Celeste Vaughan, Ken-Hou Lin, and Jennifer Hickes Lundquist. 2021. *Dating Divide: Race and Desire in the Era of Online Romance*. Oakland: University of California Press.

Danico, May Yu. 2004. "The Formation of Post-Suburban Communities: Koreatown and Little Saigon, Orange County." *International Journal of Sociology and Social Policy* 24: 15–45.

DasGupta, Sayantani. 2015. "Pregnant Women Are Now Targets: The Tragedy of Purvi Patel." *Salon*, April 26. https://www.salon.com/2015/04/26/a_terrifying_floodgate_for_prosecuting_women_why_purvi_patel_is_not_a_terrorist_partner/.
Dass, Sujan, ed. 2010. *Black Rebellion: Eyewitness Accounts of Major Slave Revolts.* Atlanta: Two Horizons Press.
Davis, Dána-Ain, and Christa Craven. 2011. "Revisiting Feminist Ethnography: Methods and Activism at the Intersection of Neoliberal Policy." *Feminist Formations* 23(2): 190–208.
De Jong, Gordon F., and Anna B. Madamba. 2001. "A Double Disadvantage? Minority Group, Immigrant Status, and Underemployment in the United States." *Social Science Quarterly* 82(1): 117–30.
Delgado-Gaitan, Concha. 2001. *The Power of Community: Mobilizing for Family and Schooling*. Lanham, MD: Rowman & Littlefield.
D'Emilio, John, and Estelle B. Freedman. 2012. *Intimate Matters: A History of Sexuality in America*, 3rd ed. Chicago: University of Chicago Press.
Derous, Eva, and Ann Marie Ryan. 2019. "When Your Resume Is (Not) Turning You Down: Modelling Ethnic Bias in Resume Screening." *Human Resource Management Journal* 29(2): 113–30.
Dhingra, Pawan. 2020. *Hyper Education: Why Good Schools, Good Grades, and Good Behavior Are Not Enough.* New York: NYU Press.
Dika, Sandra L., and Kusum Singh. 2002. "Applications of Social Capital in Educational Literature: A Critical Synthesis." *Review of Educational Research* 72(1): 31–60.
Dill, Bonnie Thornton. 1994. "Fictive Kin, Paper Sons, and Compadrazgo: Women of Color and the Struggle for Family Survival." In *Families in the U.S: Kinship and Domestic Politics*, edited by K. V. Hansen and A. I. Garey. Philadelphia: Temple University Press.
Dow, Dawn Marie. 2019. *Mothering While Black: Boundaries and Burdens of Middle-Class Parenthood.* Oakland: University of California Press.
Du Bois, W. E. B. 1903. *The Souls of Black Folk: Essays and Sketches.* Amherst: University of Massachusetts Press.
Duckworth, Kiera D., and Mary Nell Trautner. 2019. "Gender Goals: Defining Masculinity and Navigating Peer Pressure to Engage in Sexual Activity." *Gender & Society* 33(5): 795–817. https://doi.org/10.1177/0891243219863031.
Duncan, Greg J., and Katherine A. Magnuson. 2005. "Can Family Socioeconomic Resources Account for Racial and Ethnic Test Score Gaps?" *The Future of Children* 15(1): 35–54.

Eagan, Margery. 2018. "The Sting of the Tiger Mother." *Boston Globe*, March 5. https://www.bostonglobe.com/opinion/2018/03/05/the-sting-tiger-mother/8EjsAufcL8bSb2rAhsa4GI/story.html.

Eisenberg, Marla E., Debra H. Bernat, Linda H. Bearinger, and Michael D. Resnick. 2008. "Support for Comprehensive Sexuality Education: Perspectives from Parents of School-Age Youth." *Journal of Adolescent Health* 42(4): 352–59.

Eligon, John. 2018. "They Left China to Chase the American Dream. Now They're Fighting Affirmative Action." *New York Times*, August 9.

England, Paula, Jonathan Bearak, Michelle J. Budig, and Melissa J. Hodges. 2016. "Do Highly Paid, Highly Skilled Women Experience the Largest Motherhood Penalty?" *American Sociological Review* 81(6):1161–89.

Epstein, Debbie. 1995. "In Our (New) Right Minds: The Hidden Curriculum and the Academy." In *Feminist Academics: Creative Agents for Change*, edited by L. Morley and V. Walsh. London ; Bristol, PA: Routledge.

Espinosa, Lorelle L., Jonathan M. Turk, Morgan Taylor, and Hollie M. Chessman. 2019. *Race and Ethnicity in Higher Education: A Status Report*. Washington DC: American Council on Education.

Espiritu, Yen. 2003. *Home Bound: Filipino American Lives Across Cultures, Communities, and Countries*. Berkeley: University of California Press.

Ferguson, Ann Arnett. 2001. *Bad Boys: Public Schools in the Making of Black Masculinity*. Ann Arbor: University of Michigan Press.

Fineman, Martha Albertson. 1995. *The Neutered Mother, The Sexual Family and Other Twentieth-Century Tragedies*. New York: Routledge.

Fischer, Claude S., Michael Hout, Martin Sanchez Jankowski, Samuel R. Lucas, Ann Swidler, and Kim Voss. 1996. *Inequality by Design: Cracking the Bell Curve Myth*. Princeton, NJ: Princeton University Press.

Flavin, Jeanne. 2010. *Our Bodies, Our Crimes: The Policing of Women's Reproduction in America*. New York: NYU Press.

Foner, Phillip S., and Daniel Rosenberg. 1993. *Racism, Dissent, and Asian Americans from 1850 to the Present: A Documentary History*. Westport, CT: Greenwood.

Foucault, Michel. 1979. *Discipline and Punish*. New York: Vintage Books.

Francisco-Menchavez, Valerie. 2024. *Caring for Caregivers: Filipina Migrant Workers and Community Building during Crisis*. Seattle: University of Washington Press.

Freedman, Estelle B. 1982. "Sexuality in Nineteenth-Century America: Behavior, Ideology, and Politics." *Reviews in American History* 10(4): 196–215.

Fried, Marlene, and Loretta Ross. 2025. *Abortion and Reproductive Justice: An Essential Guide for Resistance*. Oakland: University of California Press.
Fujiwara, Lynn. 2008. *Mothers without Citizenship: Asian Immigrant Families and the Consequences of Welfare Reform*. Minneapolis: University of Minnesota Press.
Fujiwara, Lynn, and Shireen Roshanravan, eds. 2018. *Asian American Feminisms and Women of Color Politics*. Seattle: University of Washington Press.
Fussell, Elizabeth. 2014. "Warmth of the Welcome: Attitudes Toward Immigrants and Immigration Policy in the United States." *Annual Review of Sociology* 40(1): 479–98.
Gadsden, Vivian L., Morgan Ford, and Heather Breiner. 2016. "Parenting Knowledge, Attitudes, and Practices." In *Parenting Matters: Supporting Parents of Children Ages 0–8*, edited by H. Breiner, M. Ford, and V. L. Gadsden. Washington, DC: National Academies Press.
Gambol, Brenda. 2023. "Multi-Dimensional Hyper-Selectivity and Divergent Mobilities: Second-Generation Filipinos and Chinese." *Ethnic and Racial Studies* 46(5): 898–920.
Gans, Herbert J. 2007. "Acculturation, Assimilation and Mobility." *Ethnic and Racial Studies* 30(1): 152–64.
Garbes, Angela. 2022. *Essential Labor: Mothering as Social Change*. New York: Harper.
Gastelum, Amy. 2015. "Purvi Patel Faces 20 Years in Prison for Feticide and Child Neglect." *The World*, PRX, March 30. https://theworld.org/stories/2015/03/30/purvi-patel-faces-20-years-prison-feticide-and-child-neglect.
Geasler, Margie J., Linda L. Dannison, and Connie J. Edlund. 1995. "Sexuality Education of Young Children: Parental Concerns." *Family Relations* 44(2): 184–88.
Gee, Buck, and Janet Wong. 2016. "Lost in Aggregation: The Asian Reflection in the Glass Ceiling." AAPI Data, blog, October 7. http://aapidata.com/blog/lost-in-aggregation-the-asian-reflection-in-the-glass-ceiling/.
Geertz, Clifford. 1973. *The Interpretation of Cultures*. New York: Basic Books.
Gelb, Steven A. 2013. "Problems with Christmas Curriculum." *Learning for Justice*, April 16. Repr. from *Childhood Education*, October 1987. https://archive.learningforjustice.org/magazine/problems-with-christmas-curriculum
Germann Molz, Jennie. 2017. "Learning to Feel Global: Exploring the Emotional Geographies of Worldschooling." *Emotion, Space and Society* 23: 16–25.
Gidney, Catherine. 2019. *Captive Audience: How Corporations Invaded Our Schools*. Toronto: Between the Lines Publishing.

Giroux, Henry A., and Anthony N. Penna. 1979. "Social Education in the Classroom: The Dynamics of the Hidden Curriculum." *Theory & Research in Social Education* 7(1): 21–42.

Gissmer, David, and Elizabeth Eiseman. 2008. "Can Gaps in the Quality of Early Environments and Noncognitive Skills Help Explain Persisting Black-White Achievement Gaps?" In *Steady Gains and Stalled Progress: Inequality and the Black-White Test Score Gap*, edited by K. Magnuson and J. Waldfogel. New York: Russell Sage Foundation.

Glenn, Evelyn Nakano. 1992. "From Servitude to Service Work: Historical Continuities in the Racial Division of Paid Reproductive Labor." *Signs* 18: 1–43.

Glenn, Evelyn Nakano. 1993. "Social Constructions of Mothering: A Thematic Overview." In *Mothering: Ideology, Experience, and Agency*, edited by E. N. Glenn, G. Chang, and L. R. Forcey. New York: Routledge.

Goldberg, Joel. 2016. "It Takes A Village To Determine The Origins Of An African Proverb." NPR, July 30. https://www.npr.org/sections/goatsand-soda/2016/07/30/487925796/it-takes-a-village-to-determine-the-origins-of-an-african-proverb.

Goldman, Juliette D. G. 2008. "Responding to Parental Objections to School Sexuality Education: A Selection of 12 Objections." *Sex Education* 8(4): 415–38.

Goldstein, Dana. 2015. "Inexcusable Absences." *The New Republic*, March 6. https://newrepublic.com/article/121186/truancy-laws-unfairly-attack-poor-children-and-parents.

Gordon, Milton. 1964. *Assimilation in American Life*. New York: Oxford University Press.

Gover, Angela R., Shannon B. Harper, and Lynn Langton. 2020. "Anti-Asian Hate Crime During the COVID-19 Pandemic: Exploring the Reproduction of Inequality." *American Journal of Criminal Justice* 45(4): 647–67.

Guevarra, Anna Romina. 2009. *Marketing Dreams, Manufacturing Heroes: The Transnational Labor Brokering of Filipino Workers*. New Brunswick, NJ: Rutgers University Press.

Gumbs, Alexis Pauline. 2016. "m/other ourselves: a Black queer feminist genealogy for radical mothering." In *Revolutionary Mothering: Love on the Front Lines*, edited by A. P. Gumbs, C. Martens, and M. Williams. Oakland, CA: PM Press.

Gumbs, Alexis Pauline, China Martens, and Mai'a Williams, eds. 2016. *Revolutionary Mothering: Love on the Front Lines*. Oakland, CA: PM Press.

Gunio, Melanie Joy. 2021. "Determining the Influences of a Hidden Curriculum on Students' Character Development Using the Illuminative Evaluation Model." *Journal of Curriculum Studies Research* 3(2): 194–206.

Guo, Karen. 2013. "Ideals and Realities in Chinese Immigrant Parenting: Tiger Mother Versus Others." *Journal of Family Studies* 19(1): 44–52.

Hall, Lisa Kahaleole. 2015. "Which of These Things Is Not Like the Other: Hawaiians and Other Pacific Islanders Are Not Asian Americans, and All Pacific Islanders Are Not Hawaiian." *American Quarterly* 67(3): 727–47.

Haney López, Ian. 1996. *White by Law: The Legal Construction of Race*. New York: NYU Press.

Hanson, Kait. 2021. "Asian American Parents Say They're Afraid to Take Their Kids Out in Public." *Today*, NBC News, April 7. https://www.nbcnews.com/news/asian-america/asian-american-parents-say-afraid-take-kids-public-rcna625.

Hartlep, Nicholas D., and Daniel P. Scott. 2016. *Asian/American Curricular Epistemicide: From Being Excluded to Becoming a Model Minority*. Rotterdam: Sense Publishers.

Hartman, Saidiya. 2020. "Intimate History, Radical Narrative." *Black Perspectives* (blog), African American Intellectual History Society, May 22. https://www.aaihs.org/intimate-history-radical-narrative/.

Hays, Sharon. 1998. *The Cultural Contradictions of Motherhood*. New Haven: Yale University Press.

He, Fang. 2017. "'Golden Lilies' across the Pacific: Footbinding and the American Enforcement of Chinese Exclusion Laws." In *Gendering the Trans-Pacific World*, edited by C. C. Choy and J. T.-C. Wu. Boston: Brill.

Healy, Jack. 2021. "For Asian Americans Wary of Attacks, Reopening Is Not an Option." *New York Times*, June 8. https://www.nytimes.com/2021/06/08/us/asian-american-attacks.html.

Hersey, John. 1988. "Behind Barbed Wire." *New York Times Magazine*, September 11. https://www.nytimes.com/1988/09/11/magazine/behind-barbed-wire.html.

Higginbotham, A. Leon, Jr., and Barbara K. Kopytoff. 2003. "Racial Purity and Interracial Sex in the Law of Colonial and Antebellum Virginia." In *Mixed Race America and the Law: A Reader*, edited by K. R. Johnson. New York: NYU Press.

Hill, Shirley A., and Joey Sprague. 1999. "Parenting in Black and White Families: The Interaction of Gender with Race and Class." *Gender and Society* 13(4): 480–502.

Hing, Bill Ong. 2004. *Defining America Through Immigration Policy*. Philadelphia: Temple University Press.

Hinnershitz, Stephanie. 2020. *A Different Shade of Justice: Asian American Civil Rights in the South*. Chapel Hill: University of North Carolina Press.

Hirschman, Charles. 2013. "The Contributions of Immigrants to American Culture." *Daedalus* 142(3): 26–47.

Ho, Wendy. 1999. *In Her Mother's House: The Politics of Asian American Mother-Daughter Writing*. Walnut Creek, CA: AltaMira Press.

Hochschild, Arlie. 1989. *The Second Shift: Working Parents and the Revolution at Home*. New York: Avon Books.

Hong, Cathy Park. 2020. *Minor Feelings: An Asian American Reckoning*. London: One World.

Hong, Joann, and Pyong Gap Min. 1999. "Ethnic Attachment Among Second-Generation Korean Adolescents." *Amerasia Journal* 25(1): 165–79.

Horvat, Erin McNamara, Elliot B. Weininger, and Annette Lareau. 2003. "From Social Ties to Social Capital: Class Differences in the Relations Between Schools and Parent Networks." *American Educational Research Journal* 40(2): 319–51.

Hoshino, Mayu. 2018. "Demythologizing the 'Tiger Mother': Towards a Fairer Understanding." Short diss., University of St. Andrews. https://www.academia.edu/38006203/Demythologizing_the_Tiger_Mother_Towards_a_Fairer_Understanding.

Hou, Feng, Grant Schellenberg, and John Berry. 2018. "Patterns and Determinants of Immigrants' Sense of Belonging to Canada and Their Source Country." *Ethnic and Racial Studies* 41(9): 1612–31.

Hsiao, An-Fu, Mitchell D. Wong, Michael S. Goldstein, Lida S. Becerra, Eric M. Cheng, and Neil S. Wenger. 2006. "Complementary and Alternative Medicine Use Among Asian-American Subgroups: Prevalence, Predictors, and Lack of Relationship to Acculturation and Access to Conventional Health Care." *The Journal of Alternative and Complementary Medicine* 12(10): 1003–10.

Hsu, Madeline Y. 2017. *The Good Immigrants: How the Yellow Peril Became the Model Minority*. Princeton, NJ: Princeton University Press.

Hune, Shirley, and Gail M. Nomura, eds. 2020. *Our Voices, Our Histories: Asian American and Pacific Islander Women*. New York: NYU Press.

Iacovetta, Franca. 2006. *Gatekeepers: Reshaping Immigrant Lives in Cold War Canada*. Toronto: Between the Lines.

Iwamura, Jane Naomi, Khyati Y. Joshi, Sharon Suh, and Janelle Wong. 2014. "Reflections on the Pew Forum on Religion and Public Life's Asian Americans: A Mosaic of Faiths Data and Report." *Amerasia Journal* 40(1): 1–16.

Jackson, Pamela Braboy, Peggy A. Thoits, and Howard F. Taylor. 1995. "Composition of the Workplace and Psychological Well-Being: The Effects of Tokenism on America's Black Elite." *Social Forces* 74(2): 543–57.

Jackson, Philip W. (1968) 1990. *Life in Classrooms*. New York: Teachers College Press.

Jacobs, Margaret D. 2011. *White Mother to a Dark Race: Settler Colonialism, Maternalism, and the Removal of Indigenous Children in the American West and Australia, 1880–1940*. Lincoln: University of Nebraska Press.

Jegatheesan, Brinda. 2009. "Cross-Cultural Issues in Parent-Professional Interactions: A Qualitative Study of Perceptions of Asian American Mothers of Children with Developmental Disabilities." *Research and Practice for Persons with Severe Disabilities* 34(3–4): 123–36.

Jeung, Russell, Carolyn Chen, and Jerry Z. Park. 2012. "Introduction: Religious, Racial, and Ethnic Identities of the New Second Generation." In *Sustaining Faith Traditions: Race, Ethnicity, and Religion among the Latino and Asian American Second Generation*, edited by C. Chen and R. Jeung. New York: NYU Press.

Jin, Michael R. 2022. *Citizens, Immigrants, and the Stateless: A Japanese American Diaspora in the Pacific*. Stanford, CA: Stanford University Press.

Jones, Jacqueline. 1982. "'My Mother Was Much of a Woman': Black Women, Work and the Family Under Slavery." *Feminist Studies* 2: 237–349.

Jorawar, Shivana. 2015. "Miscarriage of Justice: Asian-American Women Targeted—and All Women Threatened—by Feticide Laws Like Indiana's." *The American Prospect*, April 3. https://prospect.org/api/content/d313ab08-80f8-5032-92e1-2dcbcfb542da/.

Jung, Moon-Ho. 2008. *Coolies and Cane: Race, Labor, and Sugar in the Age of Emancipation*. Baltimore: Johns Hopkins University Press.

Kandaswamy, Priya. 2018. "Race, Reproductive Justice, and the Criminalization of Purvi Patel." In *Asian American Feminisms and Women of Color Politics*, edited by L. Fujiwara and S. Roshanravan. Seattle: University of Washington Press.

Kang, Laura Hyun Yi. 2002. *Compositional Subjects: Enfiguring Asian/American Women*. Durham, NC: Duke University Press Books.

Kang, Miliann. 2015 a. "From Tiger Mothers to Fresh Off the Boat : Eddie Huang's Mom Is Not Every Asian-American Mom." *HuffPost*, February 27. https://www.huffpost.com/entry/from-tiger-mothers-to-fre_b_6773744.

Kang, Miliann. 2015b. "Are Second-Generation Korean American Women Tiger Mothers? Strategic, Transnational, and Resistant Responses to Racialized Mothering." Pp. 227–47 *in Second-Generation Korean Experiences in the United States and Canada*, edited by P.G. Min and S. Noh. Lexington Books.

Kang, Miliann. 2020a. "Getting the American Dirt on the Tiger Mother—or What Asian Americans Can Learn From Latinx Writers about Challenging Misrepresentation." *Tropics of Meta*, April 6. https://tropicsofmeta.com/2020/04/06/getting-the-american-dirt-on-the-tiger-mother-or-what-asian-americans-can-learn-from-latinx-writers-about-challenging-misrepresentation/.

Kang, Miliann. 2020b. "Reproducing Asian American Studies: Rethinking Asian Exclusion as Reproductive Exclusion." *Amerasia Journal* 46(2): 136–46.

Kang, Miliann. 2021. "Why Are Perpetrators' Motives Given More Importance Than the Lives They Take?" *Ms.*, March 22. https://msmagazine.com/2021/03/22/asian-women-atlanta-victims-names-violence-racism-massage-parlor/.

Kang, Miliann. 2023. "Cripping the Model Minority Mother: Race, Disability, and Reproductive Exclusion in Asian American Families." In *Disciplinary Futures: Sociology in Conversation with American, Ethnic, and Indigenous Studies*, edited by N. Y. Y. Kim and P. Dhingra. New York: NYU Press.

Kang, Miliann, and C. N. Le. 2022. "Asian American Mothers Confront Multiple Crises of Pandemic, Anti-Asian Hate and Caregiving." *The Conversation*, March 25. http://theconversation.com/asian-american-mothers-confront-multiple-crises-of-pandemic-anti-asian-hate-and-caregiving-179162.

Kanter, Rosabeth Moss. 1977. *Men and Women of the Corporation*. New York: Basic Books,.

Kawash, Samira. 2011. "New Directions in Motherhood Studies." *Signs: Journal of Women in Culture and Society* 36(4): 969–1003.

Khúc, Mimi. 2024. *Dear Elia: Letters from the Asian American Abyss*. Durham: Duke University Press.

Kim, Jina B. 2021. "Cripping the Welfare Queen: The Radical Potential of Disability Politics." *Social Text* 39(3 (148): 79–101.

Kim, Pan Suk, and Gregory B. Lewis. 1994. "Asian Americans in the Public Service: Success, Diversity, and Discrimination." *Public Administration Review* 54: 285–90.

Kim, Su Yeong, Yijie Wang, Diana Orozco-Lapray, Yishan Shen, and Mohammed Murtuza. 2013. "Does 'Tiger Parenting' Exist? Parenting Profiles of Chinese Americans and Adolescent Developmental Outcomes." *Asian American Journal of Psychology* 4(1): 7–18.

Kingston, Maxine Hong. 1989. *The Woman Warrior: Memoirs of a Girlhood Among Ghosts*. New York: Vintage Books.

Kinser, Amber E. 2008. *Mothering in the Third Wave*. Toronto: Demeter Press.

Ko, Lisa. 2018. *The Leavers: A Novel*. Chapel Hill, NC: Algonquin Books.

Koshy, Susan. 2005. *Sexual Naturalization: Asian Americans and Miscegenation*. Palo Alto: Stanford University Press.

Koshy, Susan. 2013. "Neoliberal Family Matters." *American Literary History* 25(2): 344–80.

Kosman, Josh. 2023. "How NYC Mom Wai Wah Chin Helped End Affirmative Action." *New York Post*, August 20. https://nypost.com/2023/08/20/how-nyc-mom-wai-wah-chin-helped-end-affirmative-action/.

Kramer, Andie. 2020. "Why Asian-American Women Aren't Advancing into Senior Leadership Positions." *Forbes*, January 22. https://www.forbes.com/sites/andiekramer/2020/01/22/why-asian-american-women-arent-advancing-into-senior-leadership-positions/.

Lan, Pei-Chia. 2018. *Raising Global Families: Parenting, Immigration, and Class in Taiwan and the US*. Palo Alto: Stanford University Press.

Lareau, Annette. 2000. *Home Advantage: Social Class and Parental Intervention in Elementary Education*. Lanham, MD: Rowman & Littlefield.

Le, C. N. 2007. *Asian American Assimilation: Ethnicity, Immigration, and Socioeconomic Attainment*. New York: LFB Scholarly.

Le, Danvy, Maneesh Arora, and Christopher Stout. 2020. "Are You Threatening Me? Asian-American Panethnicity in the Trump Era." *Social Science Quarterly* 101(6): 2183–92.

Lee, Catherine. 2010. "'Where the Danger Lies': Race, Gender, and Chinese and Japanese Exclusion in the United States, 1870–1924." *Sociological Forum* 25(2): 248–71.

Lee, Erika. 2015. *The Making of Asian America: A History*. New York: Simon & Schuster.

Lee, Erika, and Judy Yung. 2010. *Angel Island: Immigrant Gateway to America*. Oxford: Oxford University Press.

Lee, Eunjung, Joya Misra, and Marta Murray-Close. 2019. "Motherhood Penalties in the U.S., 1986–2014." *Journal of Marriage and Family* 81(2): 434–49.

Lee, Jennifer. 2016. "Ask a Sociologist: Jennifer Lee on Naming Success." *Contexts*, January 14. https://contexts.org/blog/names-and-bias/.

Lee, Jennifer. 2021. "Reckoning with Asian America and the New Culture War on Affirmative Action." *Sociological Forum* 36(4): 863–88.

Lee, Jennifer C., and Samuel Kye. 2016. "Racialized Assimilation of Asian Americans." *Annual Review of Sociology* 42(1): 253–73.

Lee, Jennifer, and Karthick Ramakrishnan. 2021. "From Narrative Scarcity to Research Plenitude for Asian Americans." *RSF: The Russell Sage Foundation Journal of the Social Sciences* 7(2): 1–20.

Lee, Jennifer, and Min Zhou. 2015. *The Asian American Achievement Paradox*. New York: Russell Sage Foundation.

Lee, Julia H. 2016. "Model Maternity: Amy Chua and Asian American Motherhood." In *Global Asian American Popular Cultures*, edited by S. Dave, L. Nishime, and T. G. Oren. New York: NYU Press.

Lee, Robert. 1999. *Orientals: Asian Americans in Popular Culture*. Philadelphia: Temple University Press.

Lee, Sharon M., and Monica Boyd. 2008. "Marrying Out: Comparing the Marital and Social Integration of Asians in the US and Canada." *Social Science Research* 38(1): 311–29.

Lee, Stacey J., and Lois Weis. 2005. *Up Against Whiteness: Race, School, and Immigrant Youth*. New York: Teachers College Press.

Leong, Russell C., A. Nehira, W. Furutani et al. 1981. "The Commission on Wartime Relocation and Internment of Civilians: Selected Testimonies from the Los Angeles and San Francisco Hearings." *Amerasia Journal* 8(2): 53–1025.

Letherby, Gayle. 1999. "Other Than Mother and Mothers as Others: The Experience of Motherhood and Non-Motherhood in Relation to 'Infertility' and 'Involuntary Childlessness.'" *Women's Studies International Forum* 22(3): 359–72.

"Letters to the Editor: Were the Stories about Japanese Internment during World War II Unbalanced? Two Letter Writers Think So." 2016. *Los Angeles Times*, December 11. https://www.latimes.com/travel/la-tr-letters-20161211-story.html.

Lewis, Oscar. 1959. *Five Families: Mexican Case Studies in the Culture of Poverty*. New York: Basic Books.

Li, Yao, and Harvey L. Nicholson. 2021. "When 'Model Minorities' Become 'Yellow Peril'—Othering and the Racialization of Asian Americans in the COVID-19 Pandemic." *Sociology Compass* 15(2). https://www.ncbi.nlm.nih.gov/pmc/articles/PMC7995194/.

Lin, Jami Nakamura. 2020. "Does My Child's Name Erase My Identity?" *New York Times*, May 5.

Lipschutz, Marion, Rose Rosenblatt, and Angie Wang, dirs. 2019. *Bei Bei*. Cine Qua Non.

Litam, Stacey Diane Arañez, and Christian D. Chan. 2021. "Grounded Theory of Asian American Activists for #BlackLivesMatter." *Professional Counselor* 11(4): 400–422.

Loh, Sandra Tsing. 2011. "Sympathy for the Tiger Moms." *The Atlantic*, April. https://www.theatlantic.com/magazine/archive/2011/04/sympathy-for-the-tiger-moms/308399/.

Lopez, William D. 2019. *Separated: Family and Community in the Aftermath of an Immigration Raid*. Baltimore: Johns Hopkins University Press.

Lorenzo-Blanco, Elma I., Cristina B. Bares, and Jorge Delva. 2013. "Parenting, Family Processes, Relationships, and Parental Support in Multiracial and Multiethnic Families: An Exploratory Study of Youth Perceptions." *Family Relations* 62(1): 125–39.

Lubiano, Wahneema. 1992. "Black Ladies, Welfare Queens, and State Minstrels: Ideological War by Narrative Means." in *Race-ing Justice, En-Gendering Power: Essays on Anita Hill, Clarence Thomas, and the Construction of Social Reality*, edited by T. Morrison. New York: Knopf Doubleday Publishing Group.

Lui, P. Priscilla, and David Rollock. 2013. "Tiger Mother: Popular and Psychological Scientific Perspectives on Asian Culture and Parenting." *American Journal of Orthopsychiatry* 83(4): 450–56.

Lundquist, Jennifer H., and Ken-Hou Lin. 2015. "Is Love (Color) Blind? The Economy of Race among Gay and Straight Daters." *Social Forces* 93(4): 1423–49.

Lundquist, Jennifer, Ken-Hou Lin, and Celeste Curington. 2024. "Interracial Unions and Racial Assortative Mating in an Age of Growing Diversity, Shifting Intimate Relationships, and Emerging Technologies." *Annual Review of Sociology* 50: 431–53.

Luthra, Renee, Thomas Soehl, and Roger Waldinger. 2018. "Reconceptualizing Context: A Multilevel Model of the Context of Reception and Second-Generation Educational Attainment." *International Migration Review* 52(3): 898–928.

Ly, Louise H. 2025. "Asian Americans as Objects of Desire: Gendered Racialized Attraction among White Spouses Married to East Asians." *Sociology of Race and Ethnicity* 12(1). https://doi.org/10.1177/23326492251334304.

Lydall, Jean. 1998. "From Being 'Other' to Being 'Mother': An Ethnographer's Experience of Otherness." *Paideuma* 44: 69–75.

Lye, Colleen. 2004. *America's Asia: Racial Form and American Literature, 1893–1945*. Princeton, NJ: Princeton University Press.

Lyon, Cherstin M. 2020. "Mothers of Topaz." *Densho Encyclopedia*, last updated August 24. https://encyclopedia.densho.org/Mothers_of_Topaz/.

Ma, Grace Xueqin. 1999. "Between Two Worlds: The Use of Traditional and Western Health Services by Chinese Immigrants." *Journal of Community Health* 24(6): 421–37.

Mabute-Louie, Bianca. 2025. *Unassimilable: An Asian Diasporic Manifesto for the Twenty-First Century*. New York: HarperCollins.

Maddox, Shelley. 2024. "M/Other Your Politics: A Praxis for the Next Iterations of Humanity." Ph.D. diss., Loyola University Chicago.

Manjikian, Mary. 2011. "'Tiger Mother' Isn't about Parenting. It's about Declining American Exceptionalism." *Christian Science Monitor*, January 25. https://www.csmonitor.com/Commentary/Opinion/2011/0125/Tiger-Mother-isn-t-about-parenting.-It-s-about-declining-American-exceptionalism.

Marchetti, Gina. 1993. *Romance and the "Yellow Peril" Race, Sex, and Discursive Strategies in Hollywood Fiction*. Berkeley: University of California Press.

Mason, Melanie, and Michael Finnegan. 2019. "Kamala Harris Regrets California Truancy Law That Led to Arrest of Some Parents." *Los Angeles Times*, April 17. https://www.latimes.com/politics/la-na-pol-kamala-harris-truancy-20190417-story.html.

Massey, Douglas, and Nancy Denton. 1993. *American Apartheid: Segregation and the Making of the Underclass*. Cambridge, MA: Harvard University Press.

Massey, Douglas S., and Magaly R. Sanchez. 2012. *Brokered Boundaries: Immigrant Identity in Anti-Immigrant Times*. New York: Russell Sage Foundation.

Mayer, Ruth. 2013. *Serial Fu Manchu: The Chinese Supervillain and the Spread of Yellow Peril Ideology*. Philadelphia: Temple University Press.

McGirt, Ellen. 2018. "The Asian Glass Ceiling: Studying the Model Minority Myth." *Fortune*, June 4. http://fortune.com/2018/06/04/asian-americans-model-minority-asian-glass-ceiling/.

McKenna, Rebecca Tinio. 2017. *American Imperial Pastoral: The Architecture of US Colonialism in the Philippines*. Chicago: University of Chicago Press.

McNeal, Ralph B., Jr. 1999. "Parental Involvement as Social Capital: Differential Effectiveness on Science Achievement, Truancy, and Dropping Out." *Social Forces* 78(1): 117–44.

Merriam-Webster Dictionary. 2023. "Coolie." https://www.merriam-webster.com/dictionary/coolie.

Min, Pyong Gap, and Thomas Chung, eds. 2016. *Younger-Generation Korean Experiences in the United States: Personal Narratives on Ethnic and Racial Identities*. New York: Lexington Books.

Min, Pyong Gap, and Chigon Kim. 2009. "Patterns of Intermarriages and Cross-Generational In-Marriages among Native-Born Asian Americans." *International Migration Review* 43(3): 447–70.

Minero, Emelina. 2020. "The Christmas Dilemma." *Edutopia*, December 19. https://www.edutopia.org/article/christmas-dilemma.

Mireles-Rios, Rebeca, Victor M. Rios, and Augustina Reyes. 2020. "Pushed Out for Missing School: The Role of Social Disparities and School Truancy in Dropping Out." *Education Sciences* 10(4): 108.

Mishra, Neha. 2018. "Asian Americans: Eurogamy by Asian Women." *American Behavioral Scientist* 62(14): 1988–2006.

Molnar, Alex. 1996. *Giving Kids The Business: The Commercialization Of America's Schools*. Boulder, CO: Westview Press.

Moon, Kat. 2021. "How Black-Asian Solidarity Is Taking on White Supremacy." *Time*, March 25. https://time.com/5949926/black-asian-solidarity-white-supremacy/.

Moran, Rachel F. 2001. *Interracial Intimacy: The Regulation of Race and Romance*. Chicago: University of Chicago Press.

Morris, Monique, Mankaprr Conteh, and Melissa Harris-Perry. 2018. *Pushout: The Criminalization of Black Girls in Schools*. New York: New Press.

Mowen, Thomas J. 2017. "The Collateral Consequences of 'Criminalized' School Punishment on Disadvantaged Parents and Families." *Urban Review* 49(5): 832–51.

Moynihan, Daniel Patrick, and Office of Policy Planning and Research, Department of Labor. 1965. *The Moynihan Report: The Negro Family—The Case for National Action*. New York: Cosimo Reports.

Museus, Samuel D., Amy C. Wang, Hannah Hyun White, and Vanessa S. Na. 2019. "A Critical Analysis of Media Discourse on Affirmative Action and Asian Americans." *New Directions for Higher Education* 2019(186): 11–24.

Myers, Michal Elaine, and Barbara Kimes Myers. 2001. "Holidays in the Public School Kindergarten an Avenue for Emerging Religious and Spiritual Literacy." *Childhood Education* 78(2): 79–83.

Napierski-Prancl, Michelle. 2019. *Mothers Work: Confronting the Mommy Wars, Raising Children, and Working for Social Change*. Lanham, MD: Lexington Books.

National Archives. 2023. "Restricting Immigration from Asia and the Pacific, 1870s to 1950s." https://www.archives.gov/research/aapi/immigration.

"National Asian Pacific American Women's Forum Denounces Attack on Pregnant Women's Rights." 2016. Press release, May 22. https://www.napawf.org/press-releases/052216.

Ng, Celeste. 2022. *Our Missing Hearts*. New York: Penguin Books.

Ngai, Mae. 2007. "The Architecture of Race in American Immigration Law: A Reexamination of the Immigration Act of 1924." In *Race, Law and Society*, edited by I. Haney López. Routledge.

Ngai, Mae. 2014. *Impossible Subjects: Illegal Aliens and the Making of Modern America*. Princeton, NJ: Princeton University Press.

Nguyen, Huong H. 2011. *Culture in Context: The Acculturation and Adjustment of Mexican and Vietnamese Youth*. New York: LFB Scholarly Publishing.

Nguyen, Linh Thuy. 2024. *Displacing Kinship: The Intimacies of Intergenerational Trauma in Vietnamese American Cultural Production*. Philadelphia: Temple University Press.

Nguyen, Tony, Paul P. W. Chang, and Jennifer M. Loh. 2014. "The Psychology of Vietnamese Tiger Mothers: Qualitative Insights into the Parenting Beliefs and Practices of Vietnamese-Australian Mothers." *Journal of Family Studies* 20(1): 48–65.

Nguyen, Viet Thanh. 2002. *Race and Resistance: Literature and Politics in Asian America*. Oxford: Oxford University Press.

Nguyen, Viet Thanh. 2018. "Asian-Americans Need More Movies, Even Mediocre Ones." *New York Times*, August 21. http://www.nytimes.com/2018/08/21/opinion/crazy-rich-asians-movie.html.

Ninh, erin Khuê. 2011a. "Advice on How Not to Misread the Tiger Mother." *Amerasia Journal*, September 22. http://www.amerasiajournal.org/blog/?p=1540.

Ninh, erin Khuê. 2011b. *Ingratitude: The Debt-Bound Daughter in Asian American Literature*. New York: New York University Press.

Ocampo, Anthony Christian. 2016. *The Latinos of Asia: How Filipino Americans Break the Rules of Race*. Palo Alto: Stanford University Press.

Okamoto, Dina G. 2007. "Marrying Out: A Boundary Approach to Understanding the Marital Integration of Asian Americans." *Social Science Research* 36(4): 1391–1414.

Okihiro, Gary Y. 1994. *Margins and Mainstreams: Asian in American History and Culture*. Seattle: University of Washington Press.

Okura, Keitaro. 2022. "Stereotype Promise: Racialized Teacher Appraisals of Asian American Academic Achievement." *Sociology of Education* 95(4): 302–19.

Oliveira, Gabrielle. 2018. *Motherhood across Borders: Immigrants and Their Children in Mexico and New York*. New York: NYU Press.

Ordover, Nancy. 2003. *American Eugenics: Race, Queer Anatomy, and the Science of Nationalism*. Minneapolis: University of Minnesota Press.

O'Reilly, Andrea. 2021. *Maternal Theory: Essential Readings* (2nd ed.). Bradford, ON, Canada: Demeter Press.

O'Reilly, Andrea. 2023. *Normative Motherhood: Regulations, Representations, and Reclamations*. Coe Hill, ON: Demeter Press.

Oreopoulos, Philip. 2011. "Why Do Skilled Immigrants Struggle in the Labor Market? A Field Experiment with Thirteen Thousand Resumes." *American Economic Journal: Economic Policy* 3(4): 148–71.

Osburg, John L. 2008. "Engendering Wealth: China's New Rich and the Rise of an Elite Masculinity." Diss., University of Chicago, Department of Anthropology.

Page, Horace F. 1875. Page Act of 1875. Vol. 18, Stat. 477.

Page, Horace F. 1882. An Act to Execute Certain Treaty Stipulations Relating to Chinese. 22 Stat. 58, Chap. 126.

Palumbo-Liu, David. 1999. *Asian/American: Historical Crossings of a Racial Frontier*. Palo Alto: Stanford University Press.

Pang, Valerie Ooka. 2006. "Fighting the Marginalization of Asian American Students with Caring Schools: Focusing on Curricular Change." *Race Ethnicity and Education* 9(1): 67–83.

Paris, Katie. 2020. "Democrats Should Take the 'Wine Moms' Seriously." The Forge, December 15. https://forgeorganizing.org/article/democrats-should-take-wine-moms-seriously/.

Park, Jerry Z., and Elaine Howard Ecklund. 2007. "Negotiating Continuity: Family and Religious Socialization for Second-Generation Asian Americans." *Sociological Quarterly* 48(1): 93–118.

Park, John S. 2004. *Elusive Citizenship: Immigration, Asian Americans, and the Paradox of Civil Rights*. New York: New York University Press.

Parreñas, Rhacel S. 2015. *Servants of Globalization: Women, Migration, and Domestic Work*. Palo Alto: Stanford University Press.

Pascoe, C. J. 2007. *Dude, You're a Fag: Masculinity and Sexuality in High School*. Berkeley: University of California Press.

Pascoe, Peggy. 1996. "Miscegenation Law, Court Cases, and Ideologies of 'Race' in Twentieth-Century America." *Journal of American History* 83(1): 44–69.

Peffer, George. 1999. *If They Don't Bring Their Women Here: Chinese Female Immigration Before Exclusion*. Champaign-Urbana: University of Illinois Press.

Peskowitz, Miriam. 2005. *The Truth Behind the Mommy Wars: Who Decides What Makes A Good Mother?* Emeryville, CA: Seal Press.

Peters, Eleanor. 2012. "I Blame the Mother: Educating Parents and the Gendered Nature of Parenting Orders." *Gender and Education* 24(1): 119–30.

Phelan, James D. 1901. "Why the Chinese Should Be Excluded." *North American Review* 173(540): 663–76.

Pilkington, Ed. 2012. "Indiana Prosecuting Chinese Woman for Suicide Attempt That Killed Her Foetus." *The Guardian*, May 30. https://www.theguardian.com/world/2012/may/30/indiana-prosecuting-chinese-woman-suicide-foetus.

Pollitt, Katha. 2012. "Protect Pregnant Women: Free Bei Bei Shuai." *The Nation*, March 26. https://www.thenation.com/article/archive/protect-pregnant-women-free-bei-bei-shuai/.

Poon, OiYan A. 2011. "Ching Chongs and Tiger Moms: The 'Asian Invasion' in U.S. Higher Education." *Amerasia Journal* 37(2): 144–50.

Poon, OiYan A., Megan S. Segoshi, Lilianne Tang, Kristen L. Surla, Caressa Nguyen, and Dian D. Squire. 2019. "Asian Americans, Affirmative Action, and the Political Economy of Racism: A Multidimensional Model of Raceclass Frames." *Harvard Educational Review* 89(2): 201–26.

Portes, Alejandro, and Ruben Rumbaut. 2001. *Legacies: The Story of the Immigrant Second Generation*. Berkeley: University of California Press.

Portes, Alejandro, and Ruben Rumbaut. 2006. *Immigrant America: A Portrait*, 3rd ed. Berkeley: University of California Press.

Purinton, Ted, and Vicki Gunther. 2011. "Closing School for the Holidays—Whose Holidays?" *Phi Delta Kappan* 93(4): 33–37.

Pyke, Karen, and Tran Dang. 2003. "'F.O.B.' and 'Whitewashed': Identity and Internalized Racism among Second Generation Asian Americans." *Qualitative Sociology* 26(2): 147–72.

Qian, Zhenchao, and Yue Qian. 2020. "Generation, Education, and Intermarriage of Asian Americans." *Journal of Ethnic and Migration Studies* 46(14): 2880–95.

Quillian, Lincoln, John J. Lee, and Mariana Oliver. 2020. "Evidence from Field Experiments in Hiring Shows Substantial Additional Racial Discrimination after the Callback." *Social Forces* 99(2): 732–59.

Raza, Fizza, and Arthur Sakamoto. 2024. "Socioeconomic Attainments of Second-Generation South Asian Americans: Evidence from the American Community Survey, 2014-2018." *Population Research and Policy Review* 43(28). https://link.springer.com/article/10.1007/s11113-024-09879-2.

Reeves, Richard. 2016. *Infamy: The Shocking Story of the Japanese American Internment in World War II*. New York: Picador.

Renold, Emma. 2005. *Girls, Boys and Junior Sexualities: Exploring Children's Gender and Sexual Relations in the Primary School*. New York: Routledge.

Reny, Tyler T., and Matt A. Barreto. 2020. "Xenophobia in the Time of Pandemic: Othering, Anti-Asian Attitudes, and COVID-19." *Politics, Groups, and Identities* 10(2): 209–32.

Rhee, Jeong-eun. 2013. "The Neoliberal Racial Project: The Tiger Mother and Governmentality." *Educational Theory* 63(6): 561–80.

Rich, Adrienne. 1995. *Of Woman Born: Motherhood as Experience and Institution*. New York: W. W. Norton & Company.

Robelen, Erik W. 1998. "Commercialism in Schools: Supporting Students or Selling Access?" *ASCD Infobrief* no. 15, November. http://www.ascd.org/publications/newsletters/policy-priorities/nov98/num15/toc.aspx.

Roberts, David. 2005. *The Pueblo Revolt: The Secret Rebellion That Drove the Spaniards Out of the Southwest*. New York: Simon & Schuster.

Roberts, Dorothy E. 1997. *Killing the Black Body: Race, Reproduction, and the Meaning of Liberty*. New York: Pantheon Books.

Robinson, Greg. 2015. "Exclusion." In *Keywords for Asian American Studies*, edited by C. J. Schlund-Vials, L. Trinh Vo, and K. S. Wong. New York: NYU Press.

Rock, Lindsey. 2007. "The 'Good Mother' vs. the 'Other Mother': The Girl-Mom." *Journal of the Motherhood Initiative for Research and Community Involvement* 9(1). https://jarm.journals.yorku.ca/index.php/jarm/article/view/5132.

Rodriguez, Robyn Magalit. 2010. *Migrants for Export: How the Philippine State Brokers Labor to the World*. Minneapolis: University of Minnesota Press.

Rogin, Michael. 1984. "Kiss Me Deadly: Communism, Motherhood, and Cold War Movies." *Representations* 6: 1–36.

Ross, Loretta, and Rickie Solinger. 2017. *Reproductive Justice: An Introduction*. Berkeley: University of California Press.

Rothstein, Richard. 2004. *Class and Schools: Using Social, Economic, and Educational Reform to Close the Black-White Achievement Gap*. New York: Economic Policy Institute and Teachers College.

Ruiz, Neil G., Ziyao Tian, and Jens Manuel Krogstad. 2023. "Asian Americans Hold Mixed Views Around Affirmative Action." Pew Research, June 8. https://www.pewresearch.org/race-and-ethnicity/2023/06/08/asian-americans-hold-mixed-views-around-affirmative-action/.

Rumbaut, Rubén G. 2008. "The Coming of the Second Generation: Immigration and Ethnic Mobility in Southern California." *Annals of the American Academy of Political and Social Science* 620(1): 196–236.

Ryan, William. 1971. *Blaming the Victim*. New York: Vintage Books.

Saavedra, J. Abigail, and Hyung Chol Yoo. 2023. "Translating Critical Reflection into Collective Action: The Mediating Role of Asian American Racial Identity Ideological Values." *American Journal of Community Psychology* 72(1–2): 60–74.

Said, Edward. 1979. *Orientalism*. New York: Vintage Books.

Saito, Natsu Taylor. 1997. "Alien and Non-Alien Alike: Citizenship, Foreignness, and Racial Hierarchy in American Law Symposium: Citizenship and Its Discontents: Centering the Immigrant in the Inter/National Imagination: Part I." *Oregon Law Review* 76(2): 261–346.

Sakamoto, Arthur, and Li Hsu. 2020. "Do Second-Generation Asian Americans Face a Systematic Disadvantage in Occupational Attainment? Comment on Tran, Lee and Huang." *Ethnic and Racial Studies* 43(3): 516–32.

Schrum, Lynne. 2002. "Education and Commercialization: Raising Awareness and Making Wise Decisions." *Contemporary Issues in Technology and Teacher Education* 2(2): 170–77.

Schweitzer, Jeff. 2015. "A War on Reason, Not on Christmas." *HuffPost*, December 3. https://www.huffpost.com/entry/a-war-on-reason-not-on-ch_b_6265932.

Senior, Jennifer. 2015. *All Joy and No Fun: The Paradox of Modern Parenthood*. London: Virago Press.

Shapiro, Eliza. 2019. "Racist? Fair? Biased? Asian-American Alumni Debate Elite High School Admissions." *New York Times*, February 6. https://www.nytimes.com/2019/02/06/nyregion/nyc-specialized-high-school-test.html.

Shapiro, Eliza, and K. K. Rebecca Lai. 2019. "How New York's Elite Public Schools Lost Their Black and Hispanic Students." *New York Times*, June 3. https://www.nytimes.com/interactive/2019/06/03/nyregion/nyc-public-schools-black-hispanic-students.html.

Shen, Hsiu-Hua. 2005. "'The First Taiwanese Wives' and 'the Chinese Mistresses': The International Division of Labour in Familial and Intimate Relations across the Taiwan Strait." *Global Networks* 5(4): 419–37.

Silliman, Jael, Marlene Gerber Fried, Loretta Ross, and Elena Gutiérrez. 2016. *Undivided Rights: Women of Color Organizing for Reproductive Justice*. Chicago: Haymarket Books.

Sister Song. 2026. "Reproductive Justice." *Sister Song*. https://www.sistersong.net/reproductive-justice.
Small, Mario Luis. 2009. "'How Many Cases Do I Need?': On Science and the Logic of Case Selection in Field-Based Research." *Ethnography* 10(1): 5–38.
Smearman, Claire A. 2009. "Second Wives' Club: Mapping the Impact of Polygamy in U.S. Immigration Law." *Berkeley Journal of International Law* 27(2): 382–447.
Sohoni, Deenesh. 2007. "Unsuitable Suitors: Anti-Miscegenation Laws, Naturalization Laws, and the Construction of Asian Identities." *Law & Society Review* 41(3): 587–618.
Spillers, Hortense J. 1987. "Mama's Baby, Papa's Maybe: An American Grammar Book." *Diacritcs* 17(2): 64–81.
Steiner, Leslie Morgan. 2006. *Mommy Wars: Stay-at-Home and Career Moms Face Off on Their Choices, Their Lives, Their Families*. New York: Random House.
Stone, Pamela. 2007. *Opting Out? Why Women Really Quit Careers and Head Home*. Berkeley: University of California Press.
Subramaniam, Banu. 2019. *Holy Science: The Biopolitics of Hindu Nationalism*. Seattle: University of Washington Press.
Suissa, Judith. 2013. "Tiger Mothers and Praise Junkies: Children, Praise and the Reactive Attitudes." *Journal of Philosophy of Education* 47(1): 1–19.
Swidler, Ann. 1986. "Culture in Action: Symbols and Strategies." *American Sociological Review* 51(2): 273–86.
Szirom, Tricia. 2018. *Teaching Gender?: Sex Education and Sexual Stereotypes*. New York: Routledge.
Takei, George. 2012. "Remembrance Project—Fumiko Emily Takei." Japanese American National Museum. http://remembrance-project.janm.org/tributes/fumiko-emily.html.
Takei, George. 2019. *They Called Us Enemy*. Marietta, GA: Top Shelf Productions.
Takševa, Tatjana. 2019. "One Is Not Born But Rather Becomes a Mother: Claiming the Maternal in Women and Gender Studies." *Journal of the Motherhood Initiative for Research and Community Involvement* 10(1–2).
Tam, Siumi Maria. 1996. "Normalization of 'Second Wives': Gender Contestation in Hong Kong." *Asian Journal of Women's Studies* 2(1): 113–32.
Tam, Siumi Maria. 2005. "We-Women and They-Women: Imagining Mistresses across the Hong Kong-China Border." In *Rethinking and Recasting Citizenship: Social Exclusion and Marginality in Chinese Societies*, edited by May Tam, Ku Hok-bun, and Travis Kong. Hong-Kong: Centre for Social Policy Studies, Hong-Kong Polytechnic University.

Tan, Amy. 1990. *Joy Luck Club*. New York: Prentice Hall.

Tchen, John Kuo Wei, and Dylan Yeats. 2014. *Yellow Peril!: An Archive of Anti-Asian Fear*. London: Verso.

Thanasombat, Siri, and John Trasviña. 2005. "Screening Names Instead of Qualifications: Testing with Emailed Resumes Reveals Racial Preferences." *AAPI Nexus: Policy, Practice and Community* 3(2): 105–15.

Thorne, Barrie. 1993. *Gender Play: Girls and Boys in School*. New Brunswick, NJ: Rutgers University Press.

Tso, Tiffany Diane. 2018. "Nail Salon Brawls and Boycotts: Unpacking the Black-Asian Conflict in America." *Refinery 29*, August 21. https://www.refinery29.com/en-us/2018/08/207533/red-apple-nails-brawl-black-asian-conflict.

Turner, Natasha. 2013. "Plea Deal Confirmed for Bei Bei Shuai." *Ms. Magazine*, August 7. https://msmagazine.com/2013/08/07/newsflash-plea-deal-confirmed-for-bei-bei-shuai/.

Vallence, Elizabeth. 1983. "Hiding the Hidden Curriculum: An Interpretation of the Language of Justification in Nineteenth-Century Educational Reform." In *The Hidden Curriculum and Moral Education: Deception or Discovery?*, edited by H. A. Giroux and D. Purpel. Berkeley, CA: McCutchan Publishing.

Valverde, Kieu Linh Caroline, and Wei Ming Dariotis, eds. 2019. *Fight the Tower: Asian American Women Scholars' Resistance and Renewal in the Academy*. New Brunswick, NJ: Rutgers University Press.

Varnham, Sally. 2014. "Getting Tough on Truancy: Punishing Parents Is Not the Answer." *The Conversation*, August 18. http://theconversation.com/getting-tough-on-truancy-punishing-parents-is-not-the-answer-30310.

Veiga, Christina. 2018. "Fair and Objective or Useless and Biased? A Chalkbeat Guide to the Case For and Against New York City's Specialized High School Test." *Chalkbeat*, August 13. https://www.chalkbeat.org/newyork/2018/8/13/21105525/fair-and-objective-or-useless-and-biased-a-chalkbeat-guide-to-the-case-for-and-against-new-york-city/.

Villalobos, Ana. 2014. *Motherload: Making It All Better in Insecure Times*. Berkeley: University of California Press.

Visweswaran, Kamala. 1997. "Histories of Feminist Ethnography." *Annual Review of Anthropology* 26: 591–621.

Vuong, Ocean. 2019. *On Earth We're Briefly Gorgeous*. New York: Penguin Press.

Vuong, Ocean. 2023. *Time Is a Mother*. New York: Penguin Books.

Waggoner, Miranda. 2017. *The Zero Trimester: Pre-Pregnancy Care and the Politics of Reproductive Risk*. Berkeley: University of California Press.

Walker, Joy. 2004. "Parents and Sex Education—Looking beyond 'the Birds and the Bees.'" *Sex Education* 4(3): 239–54.

Wallace, Nina. 2021. "Issei Mothers Played an Important—and Largely Forgotten—Role in the Japanese American Draft Resistance Movement." *Catalyst*, May 5. https://densho.org/catalyst/issei-mothers-played-important-role-in-the-japanese-american-draft-resistance-movement/.

Wallace, Sophia Jordan, and Chris Zepeda-Millán. 2020. *Walls, Cages, and Family Separation*. Cambridge: Cambridge University Press.

Wang, L. Ling-chi. 1998. "Race, Class, Citizenship, and Extraterritoriality: Asian Americans and the 1996 Campaign Finance Scandal." *Amerasia* 24: 1–21.

Wang, Sherry C., and Bianca Marie C. Santos. 2023. "At the Intersection of the Model Minority Myth and Antiblackness: From Asian American Triangulation to Recommendations for Solidarity." *Journal of Counseling Psychology* 70(4): 352–66.

Washington, Myra S. 2019. *Blasian Invasion: Racial Mixing in the Celebrity Industrial Complex*. Jackson: University Press of Mississippi.

Waters, Mary C. 1990. *Ethnic Options: Choosing Identities in America*. Berkeley: University of California Press.

Waters, Mary C. 1999. "Immigrant Dreams and American Realities: The Causes and Consequences of the Ethnic Labor Market in American Cities." *Work and Occupations* 26(3): 352–64.

Waters, Mary C., Van C. Tran, Philip Kasinitz, and John Mollenkopf. 2010. "Segmented Assimilation Revisited: Types of Acculturation and Socioeconomic Mobility in Young Adulthood." *Ethnic and Racial Studies* 33(7): 1168–93.

Watson, Denise. 2016. "Before Loving v. Virginia, There Was Naim v. Naim in Norfolk to Challenge the State's Race Laws." *Virginian-Pilot*, December 10. https://www.pilotonline.com/history/article_58459574-0ba6-5ecc-b2f3-6b8a23f7e02a.html.

Williams, Apryl. 2024. *Not My Type: Automating Sexual Racism in Online Dating*. Stanford: Stanford University Press.

Williams, Heather Andrea. 2016. *Help Me to Find My People: The African American Search for Family Lost in Slavery*. Chapel Hill: University of North Carolina Press.

Williams, Joan. 2004. "Hitting the Maternal Wall—Before They Reach a 'Glass Ceiling' in Their Careers, Women Faculty May Hit a 'Maternal Wall.'" *Academe Bulletin of the American Association of University Professors* 16. https://repository.uclawsf.edu/faculty_scholarship/1202.

Williams, Joan C., Marina Multhaup, and Rachel Korn. 2018. "The Problem with 'Asians Are Good at Science.'" *The Atlantic*, January. http://www.theatlantic.com/science/archive/2018/01/asian-americans-science-math-bias/551903/.

Williams, Joan C., Katherine W. Phillips, and Erika V. Hall. 2014. *Double Jeopardy? Gender Bias Against Women in Science*. San Francisco: The Center for WorkLife Law, University of California at Hastings. https://worklifelaw.org/publications/Double-Jeopardy-Report_v6_full_web-sm.pdf.

Willis, Paul. 1981. *Learning to Labor: How Working Class Kids Get Working Class Jobs*. New York: Columbia University Press.

Wingfield, Adia Harvey. 2010. "Are Some Emotions Marked 'Whites Only'? Racialized Feeling Rules in Professional Workplaces." *Social Problems* 57(2): 251–68.

Wong, Kristina, and Rebecca Solnit. 2021. *The Auntie Sewing Squad Guide to Mask Making, Radical Care, and Racial Justice*. Edited by M.-L. K. Hong, C. Y. Lau, and P. Sharma. Oakland: University of California Press.

Wong, Yuk-Lin Renita, and A. Ka Tat Tsang. 2004. "When Asian Immigrant Women Speak: From Mental Health to Strategies of Being." *American Journal of Orthopsychiatry* 74(4): 456–66.

Woo, Deborah. 2002. *Glass Ceilings and Asian Americans: The New Face of Workplace Barriers*. Walnut Creek, CA: AltaMira Press.

Wu, Diana Ting Liu. 1997. *Asian Pacific Americans in the Workplace*. Walnut Creek, CA: AltaMira Press.

Wu, Ellen D. 2014. *The Color of Success: Asian Americans and the Origins of the Model Minority*. New Brunswick, NJ: Princeton University Press.

Xu, An Rong, and Leslie Nguyen-Okwu. 2022. "Asian and Black Communities Have a Long History of Shared Solidarity." *New York Times*, May 30. https://www.nytimes.com/2022/05/30/opinion/asian-black-americans-community.html.

Yee, Pamela M. 2023. "Towards Narrative Plenitude: Asian Representation in Young Adult Arthurian Fantasy." *Arthuriana* 33(3): 60–85.

Yellowhorn, Eldon, and Kathy Lowinger. 2019. *What the Eagle Sees: Indigenous Stories of Rebellion and Renewal*. Toronto: Annick Press.

Yi, Jacqueline, and Nathan R. Todd. 2021. "Internalized Model Minority Myth among Asian Americans: Links to Anti-Black Attitudes and Opposition to Affirmative Action." *Cultural Diversity and Ethnic Minority Psychology* 27(4): 569–78.

Zambrana, Ruth Enid, Adia Harvey Wingfield, Lisa M. Lapeyrouse, Brianne A. Dávila, Tangere L. Hoagland, and Robert Burciaga Valdez. 2016. "Blatant, Subtle, and Insidious: URM Faculty Perceptions of Discriminatory Practices in Predominantly White Institutions." *Sociological Inquiry*, special issue, November 28. https://onlinelibrary.wiley.com/doi/10.1111/soin.12147.
Zhao, Xian, and Monica Biernat. 2017. "'Welcome to the U.S.' but 'Change Your Name'? Adopting Anglo Names and Discrimination." *Journal of Experimental Social Psychology* 70: 59–68.
Zheng, Robin. 2016. "Why Yellow Fever Isn't Flattering: A Case Against Racial Fetishes." *Journal of the American Philosophical Association* 2(3): 400–419.

Index

www.ingramcontent.com/pod-product-compliance
Ingram Content Group UK Ltd.
Pitfield, Milton Keynes, MK11 3LW, UK
UKHW012229160826
474339UK00002B/59

9 780520 356290